SCAC

D0065370

OCT - - 2020

Praise for Ira Berkow

"Ira Berkow is one of the great American writers, without limitation to the field of sports. His writing is agile, clever, and sparked by observation of perfect details." —Scott Turow

"With the keen eye of a reporter, the literary touch of a highly skilled writer, and above all a feel for the humanity in every story, Ira takes his readers to a place beyond and above what even competent sports writing generally delivers." —Bob Costas

"I follow Ira Berkow in the *Times* with unfailing interest." —Saul Bellow

"Ira Berkow over the years has regularly given us sportswriting of the most elegant kind—his work glistens with intelligence and sensitivity." —David Halberstam

"Sports at its best is a kind of music and sportswriting is a kind of libretto. Ira Berkow is among the best—a Sondheim of the sports page."—George Will

"Ira Berkow gets inside people. It can be stated as a law that the sports writer whose horizons are no wider than the outfield fences is a bad sports writer because he has no sense of proportion and no awareness of the real world around him. Ira Berkow knows that what is important about a game is not the score but the people who play it." —Red Smith, from the foreword to *Beyond the Dream*

"*Rockin' Steady* has kept me steady for several days and I have been enjoying it, particularly since I had never heard of Clyde (I live a sheltered life)." —E. B. White (for *Rockin' Steady*)

"I bought the book when I was 12 years old. I loved all the fashion stuff and how to catch flies with your bare hands." —President Barack Obama (as told to Ira Berkow, for *Rockin' Steady*)

"Ira Berkow is simply one of America's best writers, sports or otherwise." —Jim Bouton (for *Pitchers Do Get Lonely*)

"An extraordinary look into the art of pickup basketball. Who would have guessed that, along with his writing talents, Ira knows how to play the game!" —Senator Bill Bradley (for *To the Hoop*)

"Ira Berkow is one of the best sportswriters around, so it is no surprise that his basketball odyssey is one of the best sports books of this or any other year. . . . Very few sports columnists have the genius to produce a timely piece that is also timeless. Ira Berkow has that ability in spades." —George Plimpton (for *To the Hoop*)

"This book is a paean to writing. . . . Ira Berkow (is) one of America's greatest sports journalists, as good perhaps as his mentor, the supreme sports columnist Red Smith." —*The Saturday Evening Post* (for *Full Swing*)

"Few journalists on any beat—sports, politics, or war—ply their trade with the skill, insight and empathy of Ira Berkow." —Wes Lukowsky, *Booklist* (starred review, *The Minority Quarterback*)

"Nobody covered the fight game with more artistry and insight, with more compassion and humor, than he did." —Jeremy Schaap, from the foreword to *Counterpunch*

"The book is a grand portrait gallery, and in its way a historical treasure (with) terrific picaresque stories and scenes." —Richard Stern, *New York Times Sunday Book Review* (for *Maxwell Street*)

"An urban classic" —William Braden, *Chicago Sun-Times* (for *Maxwell Street*)

HOW LIFE IMITATES SPORTS

Also by Ira Berkow

It Happens Every Spring
Giants Among Men
Wrigley Field
Autumns in the Garden
Summers at Shea
Summers in the Bronx
The Corporal Was a Pitcher
Full Swing
The Minority Quarterback
Court Vision
To the Hoop
The Gospel According to Casey (with Jim Kaplan)
How to Talk Jewish (with Jackie Mason)
Hank Greenberg: The Story of My Life (editor)
Hank Greenberg: Hall-of-Fame Slugger (juvenile)
Pitchers Do Get Lonely
The Man Who Robbed the Pierre
Carew (with Rod Carew)
The DuSable Panthers
Maxwell Street
Beyond the Dream
Rockin' Steady (with Walt Frazier)
Oscar Robertson: The Golden Year

HOW LIFE IMITATES SPORTS

*A Sportswriter Recounts, Relives, and
Reckons with 50 Years on the Sports Beat*

IRA BERKOW

PULITZER PRIZE–WINNING JOURNALIST

Sports Publishing

Sports Publishing books may be purchased in bulk at special discounts for sales promotion, corporate gifts, fund-raising, or educational purposes. Special editions can also be created to specifications. For details, contact the Special Sales Department, Sports Publishing, 307 West 36th Street, 11th Floor, New York, NY 10018 or sportspubbooks@skyhorsepublishing.com.

Sports Publishing® is a registered trademark of Skyhorse Publishing, Inc.®, a Delaware corporation.

Visit our website at www.sportspubbooks.com.

10 9 8 7 6 5 4 3 2 1

Library of Congress Cataloging-in-Publication Data is available on file.

Cover design by 5mediadesign
Cover photographs courtesy of the author (main image: author with Oscar Robertson; top inset: author with Pete Rose; bottom inset: author with Archie Moore)

Print ISBN: 978-1-68358-379-0
Ebook ISBN: 978-1-68358-380-6

Printed in the United States of America

For Dolly, with Dolly knows what and Dolly knows why.

Table of Contents

Introduction

O n an airplane heading to Chicago, I was seated with Muhammad Ali, and working on a story about him. Just before takeoff, the flight attendant came by and said to the champ, "Mr. Ali, you have to put your seat belt on."

"Superman," Ali said, "don't need no seat belt."

"And Superman," she responded, "don't need no airplane, either."

The next sound heard was the click of Ali's seat belt being buckled.

One way or another, Ali was always either entertaining or the subject of news, from his conflict with the military to the Black Muslims to becoming an American icon, even celebrated by those who disdained him earlier on.

A number of his fights were classic encounters, often with cultural overtones. None more so than the first Ali-Joe Frazier fight on the night of March 8, 1971. Ali had not long before been exiled from his profession while still the world's heavyweight champion for his refusal to accept induction into the Army, but had won a unanimous decision from the United States Supreme Court, allowing him to return to the ring. In the three and a half years that he was away from the sport, Joe Frazier had been crowned the heavyweight champion. Ali was still a figure of opprobrium by many, while Frazier, a black man, was in a way viewed by some as a "White Hope" against Ali.

It was a remarkable night in Madison Square Garden. The arena was eagerly filled to capacity, with mink coats and diamond rings on pinkies in abundance in the good seats. Celebrities crowded in. Burt Lancaster was doing radio commentary, Frank Sinatra was leaning on the ring apron taking photographs for *Life* magazine.

The atmosphere was so electric that, earlier in the press room, Bill Cosby, then one of the most popular entertainers in the country, told a clutch of writers, "This is so exciting I wish it could go on forever."

Now I took my seat in the press area, second row from the ring itself. Then "Smokin' Joe" Frazier, stocky, powerfully built, but rather short for a heavyweight, climbed through the ropes and into the ring. Simple robe and trunks and boxing shoes. The working man's fighter. Few frills. In contrast, here came Ali, 6-foot-3, sleeker than Frazier, "pretty," as he self-proclaimed—in striking crimson robe and white boxing shoes with red tassels. The crowd erupted. The star of the show had come on stage. Under the bright lights, Ali bounced around in his corner and then began a little journey around the ring—and suddenly brushed up against Frazier, his back to Ali, in the far corner. It appeared that Ali threw a light, almost playful, jab at the back of Frazier's head. Frazier turned nastily, and it appeared the fight might break out right there. But the combatants did wait for the opening bell in order to pummel each other. It was a bruising fight, one for the ages, all stirring 15 rounds of it. (Frazier won by a decision.)

The event was one of many significant ones I was fortunate—indeed privileged—to cover in my 50-plus years as a sportswriter and columnist, first for the *Minneapolis Tribune* starting in 1965, then for the national feature syndicate, Newspaper Enterprise Association (750 newspaper clients), beginning in 1967, and then for *The New York Times*, beginning in 1981, until my retirement from the paper in 2007. I continue to freelance to the present.

I have covered most of the major sports events, from Super Bowls and World Series to the Olympics and March Madness and horse racing's Triple Crown, and most of the major individuals in those sports, as well as on occasion the offbeat, such as Abel Kiviat, at ninety-eight in 1991, the oldest living Olympic medal winner (a silver in a photo finish in the 1,500-meters in 1912) who, with failing eyesight, said he was seeking a companion. "She doesn't have to have teeth," he told me, "but just have to have a driver's license."

In the best of all possible worlds, the chapters in this volume comprise a part of the record of our times over this past half century, in terms of society, in terms of race and gender, in terms of politics, in terms of legal issues, and, last but perhaps not least, in terms of the fabric of our sports passions and human condition, ranging from pathos to humor, from introspection to perception.

These chapters depict some of the front-page sports events and the headline-making athletes of our time, in America and worldwide, from Ali to Jackie Robinson to O. J. Simpson to Pete Rose to Michael Jordan to Larry Bird to Jack Nicklaus to Nadia Comaneci to Tonya Harding and Billie Jean King to the tragic Munich Olympics to Arthur Ashe, LeBron James, Tiger Woods, and Roger Federer. And some who were headline makers in an earlier age—Jesse Owens, Red Grange, Joe Louis, Mark Spitz, Gordie Howe, Wilma Rudolph, Roger Bannister, Bill Shoemaker, Hank Greenberg, and Ted Williams.

I also include some lesser known athletes, such as the marathoner Kathy Spitzer and the drama that was played out with a knife at her throat while training, and a variety of sports beyond the most obvious, from discus throwing to gymnastics to pigeon racing in the midst of the NFL season. Each of the athletes—and the sports in which they participated—is portrayed from my on-the-scene reporting and then added and updated research and commentary. Some of it is personal, as in a memoir. It is hoped that these pieces not only embrace the reader's imagination, but also present each piece as a kind of historical document in the form of, essentially, nonfiction sports essays or short stories. The issues treated here are, in the author's view, both timely and timeless.

The events and the participants have shaped in a variety of significant ways how we as a nation have come to understand and perceive our culture and even our politics. They are a historical record of one significant sphere of our life and times—sports.

They are written by someone "who was there," having a ringside, or box, seat, as it were, both observing and, following, arriving at opinions, from when I began as a sportswriter with the *Minneapolis Tribune* in 1965 to Newspaper Enterprise Association from 1967 to 1976, followed by four-and-a-half years of freelancing and book writing, then from 1981 to 2007 writing on the staff of *The New York Times*, and followed, once again, by freelancing and book writing. The hope is that the reader, in a true sense, has for all these 50-plus years taken a seat beside me in the press box, or stood with me on the sidelines, or together shared a meal, as depicted in some of the pieces contained in the book, with Jackie Robinson or Joe Namath or Katarina Witt or Martina Navratilova, or was a teammate of Oscar Robertson's and when we played a pickup full-court basketball game in a Cincinnati YMCA together. And then you had to meet a deadline.

The title of the book, *How Life Imitates Sports*, is derived from that very fact, as I see it, have seen it and have experienced it. That is, we often can look into the mirror of sports and see ourselves in our daily non-athletic lives. We certainly seek pleasure in recreation, sports or otherwise, and I had hoped to portray that part of it in my work as a sports journalist. But I sought to include another, enduring aspect. How, for example, to attain and handle success, how to handle failure, how not to handle each, in 60 minutes of a football game, in nine innings of a baseball game, in a season, in a career and, to be sure, in the hurdles—variously, but surely as night follows day—met.

I believe that something the great sportswriter Red Smith once said continues to apply, and in the best of all possible worlds I tried to apply it: "Sports is not really a play world," Smith said. "I think it's the real world. The people we're writing about in professional sports, they're suffering and living and dying and loving and trying to make their way through life just as the bricklayers and politicians are.

"This may sound defensive—I don't think it is—but I'm aware that games are a part of every culture we know anything about. And often taken seriously. It's no accident that of all the monuments left of the Greco-Roman culture, the biggest is the ball park, the Colosseum, the Yankee Stadium of ancient times. The man who reports on these games contributes his small bit to the record of his time."

Of course, the title of this book could be the other way around, *How Sports Imitates Life*, but then it would undoubtedly be the same thing.

Part I: One of a Kind—Every One of Them

There are moments in all lives, some brief, some longer, or even much longer, that transform the way we live and think. Sports, being an indisputable part of life, inevitably takes its place among such moments. Following are some of those times, and the people who inspired them:

They Changed the Game

Jackie Robinson: He Led the Way

On a crisp, sunny fall afternoon, October 15, 1972, in sold-out Riverfront Stadium in Cincinnati, Jackie Robinson, at fifty-three, looking greatly older than his years—it was as if the man had lived several lifetimes in one, and in fact one could argue at that point that he had—was scheduled to throw out the ceremonial first ball to begin the second game of the World Series between the Oakland A's and the Cincinnati Reds.

The honor was to commemorate the 25th anniversary of Robinson's entrance into major-league baseball (at age twenty-eight, a relatively late age for a rookie), when, against almost inhuman obstacles—race baiting, pitches thrown at his head, intentionally spiked on the basepaths, 15 out of the 16 team owners voting to ban him (Branch Rickey, the Dodgers owner, was the one vote for him)—he alone broke the reprehensible color barrier that had prevented blacks from playing with whites on professional ball fields from coast to coast in America, the land of the free.

The dashing, pigeon-toed Jackie Robinson, the electrifying home-base stealing Jackie Robinson (he indeed stole home 19 times in his 10-year major-league career as a Brooklyn Dodger), the power-hitting, slick-fielding Jackie Robinson was no longer in sight—both from a viewer's standpoint, as well as his own. White-haired now—it seemed prematurely white—heavier in blue blazer and light-colored pants than one remembered him in his playing days, he had gone blind in one eye and was losing sight in his other eye, both due to diabetes. A few years earlier he had survived a heart attack.

Several months before that I had spoken with Satchel Paige, ancient at an indeterminate age, and he said, "Have you seen Jackie lately? His hair's white and you'd think he was my grandfather."

I remember Robinson that day in Cincinnati standing near the batting cage before that World Series game, and talking to reporters, of which I was one. I remember someone handing him a baseball to autograph and, in that unexpectedly high voice for so great a distinguished athlete, he said, "I'm sorry. I can't see it."

I remember a description of a ball he *did* see, against great odds. It was the bottom of the 12th inning of a game against the Phillies in Philadelphia on the last day of the season in 1951—the Dodgers had to win to preserve a tie with the New York Giants to gain the playoffs. In a tie game, with men on base, Phillies first baseman Eddie Waitkus smashed a line drive to the right of second base. The game would be over if the ball lands safely in center field. "The ball is a blur passing second base," wrote columnist Red Smith of the *New York Herald-Tribune*, "difficult to follow in the half light, impossible to catch, Jackie Robinson catches it. He flings himself headlong at right angles to the flight of the ball, for an instant his body is suspended in midair, then somehow the outstretched glove intercepts the ball inches off the ground. Stretched at full length in the insubstantial twilight, the unconquerable doing the impossible." Two innings later, Robinson hit a towering home run to left field that put the Dodgers ahead to stay.

Soon, in Cincinnati, Robinson and his family were out onto the field with Bowie Kuhn. Near home plate, the baseball commissioner presented Robinson, now a Hall of Famer, with a plaque for his stunning achievement of breaking the color barrier a quarter of a century earlier. Robinson, holding the plaque and, true to his courageous and combative nature and continuing civil rights activism, said into the microphone, "I'm extremely proud and pleased." He paused. "But I'm going to be tremendously more pleased and more proud when I look at that third-base coaching line one day and see a black managing in baseball."

At the time, no black had ever managed a big-league club. (Two years later, in 1974, Frank Robinson, no relation, became the first black manager, hired by the Cleveland Indians.) Then Jackie Robinson, unsteadily it seemed to me, walked off the Riverfront Stadium field. (It was later learned that the diabetes had affected his legs to the extent that he was facing a double amputation.) A few minutes later, from his front-row seat before the start of the World Series game, the aging second baseman tossed out the ceremonial first pitch to Reds catcher Johnny Bench, releasing the ball with as much natural grace as in his playing days when he'd thrown out a runner at first base.

Nine days later Jackie Roosevelt Robinson was dead. He had suffered a heart attack in his home in Stamford, Connecticut.

Five days later, on October 29, I along with some 2,500 people— from old Dodgers teammates like Roy Campanella in a wheelchair to Henry Aaron to Joe Louis to Bill Russell to civil rights leader A. Philip Randolph to future Vice President Nelson Rockefeller—attended the funeral for Robinson at the Riverside Church on the Upper West Side of Manhattan. I sat in the balcony, not far from the Oakland A's pitcher

Vida Blue—the only active major-league player that attended Robinson's funeral, as far as I could see. It was striking to me that in this offseason, in late October, more current black players didn't show up (and some, like St. Louis Cardinals outfielder Vince Coleman, some twenty years later, when asked about Robinson, said, "I don't know nothin' about no Jackie Robinson.")

We heard the Reverend Jesse Jackson deliver a moving eulogy that rang through the great vaulted cathedral. Jackson compared Robinson to Louis Pasteur and Gandhi and Martin Luther King and Jesus, as a man who gave others hope by example. "No grave can hold his body down," Jackson concluded. "It belongs to the ages. His spirit is perpetual. And we are all better because a man with a mission passed our way."

Four years earlier, in 1968, I met Jackie Robinson for the first time. I was then a sports columnist for the national newspaper syndicate Newspaper Enterprise Association. I had arranged a lunch date with him, and that afternoon I came by his midtown Manhattan office. He was then a vice president of Chock Full o' Nuts, a popular chain of coffee shops. He was on the phone, legs up on his desk, talking to some friend about a celebrity golf event to which, that year, he had not been invited. Robinson had gone to several previous tournaments in the series.

Robinson asked the friend to find out why there was no invitation. Did it have anything to do with some of his recent controversial remarks about "racism in America?" "We'll give it a good fight," Robinson said, with a smile. He had the shaft of his glasses in his teeth. Jackie Robinson, it seemed to me, *enjoyed* the fight—or at minimum wished to confront an apparent racial slight. Even then, at age forty-nine, with that wide variety of illnesses and, at home, dealing with the drug addiction of his son, Jackie Jr., he remained a staunch advocate.

I told Robinson that day that I had recently been in Chicago and had talked casually with a black shoeshine boy in his early teens. I asked who his favorite baseball player was.

"Ernie Banks," the bootblack said. "Willie Mays, too. Yeah, I wanna be a ballplayer, like him."

I asked the fellow if he wanted to be a ballplayer like Jackie Robinson, too?

"Who?" he asked, seriously. "Never heard of him."

This was neither sad nor surprising to Robinson. He dealt in realities.

"It's true that many black kids have never heard of me," he said. "But they haven't heard of the Montgomery bus boycott in 1956, either. And that was the beginning of Dr. King's nonviolent movement. They don't get any kind of black history in their books. They want it. They read only about white society. They're made to feel like nonpersons. This is frustrating. It's up to the power structure of this country to understand these kids. Then the burnings, the muggings, the dope, the despair, much of what plagues this country will be lessened.

"Black athletes playing today carry prestige. They can be very significant in explaining the problems and encouraging the kids. But I've been out of baseball for twelve years. The kids look at me like I'm an old-timer."

What is often overlooked is that "the old-timer" was perhaps the greatest all-around athlete in organized sports in American history, "the Jim Thorpe of his race," according to the sportswriter Vincent X. Flaherty. In *Baseball's Great Experiment: Jackie Robinson and His Legacy* by Jules Tygiel, Tygiel wrote:

> In 1940 and 1941, after transferring to UCLA from a junior college, [Robinson] emerged as the school's first four-letter man, starring in football, basketball, track and baseball. Twice he led the Pacific Coast Conference in scoring, leading one coach to call him "the best basketball player in the United States." (He also was a standout later in the West

Coast professional basketball league.) In his junior year, he averaged eleven yards a carry in football. "He is probably the greatest ball carrier on the gridiron today," wrote Maxwell Stiles in *Sports Weekly*. Robinson, who held the national junior college broad jump record, was the NCAA champion in that event in 1940. (Because of the war raging in Europe, the Olympic Games were cancelled and so Robinson was denied the chance for an Olympic medal, unlike his older brother, Mack Robinson, who won a silver medal in the 1936 Berlin Olympics, breaking the 200 meter world record but still finishing second to Jesse Owens.) During his college years, baseball was one of Jackie's lesser sports . . .

Robinson had not confined his competitive fires to the major college sports. All athletic events came within his realm. He tried his hand at golf and won the Pacific Coast intercollegiate golf championship; he won swimming championships at UCLA; in tennis he reached the semifinals of the national Negro tournament. It is probable that no other athlete, including Jim Thorpe, has ever competed as effectively in as broad a range of sports.

Pee Wee Reese once told me that in ping-pong competition among the Brooklyn Dodgers players in spring training, among these outstanding professional athletes, Robinson was the undisputed champion.

It is little remembered that, as he battled racial prejudice in breaking the color barrier in Organized Baseball, he did so while at the same time having to master three different positions on the field. Playing for Kansas City in the Negro Leagues, Robinson was a shortstop. When in 1946 he joined the Triple A Montreal Royals in the International League—the first black to play in that league—he had to play second base because the team had an established shortstop, Al Campanis. He then led Montreal to IL championship, and led the league in batting at .349 as well as stolen bases with 40.

The next season he moved up to the Dodgers and was also required to play first base, since the Dodgers had the double-play combination of Pee Wee Reese at short and Eddie Stanky at second.

There had been resistance from some of the white players, especially those from the South, about having to play with a black man. But they relented. "Players are concerned with money and with winning," Robinson told me. "Do you know who the first player on the Dodgers was to give me tips? Dixie Walker—from Birmingham, Alabama! And he had been the staunchest opponent to my joining the Dodgers. I'll never forget that first time. It was early in the season of my rookie year. We were in Boston. I was on the rubbing table and Walker came over and started telling me the best way to hit behind the runner with no outs and a man on second base."

Robinson was named Rookie of the Year with a .297 batting average and led the league with 29 stolen bases, and the Dodgers won the National League pennant. When Stanky was traded to the Boston Braves in 1948, Robinson became the team's second baseman. (In later years, Robinson also played third base, shortstop, and left field for the Dodgers.)

In 1949, he again led the Dodgers to the league pennant and was named the National League's Most Valuable Player, with a league-leading .342 batting average and a major-league-leading 37 stolen bases.

While that black teenage shoeshiner in Chicago in 1968 had never heard of Jackie Robinson, others, to be sure, had. One of them was the future major-league third baseman Ed Charles.

"I owe so much to Jackie Robinson," Charles once told me. "All black players do. We tend to forget. I never will. When Jackie Robinson came through my hometown with the Dodgers in 1947, it was the biggest day of my life. It was the biggest day of all our lives."

Charles was a thirteen-year-old boy living in Daytona Beach, where discrimination in the state was rife, and lynching of blacks still occurred (the last one recorded in Florida was in nearby Orange County, in 1951).

"Seeing Jackie," Charles continued, "I realized that it was possible that I could play in the major leagues. They pushed the old people to the ballpark in wheelchairs and some came on crutches and a few blind people were led to the park.

"When it was over, we chased the Dodger train as far as we could with Robinson waving to us from the back. We ran until we couldn't hear the sound any more. We were exhausted but we were never so happy."

* * *

In my mind's eye, going back to when I was fifteen years old, in 1955, I can still vividly see Jackie Robinson in that dramatic, base-daring style of his—arms flapping, feet dancing—challenging the Yankees' rookie left fielder, the first black Yankee, Elston Howard. I had skipped school that afternoon—I was a sophomore at Sullivan High School on the North Side of Chicago—to watch on television the Brooklyn Dodgers and New York Yankees in a World Series game.

Robinson, in my recollection, had taken a wide turn after rounding second base—I didn't remember how he had arrived there, but I assumed over the years that he had gotten to first base on a hit or walk or error and then advanced from first on a teammate's base hit to left.

I had never written the story, nor spoken about it on television or in radio interviews, until my appearance on a show on the Major League Baseball network, in 2018. In conversation at one point the television host, Brian Kenny, asked me about Jackie Robinson. I mentioned that

'55 Series moment and set the scene for him, to the best of my memory, though I didn't remember exactly in which game it occurred.

"Jackie had rounded second and gone about halfway down the basepath between second and third, as I remember it," I said. "And then he turned toward Howard and seemed to be saying, 'Okay, you're here because I opened a door for you, now you're on your own. It's the big leagues. Which base are you going to throw to?' Time stood still. And then in my mind's eye I see Robinson making a shoulder move to second base. Howard throws to second to erase a surely sliding Robinson—but no, Robinson trots into third standing up. He had faked poor Howard out. Or so I remembered." In hindsight, Robinson was certainly aware that Howard was primarily a catcher, but Yogi Berra was still behind the plate for the Yankees and Yankees manager Casey Stengel wanted both their bats in the lineup, so he put Howard in the fairly, for him, unfamiliar outfield position.

Robinson, then at age thirty-six, and in the penultimate season of his remarkable career that not only saw him break the color barrier in the major leagues but also play so spectacularly that he was elected to the National Baseball Hall of Fame, was yet a force on the basepaths. Indeed, in that Series he even stole home, off Whitey Ford, despite the hopping-mad protest to the umpire by Berra that he was tagged out.

Robinson retired from baseball after the 1956 season. Some twelve years later, now a sports columnist for Newspaper Enterprise Association, a national feature syndicate, I had lunch with Robinson. I was eager to recall that moment that I had, well, recalled.

After explaining it all to him, complete with my theory, he gave it some thought. "I don't remember it that way," he said, rather graciously. "I most likely would not have been thinking about any historical aspect at that moment. All I'd be thinking about was getting the extra base."

Well, sure, ever the competitor. However, I still liked my version of it. Yet following my appearance on *MLB Now*, I even wondered if I had only imagined that Robinson had tricked the outfield novice Howard. Stengel used to say about a point he was making, "You could look it up." And so, after sixty-two years, I sought to "look it up."

The 1955 World Series went the full seven games. The first game was on Wednesday, September 28, in Yankee Stadium. And the two teams, in this subway series, played on seven consecutive days. So I wouldn't have to check the two weekend games, when I was legitimately home from school.

I Googled the Game One box score and play-by-play, which had an insertion after each at-bat with "play description": Robinson got one hit in four at-bats, but scored two runs (one was the steal of home). The hit was a triple. Could this be what I was remembering? Somehow I didn't think so—the play I was exploring didn't *seem* like a triple. Turns out Robinson also got to second base on an error, but stopped there because the runner ahead of him, Carl Furillo, stopped at third. So that wasn't it.

Game Two, at Yankee Stadium: Robinson 0-for-2, but with one walk. Following the walk, he went to second on a single by Don Zimmer. So that wasn't it.

Game Three, at Ebbets Field: Robinson goes 2-for-5. In the second inning, Robinson singles. Goes to second when Sandy Amoros is hit by a pitch. So that wasn't it. Meanwhile, Howard had started this game in right field, but switched to left in the second inning.

And then . . . ! After Gil Hodges flied out to lead off the bottom of the seventh inning, with the Dodgers ahead 6–3, and behind in the Series, two games to none, the play description, with Tom Sturdivant pitching, reads for "Robinson": "Double to LF; Robinson to 3B/Adv. on throw to 2B." Below, in an "Explanation" of the play-by-plays, it reads: "Advancement of baserunners is given in cases where advancement is not easily deduced or obvious from the play."

And so it happened, perhaps not in the way I had conjured the silent challenge of Robinson, but he indeed had faked out the young left fielder Howard. The Dodgers went on to win their first ever World Series, and Howard went on to play 13 outstanding seasons with the Yankees, becoming the regular catcher in 1960, and making nine American League All-Star teams overall.

While some things are lost in the mists of time and memory, some things unaccountably and indelibly remain. Fast forward to the present: I recently phoned someone about a matter and the fellow said he'd have to call me back. He asked for my number. It took me a few moments to remember it.

In 1962, Jackie Robinson became the first African American elected to the National Baseball Hall of Fame in Cooperstown, New York, with a lifetime batting average of .311. In 1997, on the 70th anniversary of Robinson's breaking the color barrier, the number 42 that he wore with the Dodgers was retired across Major League Baseball and remains the only jersey number retired across the league.

"I have often stated that baseball's proudest moment and its most powerful social statement came on April 15, 1947 when Jackie Robinson first set foot on a Major League Baseball field," said former MLB commissioner Bud Selig upon establishing the "42" jersey tradition. "On that day, Jackie brought down the color barrier and ushered in the era in which baseball became the true national pastime."

Billie Jean King, Bobby Riggs, and Chris Evert: The Unexpected

It was difficult for many of us, I believe—by "us" I include myself first and foremost—to fathom the significance early on of the tennis match between Billie Jean King and Bobby Riggs, in relation to who we were as a nation on gender equality and gender status. So what if a woman could beat a guy at a game? And so what if the guy could beat her? How wrong I was. And this coming from a writer—me—who a few years earlier had joked in print about "female jocks" playing softball seriously. I would now look into who these two people, King and Riggs, were, what their intentions and motivations were, and what, eventually, was the meaning of their truly historic meeting, dubbed "The Battle of the Sexes," in all its flamboyant pageantry.

Billie Jean King: A Model for Our Times

October 11, 1974

Buoyantly, Billie Jean Moffitt King said, "These are great times for women, and getting greater. We're gaining more acceptance and appreciation and opportunity. Five years from now it will be changed even more drastically, and girls being born now—wow! It's thrilling for me to know that I was at the beginning of it."

And then this historic personage, this heroine of the women's movement, this Joan of Arc in Adidas, wagged her head and stuck out Her tongue, not in petulance, to be sure, but in, like wow!

Billie Jean King has seemingly few airs. She reminds one of something Muhammad Ali recently said, "No, I don't pass through life. Life passes through me." Passivity is not her niche. Nor is demureness. She has, however, been blessed with gusto.

With her tennis racket the symbolic axe, she busted barriers the way Carrie Nation pummeled Demon Rum.

Billie Jean King, recent US Open women's champ—and number one in the world for five years up to now, starting in 1966, as well as winner of each of the four Grand Slams, a few on numerous occasions—fought to get women equal tournament money with men players. Her battle against the hypocrisy of amateur tennis resulted in part in the successful tennis tour. Her earnings of $100,000 (the first woman athlete to reach this peak) established women in this capitalistic society as serious athletes, as never before. She was one of the leaders of the revolutionary conception, World Team Tennis. She helped finance a new magazine, *WomenSports*.

The twenty-nine-year-old, 5-foot-4 ½, 130-pound Billie Jean King proved an inspiration to many women in all this, but nothing was more exulting or more important in her crusade-of-sorts than that zany, carny night when she beat the baggy pants off Bobby Riggs, in three sets.

The impact was enormous. The next day, for example, some women reportedly stalked into their boss' office demanding raises in pay, after Billie Jean King had in fact raised their own self-esteem.

Her Riggs match, $100,000 winner-take-all, was played on the night of September 20, 1972, in the Houston Astrodome, before 30,472 in the stands and an estimated 90 million more watching on national television.

Her short dark hair matted with sweat, her eyeglasses agleam, her sleeveless white-and-blue tennis dress and blue tennis shoes sometimes a blur, King's one-sided victory was so sensational that, one year later, it remained a topic of conversation. And few remember that only four months earlier, on Mother's Day yet, the spindly, thickly sideburned showman, the fifty-five-year-old, years-ago US Open and Wimbledon champ Riggs, viewing the court through thick glasses, solidly whipped a nervous Margaret Court—one of the two great tennis players of her time, along with King—and won, temporarily at least, his pseudo-argument for Male Chauvinism (and Riggs's Pigs, as he called his followers).

"When I saw that Court match, I went bananas," said Billie Jean, sitting recently in the lounge of a New York tennis club. "Right then and there I said, 'That's it. I've got to play him.'"

Women now approach her on the street and tell her what she has meant to their self-image.

It is a strange posture for her—one which she likes and dislikes. She says she has few friends on the tour itself. Fellow players, she believes, are often envious of her success and publicity and riches. (She recalls one of them saying to her, "Billie Jean, you're overpaid.")

She admits to selfishness. Where Billie Jean was a teenage prodigy, in fact, Maureen Connolly, a great tennis player as well, "blasted me for thinking too much of myself."

King, however, says that tennis is an individualistic game, and to become Number One—and then to defend that position—takes a staunch and healthy ego.

"I'm a realist," she said, adjusting her aviatrix glasses while the thin silver and gold bracelets on her strong left arm jangle. "Or I try to be a realist. I know what it takes to get to the top, to try to fulfill my dreams. Some women take me for a role model. I think that's good, if taken in the right way. I mean, if they try to be a tennis champion without a lot of ability, that's not good.

"But if they try to do the best they can at what they are interested in, and enjoy themselves while doing it, that's terrific."

Role models, she believes, are important. She said that she had no women models growing up in Long Beach, California. "I wanted to be an athlete," she said. "People put it down. And the only hero I had was Mickey Mantle, whose averages I used to figure out. But really, the media never gave women much coverage. And when they did write about women athletes, it was condescending. They'd write about how cute they looked."

Strange how times change. Now, some write that Billie Jean is "beautiful." But in the 1970s, that word does not necessarily have to do with looks. It's how, with quickness and skill and spirit and, yes, that fierce backhand, she appears wielding a racquet on the tennis court.

* * *

Some eight years later I met with Bobby Riggs, who remembered the match in detail.

Bobby Riggs Sees Double

July 27, 1982 / South Orange, New Jersey

No knight errant, Bobby Riggs, at age sixty-four, still seems the enfant terrible. The conqueror of Margaret Court and the victim of Billie Jean King—in the two mixed-sexes matches of nearly a decade ago that gave him, as he says, "instant celebrity"—Riggs remains on the prowl for a new hustle. And he has one. He calls it a "godfather deal," so compelling it can't be refused.

Riggs, his thick glasses sparkling in the sunlight so one couldn't quite see his eyes, was talking about it at the Orange Lawn Tennis Club in South Orange, New Jersey, where he competed recently in the Almaden Grand Masters tournament. He was a symphony in yellow, wearing yellow shorts, yellow-orange bleached hair coiffed like Dennis the Menace, and a yellow jacket with "Sugar Daddy" on the back.

It was the same jacket he wore on September 20, 1973, when he rode into the Houston Astrodome in a chariot to meet Billie Jean King in a modern-day Roman spectacle that brought 30,000-plus people into the arena and 90 million more to their television sets around the world. They watched the professed world's greatest male chauvinist—he called himself "Jane L. Sullivan" after beating Margaret Court five months before—play the leading feminist athlete.

He presented Billie Jean with a giant "Sugar Daddy" lollipop, and she responded by giving him a piglet, and a whipping in three straight sets.

"I'm thinking doubles now," said Riggs. "A challenge match with Pancho Segura and me—we're a combined age of 125—against the winners of the women's US Open doubles in September. It would probably be Martina Navratilova and Pam Shriver, they won Wimbledon.

"I think the TV networks will go for it big, and I'm sure sponsors will. It's up to the girls. They'd make $50,000 to $100,000 apiece. Right now, they get $7,500 for winning in doubles. Pretty tempting, isn't it?"

Flim-flam man extraordinaire, Riggs has a knack for making deals appealing. He has played opponents while carrying a bucket of water, wearing divers' flippers, putting park benches on his side of the court, and teaming up with such peculiar partners as an elephant, a donkey and a lion. He had to hold them all on a leash while playing. He said the donkey was the most difficult; it balked at following him. The lion—a one-year-old cub—was the best: Riggs threatened that if his opponent came to the net, he'd unleash the beast.

Generally, he won. Despite his age, he remains a very fine tennis player. He twice won the US National in 1939 and 1941, and also won Wimbledon in '39. He turned pro and was outstanding. When Big Bill Tilden, the great player of the 1920s, was asked who he thought was the best modern player, he said simply, "Riggs." Today, Riggs, who doesn't quite cover the court the way he once did, is the defending titleholder in the over-sixty clay-court division.

"But wherever I go, the thing people are always bringing up is my match against Billie Jean King" he said. He was beaten decisively, 6–4, 6–3, 6–3. "It was meant to be fun, but it also had its dramatic side. Women were angry that I had beaten Margaret. I got a lot of hate letters. I couldn't hardly get a date. The women's liberation movement was growing and it was embarassing, a fifty-five-year-old man beating one of their star players.

"Women were struggling for equal pay, in offices and in the tennis tournaments. And Billie Jean was the leader in tennis. So she accepted my challenge and came to the rescue for the sake of the crusade.

"I have to admit, I underestimated Billie Jean and overestimated myself. I was embarrassed and shocked.

"But I think that it helped give women's tennis credibility—Billie Jean beats a former men's world champion, and our match contributed to women's prize money going up. It generated greater interest in tennis. More people started playing it.

"Now girls saw me and thought I was great, a good sport, and they ran their hands through my hair and invited me home for chicken dinner.

"But some guys were mad. They felt I had disgraced them, that I had disgraced the cause of men, and especially older guys—the over-the-hill gang. Some even accused me of throwing the match. Throwing it! I had expected to make it an annual affair, by beating the women's champion for the next five years or so, until I got so old one of them could beat me. Losing cost me money. Sure, I made $1.5 million on the match—after endorsements, personal appearances and TV rights—but I might've made more."

Riggs believes he has another chance at a financial boon with the mixed-sexes doubles offer. Will it be accepted?

"It all depends if the girls think it'll help the cause or not," he said.

For Riggs, meanwhile, the beat of the hustle goes on. It recalls the song of mehitabel the cat in Don Marquis's lower-case poem, "archy and mehitabel." "toujours gai, toujours gai" she crooned, "there's a dance in the old dame yet."

* * *

Two years before the Riggs match, King competed in the US Open and met young Chris Evert in the semis. It was the first time I had seen Evert play. And three years later I recalled that event—when the tennis world learned "officially" that a star was surely on the horizon, or, as Evert would say, "It was my 'coming-out party' on the national stage."

Chris Evert's Rite of Passage

October 11, 1974

It was inconceivable on that pleasant late summer afternoon that this sixteen-year-old girl, her blond hair caught in a white ribbon, wearing a demure white dress on her slim frame, and walking with head modestly bowed as the 15,000 fans in the West Side tennis club applauded her entrance to center court—it was inconceivable then that Chrissie Evert could ever be booed.

Three years later she was booed.

Chrissie Evert is no longer the sweetheart of America. She is a competitor, a corporation, a pro.

Three years ago, she came out of relative obscurity, unseeded, to reach the semifinals of the US Open at Forest Hills. And when she emerged onto the center court to play the Queen Bee, Billie Jean King, at twenty-seven, and a former Open champ, the kid was easily the sentimental favorite.

Evert was still an amateur, a high-school junior. She had a peculiar two-handed backhand. She did not rush the net, but patiently stayed back at the baseline and allowed her opponent to make the mistake. "Just darling," was a phrase not infrequently heard about her.

Something else was demonstrated by Chrissie under those evenly overcast skies that September afternoon three years ago. Chrissie Evert had a killer instinct. She lost to Billie Jean, 6–3, 6–2, but everyone knew she'd be back.

King saw that Evert represented the future of women's tennis. "You are riding the crest of a wave," King told her afterward. Evert wasn't sure what she mean at that time, but learned. She also learned a lesson from King. "All she did was chop, slice and drop shot to throw me off my game. She knew I needed to get into a rhythm. So she just chopped me up; she didn't even play her game. She was a master."

Much has changed for Evert now that she is nineteen, now a pro for two years. She is engaged to the redoubtable Jimmy Connors, the Wimbledon and US champion. He is a fervent competitor, too, but much more demonstrative. He shouts, spins and flies into rages; sometimes he will even pull his Page Boy hairdo in anguish.

Chrissie, on the other hand, is brilliant in a mechanical way. She has in fact been labeled, "The Ice Maiden."

Once, she declined $60,000 in prize money to maintain her amateur status. Now, she had earned $150,000 in winning 55-straight matches this year, including winning Wimbledon and the French Open, up to this Forest Hills semifinals.

As a corporate entity, she receives a reported $100,000 a year from a manufacturer of tennis clothes. The manufacturer owns race horses, one named Chris Evert. It's a championship horse, too.

Perhaps all this success has soured some fans, for when, in a rare moment, she grimaced at a questionable call in the quarterfinals at Forest Hills, she was booed.

"I've noticed," she said, "that in the last few weeks the crowd roots for the underdog."

Or they boo those with whom they have become disenchanted, those who have unwittingly sullied the stuff of which the fans' dream has been fabricated.

She isn't above accepting prize money and forsaking college to travel around the world as a tennis pro. She is turning into a woman, full of all the foibles—and glories—that make up a human being.

She is an athlete of the first order, to be sure. She demonstrated this above all question in her first US Open semifinal match this year against another former Open champion Evonne Goolagong, again at center court in Forest Hills. Chris had lost the first 6–0, and was losing in the second (of best of three) 4–3, Goolagong serving when rain postponed the match.

It rained the next day. Now, on a sunny Sunday noon, the pair met again. With her careful, cool presence, Evert came back tenaciously to win the second set, 7–6.

In the third set, the fans began slowly to cheer her pluck. Evert the corporation, the betrayer of lame dreams, was deserving once again of their admiration—if not their undying love, as in days of romantic yore.

In the shade of the marquee, Pancho Segura, the white-haired old tennis great, said, "Chris is such a tough competitor you can tell because she is so patient."

Goolagong was tough today, too. Four times she had Chris at match point, four times Evert wriggled out. "Evonne didn't lose those points," said Segura."Chris won them."

Evert did not win the fifth match point, however. Chris came off the court, her blond ponytail in a white ribbon, her white dress spotless, her tan legs smooth with the glint of sweat—and she was warmly applauded, just as she had been after losing to Billie Jean King in the semifinals three years ago.

But that was when Evert was a mere girl of sixteen, a hundred years ago.

* * *

Despite the Open loss to Goolagong (King beat Goolagong in the finals), Evert would receive a Number One ranking in 1974 and stay at the top for the next six of seven years. She would win 21 Grand Slams in her career, 18 singles, including four straight US Opens, and three doubles. She retired in 1989, at forty-one. Though married three times, Jimmy

Connors was not one of her husbands. King won 39 Grand Slams—12 singles, 16 doubles, and 11 mixed doubles. She retired from singles competition in 1984, and doubles in 1990, at forty-six. Head-to-head King beat Evert the first three times they met in major competition, 1971 to 1975, but lost from there on, 10 times, ending in 1983. King divorced her husband, Larry King. She announced that she had a relationship with a woman. Her partner is Ilana Kloss. Riggs continued to enjoy the game and the hustle virtually until his death in 1995 at age seventy-seven.

Nadia Comaneci: Gold-Medal Gymnast, Worldwide Heartthrob, Courageous Defector

It was March 5, 1999, and I had been invited as a sports reporter to the White House for the premiere showing of an HBO documentary, *Dare to Compete: The Struggle of Women in Sports*, about female athletes who reached extraordinary heights in their individual sports. A number of the women who were featured in the film had been invited to attend the showing in the East Room with a buffet dinner in the State Dining Room to follow. I was standing near the entrance and was able to identify some of the women, from tennis champion Billie Jean King to basketball star Lisa Leslie to skater Dorothy Hamill.

Then in walked a very attractive brunette in a short gray dress and red pumps who I assumed was a movie actress invited simply as a guest. I was wrong. It was Nadia Comaneci, looking nothing like I had first seen her, in 1976, twenty-three years before, a 4-foot-11, slight as a ragdoll, fourteen-year-old Rumanian with soulful eyes (she still had those arresting eyes but she had grown to 5-foot-4) who stunned the world at the Montreal Olympics by registering unheard of 10s, or perfect scores—seven of them—swirling through the air on the uneven bars, the balance beam, and flipping and floating through the floor exercise, to win three gold medals.

She accomplished what was considered an impossible human feat—that kind of athletic "perfection." It was reminiscent of the "impossible feats" of Roger Bannister breaking the four-minute mile in 1954 (3:59.4 to be exact), and Bob Beamon leaping 29-2½ feet in the broad jump in the 1968 Mexico Olympics to break a record by an amazing 21½ inches, nearly two feet, or Johnny Vander Meer in June of 1938 pitching back-to-back no-hitters for the Cincinnati Reds, the first against the Boston Braves and the second, four days later, against the Brooklyn Dodgers. (Bannister's record has since been broken, but neither Beamon's nor Vander Meer's have.) Never before had a gymnast recorded a perfect 10, and the Omega SA—the traditional Olympics scoreboard manufacturer—had apparently been told that a perfect 10 was impossible, so the scoreboard was not programmed to display it. When Comaneci received a 10 the scoreboard read "1.00," the only means by which the judges could indicate that crazy score.

Comaneci at the White House now was thirty-seven years old, and a woman, fit, and no longer, to be sure, the teenager I had last seen when, at age nineteen in 1981, she had come to Madison Square Garden on an exhibition tour of Rumanian gymnasts. She was making that transition from a kid, regardless how decidedly acrobatic, to a young woman. Her lithe body, still slender, was now endowed with graceful feminine curves, yet her arms and hands were still strong enough to grasp the equipment bars with authority. When we met at the Garden and I shook her hand I was struck by the odd contrast of her carefully red-polished fingernails with the hard calluses on her palms.

I remember asking her at that time about her social life. "No special boyfriend," she said. "I have many friends—boyfriends and girlfriends." Boys, though, intrigued her even in Montreal. At that time, she was asked who her favorite actor was. "Alain Delon," she said, without hesitation. I asked her if, five years later, the French actor was still her hero. She scrunched her nose, apparently suggesting such things were for starry-eyed little girls. "No," she said. "It's Robert Redford."

At the White House, her answer to that question would be Bart Conner, the former Olympic gymnast and now her husband, and father of their son, Dylan. She was living in Oklahoma City where she and Conner ran a gymnastics school. It was ten years after her defection from Rumania, and the Communist-run authoritarianism that, she said, "I started to feel like a prisoner" in her own country—the government fearful of her possible defection of their world-renowned celebrity and thus keeping a careful and suppressive eye on her. On the night of November 27, 1989, she and a handful of other young Rumanians embarked on a dangerous overland journey (mostly on foot and at night) that took her through Hungary, Austria, and finally to the United States. She became a naturalized US citizen in 2001 but retains dual citizenship with Rumania.

I covered both the 1972 Munich Olympics and the one in Montreal four years later. And for me, the Comaneci story began in 1972 with the saga of the Soviet Union's Olga Korbut, who in 1972, at 4-foot-11, 86 pounds, and dubbed "The Sparrow of Minsk," was nearly as mesmerizing a gold-medal-winning gymnast as Comaneci would become. "It was amazing," Korbut had said. "One day I was a nobody and the next I was a star." And yet Korbut's star would swiftly diminish four years later, thanks in no small part to Comaneci's transcendence on the last days of July.

* * *

"No, I have no plans absolutely to retire," Korbut said, in the interview room of the Montreal Forum at the '76 Olympics. The Russian gymnast said this with conviction and a smile after what may have appeared a most distressing event for her. She had been outpointed and outshined in what was nearly head-to-head competition with Comaneci, who, at fourteen, was then seven years Korbut's junior. Korbut came in second to Comaneci in the balance beam, and fifth to her in the individual all-around. And now Comaneci, with her unparalleled excellence, was the newly crowned princess, the heroine, the all-around international sports heartthrob as suddenly as Korbut had been four years before in Munich when she won three gold medals (in the balance beam and the floor exercises, as well as in team competition) and a silver (in the uneven bars) in a thrilling and daring performance of somersaults, spins and twists. Her precision and strength seemed incredible for that thin, tiny, pigtailed blonde. Suddenly, Olga was in Nadia's shadow.

I remember when Korbut appeared with the Russian team at Madison Square Garden in the winter before the '76 Olympics, Korbut was introduced as "the most beloved athlete in the world." If it wasn't wholly so, it was too close to quibble.

Something obviously had changed in that dramatic night in Montreal, the final of the two-day women's team gymnastics competition. Four teams of six girls from Hungary, East Germany, Russia and Rumania competed in four events, rotating after each team completed its turn on the balance beam, the vault, the floor exercise and the uneven bars.

Although there were twenty-four of the best women gymnasts on the same brightly lighted floor of the Montreal Forum, the capacity crowds of 18,000—as fervent as sellout crowds for the hometown Montreal Canadiens National Hockey League games played there—these crowds now had eyes almost exclusively for Nadia and something less so for Olga. Comaneci made two perfect scores, one on the uneven bars and one on the balance beam. Olga did well, but less so.

When the crowd cheered, they were usually cheering for Nadia. When they gasped at a mishap, it was Olga's.

24

The scheduling called for the two girls to go through routines at about the same time on different locations on the floor. There was high anticipation in the crowd regarding this.

The difference in the two girls in age was apparent. Olga seemed so much more a woman of the world. Olga in her red uniform showed a ruddy physical maturation, whereas Nadia in white uniform is still slight as a tomboy. Olga still wore pigtails but that is one of her last concessions to the demure Olga of former days—her pigtails and her skill, that is.

Nadia had a wispy ponytail and bangs that came down, as I wrote then, "nearly to her large, impassive brown calf eyes." Her lips were normally tight. Her face was pale and pristine and she looked like the kind of small girl who would—and did—have a collection of dolls in international costumes on a shelf in her bedroom.

Olga's hazel eyes were wearier, having, unlike Nadia, been exposed to the world in the last four years. Olga's muscles were more rigidly defined, especially in the thighs. The veins in Olga's hands were quite prominent. They were nearly hidden in Nadia's.

When the girls performed on that second of the two nights in the team competition Olga began with a 9.90 score in the uneven bars. As she accepted adulation from teammates, a roar went up from the crowd. A perfect 10 for Nadia on the balance beam had just been posted on the scoreboard.

Next, Olga on the balance beam slipped at one point, but windmilled back to execute a courageous backslip. She got a 9.85, while Nadia was also obtaining a 9.85 on the floor exercise. However, a crowning humiliation was the house piano's background music. "Yes Sir, That's my Baby," as Nadia took her bow. Unfortunately, the song concluded while Olga was halfway through her routine.

Olga on the floor exercise scrambled to get a 9.95. Nadia was then receiving a 9.90 on the vault. Olga at the vault fell once but managed a 9.85 as the crowd went wild for Nadia's 10.00 on the uneven bars.

Hitting the floor after the vault, Olga scrunched her eyes and moaned softly in pain. She had twisted her ankle. She then hobbled over to the water cooler during Nadia's encores. Then Olga sat back down and gauntly sucked a lemon.

Olga's scores would not allow her to perform in two of the four events in the women's individual all-around finals two days later. Nadia qualified for all four.

Afterward when the team exchanged congratulations, Nadia and Olga shook hands. "We said we are the friends," said Nadia to a reporter through an interpreter.

Olga had no excuse. She said, no, that her ankle did not bother her. "When you are an athlete," she said, "an injury is something you just work with." She said she hoped to return to the Olympics in 1980.

A German journalist, admiring Olga's dignity, was dubious, however. "Her concentration is not like Nadia's anymore," he said with an accent. "Olga, she is getting old. She has now other `sings on her mind. But she is still touching, so?"

Amid the lovefest for Nadia, a reporter asked what her greatest wish was. "I want to go home," she said. Any plans to retire? Her eyes widened. "I'm only fourteen," she said.

Korbut retired from gymnastics competition in 1977, at age twenty-two. In the 1980 Olympics in Moscow, which were boycotted by the United States and several other countries to counter Russia's aggression in Afghanistan, Comaneci won two gold medals (balance beam and floor) and two silvers (team all-around and individual all-around). Korbut married a Belarusian singer and settled down as a housewife. But she had an independent streak and sometimes expressed criticism of the Soviet regime, especially the fact that whatever rewards that would have accrued to her, they were mostly confiscated by the Soviet regime. In 1991, Korbut moved from Canada to the United States and became a gymnastics coach, and eventually took up residence in Scotts-dale, Arizona. In 2017, she auctioned off her Olympic medals and other memorabilia. She reportedly said that she did so "to avoid going hun-gry," but later denied that remark. The auction brought her $333,500.

* * *

On March 6, 1981, I wrote my first story as a new reporter for *The New York Times* (a career there that would last twenty-six more years).

Miss Comaneci, 19, Makes a Fresh Start

March 6, 1981

Suddenly the music stopped. Nadia Comaneci turned, her body frozen still as a park statue, arms extended, balletic toe dipped, and looked over her shoulder to see what was the matter.

"Oom," explained Ghesa Pojar, choreographer for the Rumanian gymnastics team, "Yuh." He thrust his arms back and his bearded chin up.

"It must be like a bird, soaring, like wings," Pojar said, in Ruma-nian. "Not like a scared woodpecker." He stood at the edge of the blue gymnastics carpet in the Felt Forum yesterday while his star pupil prac-ticed her floor exercise routine. She was preparing for "Nadia '81," an exhibition at Madison Square Garden Sunday afternoon that includes the Rumanian Women's Olympic team and selected members of the United States men's national team, the start of a six-city tour.

As Pojar spoke, a little smile appeared on Miss Comaneci's small, pouty mouth—a surprise to those observers who remembered her as the intense fourteen-year-old with brooding eyes who rushed into fame at the 1976 Olympics in Montreal, scoring the first 10 in Olympic history, then went on to achieve six more 10s and three gold medals, before a packed crowd in the Montreal Forum and before millions on six continents watching on television.

She grew serious again when the tape of "Ciocirlia" a popular Rumanian symphonic work, again filled the relatively empty auditorium.

In a simple, black warm-up uniform, her ponytail tied in a shimmery blue ribbon, wearing eye shadow and with red polish on the fingers of her calloused hands, Miss Comaneci elegantly, buoyantly, wingedly whirled through a series of flips, spins and leaps.

"Bravo," Pojar said. "Perfect." Perfect. The word was hers well before it was Bo's. It was her glory—she gained instant international celebrity—and it was her despair. A year after the 1976 Olympics she had gained 25 pounds, going from 85 to 110, and had grown from 4-foot-11 to 5-foot-3 1/2 (she is now 5-foot-4). Changes in body size were inevitable in a girl, but the added weight seemed excessive. And shocking.

She had received great attention—from the covers of magazines to the Hero of Socialist Labor medal, the highest award granted in Rumania—and she was obviously buckling. Rumanian officials, often tight-lipped about such things, admitted to intimates that Miss Comaneci might be suffering an emotional breakdown.

And she discovered that she could no longer do things in gymnastics that, since age 6, had seemed to come to her as naturally as waking up.

"I couldn't look at myself in the mirror," she recalled yesterday, sitting in a chair in the Forum. Her once exquisitely muscled legs and arms had grown beefy. She had cried to her coach, Bela Karoli, who discovered her in a first-grade recess class, "I cannot do anything right anymore." Gently, he had assured her she would. "I had to go to the seashore for a rest," she said. She also canceled several performances and lost in meets that she was expected to win.

Gradually, she regained her form. She went on a strict diet of milk products, even abjuring her beloved Mars chocolate bars, and dropped to her present weight of 90 pounds.

"But her enthusiasm for the sport, and her concentration—that is the key—it was still there," Karoli had said.

Miss Comaneci won a gold medal in the 1977 European championship and won the all-round title in 1979. In the World Gymnastics Championships in Fort Worth in December 1979, she suffered an infected left wrist. Despite doctor's orders not to compete, she dramatically entered the stadium, and, with one hand, scored a 9.95 on the balance beam to provide the margin of victory for her team.

In the 1980 Olympics in Moscow, she won two gold medals and again scored 10's, but her experience was tainted by a long argument among the judges that tilted the decision for the all-round gold medal to the home-town Soviet entry, Yelena Davydova.

"I don't want to remember Moscow," she said. At nineteen, there is no reason for her to look back. She expects to compete in three world-class tournaments this year, and, possibly, the 1984 Olympic Games in Los Angeles, but she maintains a wait-and-see posture on that.

As a first-year student at the University of Physical Education in Bucharest, she is working hard in her studies, which include English, French, Geography, and Mathematics, and she plans to be a trainer of gymnasts.

She is a young woman now, and not the child of Montreal. Her lithe body, still slender, is endowed with graceful feminine curves. She is no longer the narrow all-consumed gymnast. She jokes with teammates, clowning through routines in casual moments, and is involved in a social life that she never had before.

And that's when she mentioned to me that it was "Robert Redford," and no longer "Alain Delon," who had captured her heart.

Her coach, Bela Karolyi, and his wife, Martha, defected to America as soon as that tour ended. That's when the Romanian government began to watch Comaneci closely and refused to let her travel out of the country, and led, eight years later, to her defection, at age twenty-seven.

* * *

In 1999, at the White House, my wife Dolly and I had the opportunity to talk with Comaneci. Her English was excellent, with only a slight accent. She was lovely, bright and engaged. She smiled readily. I told her that my grandparents had lived in Romania before coming to the United States in the early 1900s.

"Where were they from?" she asked

"A town called Focsani," I said.

"Oh, I know Focsani," she said. "I was born and raised in Onesti, which is not far from Focsani." (In fact, they are only 70 miles apart in the region known as Western Moldavia.)

"I know that the word *foc* in Romanian means "fire," I said.

"That's true," she said.

"I don't know what `sani' means," I said.

"I don't, either," she said. "Must be someone's name that the town was named for."

"How did you know *foc*?" she said.

"There is a family legend," I replied, "that when my grandparents and four of my father's oldest siblings came to America, they moved into a second-floor apartment on the West Side of Chicago in the summertime. My aunt Rose was then a sixteen-year-old buxom redhead. The story goes that a small fire started in a corner of the apartment and Aunt Rose ran to the window and, with her accent, started shouting *Foc, foc!* since it was the only word for 'fire' that she knew. And the story goes that all the guys in the neighborhood came running upstairs."

Nadia threw back her head and laughed. "Do you know any other Romanian words?" she asked.

"No," I said, "just one." She laughed again. We chatted some more and then repaired to the buffet table.

At the end of the evening, as Dolly and I were leaving, I saw Nadia, and waved good night to her. "Nadia," I said, "how many words in Romanian do you know?"

"Just one," she said. And all three of us laughed.

It was, to be sure, a night to remember, as were those incandescent nights in Montreal in 1976 when fourteen-year-old Nadia Comaneci swirled and soared and thrilled the world.

Roger Bannister: The Impossible Becomes Possible

November 3, 1996

The elderly physician and grandfather of five in the conservative gray suit and brown-rimmed spectacles and clipped British accent hardly appears now as the ultimate sports symbol, the one who achieved the impossible dream.

This is Roger Bannister, who, on May 6, 1954, a damp, windy day in Iffley, England, broke the four-minute mile—he ran the course in 3:59.4—and then, after breaking the tape and the world record, collapsed from his effort.

He was then twenty-five years old, and lean, at 6-foot-1, 158 pounds; he is now sixty-seven, and 16 pounds heavier, though still looking fit. (He no longer runs, after breaking an ankle several years ago, but he says he still walks vigorously.) And this weekend, on the eve of the New York City Marathon, and to celebrate 100 years of competitive

running—beginning with the inaugural modern Olympics in 1896—
Runner's World magazine chose his shattering of the record and pre-
conceptions forty-two years ago as "The single greatest moment in the
history of running."

"A fairly arbitrary designation," Bannister said graciously, in the
Runner's World office in Manhattan recently.

For years the barrier of four minutes for a mile seemed to many
outside of human limits. "I had analyzed scientifically that it was in fact
humanly possible," said Bannister, who was then a medical student and
is now a neurologist living in England, "and so I saw no reason not to
do it."

Sometime after that, Bannister predicted that there would one
day be a mile run in three and a half minutes. "I stick to that now," he
said, with a smile. He was well aware, of course, that the world record is
3:44.39, set in 1993 by the Algerian Noureddine Morceli.

Other track and field records are being smashed regularly; even
Bob Beamon's colossal long-jump record was bettered by Mike Powell's
29 feet 4 1/2 inches. The high-jump record is at 8-1/2, where half a century ago seven feet was considered beyond belief. (The record in 1936
was 6-8.) And the marathon mark gets ever closer to the two-hour barrier (the record is 2:06.50 by Belayneh Densimo of Ethiopia).

What, then, are the limits? There must be some. Can anyone run a
three-minute mile?

"There will never be a three-minute mile," Bannister said. "Yes,
there are human limitations. I was a physiologist before I was a neurologist, and I know the human cardiac output and know the amount of work
that has to be done and the amount of oxygen you'd have to move from
the outside air to the muscles to break down the fuel to provide energy;
and you factor in the overdraft you can take by producing lactic acid
without any oxygen, and the equation does not permit a three-minute

mile." Sir Roger—he was knighted, after all—took a deserved breath. "I'm excluding genetic engineering, of course, an abhorrent thought."

Records, though, will continue to be broken, but in much smaller increments than before, he said. (The mile record has been reduced by "about a third of a second a year," Bannister said, since he broke it.) Meanwhile, improved training methods, nutrition and a wider pool of athletes from such emerging areas as India and Africa will add to the competitive mix.

And there is the intangible of motivation to spur the athletic effort, he added, from personal circumstances to patriotism. He had finished a "singularly discontented" fourth in the 1,500-meters in the 1952 Olympics—"England's only gold medal was by a horse, Foxhunter, in show jumping," he said—and he wanted to succeed for himself as well as his country, still suffering from "rationing" after World War II. Bannister was also inspired by the climb in 1953 of Sir Edmund Hillary, the first person to scale Mount Everest. "That was considered an impossible feat, as well," Bannister said.

"But that was all on a physical level," he said. "I have been studying the brain for several years now, and I believe we will never learn all there is to know of its workings. Which is different from sport. The so-called impossible in sport is simply a recreational escape, in comparison to the larger issues in the real world. In sport, after all, at the end of the day we know that it may have been fun, but that it was unimportant."

* * *

The mile record lasted for the shortest amount of time in history. Within three weeks, John Landy of Australia ran it in 3:58. The ceiling had been broken.

"Broadway Joe" and the Greatest Super Bowl Upset

Irrepressible quarterback Joe Namath predicted a few days before Super Bowl III, on January 12, 1969, that his New York Jets, nearly three touchdown underdogs, would triumph over the Baltimore Colts. In fact, he "guaranteed" it, which drew laughter from many, if not most, followers of football. The Jets had emerged from the American Football League to the National Football League and the first two Super Bowls between their two top teams were won handily by the NFL's Green Bay Packers. In Super Bowl III, the Jets indeed upset the Colts, 16–7, and Namath was voted the MVP of the game on the strength of his command of his offense, completing 17 of 28 passes for 206 yards, though, remarkably, not throwing for a touchdown. The AFL had gained equality, and then some.

It is widely held among sports cognoscenti that this upset set the stage for the National Football League to become the dominant sports organization in this country. "The game changed the whole scope of professional football in America," Bob Lederer, author of *Beyond Broadway Joe: The Super Bowl Team That Changed Football*, told CNN Business on February 1, 2019. "It might've been the point at which football became the national pastime instead of baseball."

Joe Namath at Candlelight

February 15, 1972 / Dorado Beach, Puerto Rico

Two women circle and stop and peek, like curious kittens, and ask themselves in quiet excitement, "Is that really . . . *him*?

Joe Namath at dinner with three male companions raises a glass of wine and toasts, "Health," when the two bejeweled middle-aged women interrupt. "Joe, may we bother you for an autograph for our sons?" One extends a cloth napkin.

Namath is giggly. He pushes back his chair, slowly rises. "Want me to write something special?" he asks. He laughs shyly, like a tickled schoolboy trying to cover a giggle from the teacher. "You won't get this napkin through customs," he says. The ladies are delighted.

Namath is one of the most recognizable men in the United States, and Puerto Rico, and also one of the most controversial. Everyone seems to have an opinion on Joe Namath, and it seems almost everyone wants his autograph, too.

Namath's mood is changed now from the time two years ago in 1970 when he received a crank threat on his life. He seemed more puzzled than frightened by such a vicious response to his carefree life style. For a time, it appeared he wanted to shrink from the limelight. But Namath is too spirited to remain hunched in dark corners.

One of Namath's dinner companions said he had recently talked with George Sauer, the former Jet wide receiver who retired. "George said one reason he quit was that he was sick of people pawing and drooling over him because he was a football player," said the companion.

"George say that?" asked Namath. "Well, some people just don't want it. They don't like it. Steve Thompson wanted to go back home to work. He up and quit the Jets, too."

Namath, his black hair in bangs, bent his head and dug into a steak. He looked up and smiled again, the candlelight on the table accentuating his dimples.

"I was supposed to have a date tonight," he said. "I met this beautiful blonde last night in the hotel casino here. I mean bee-yoo-tee-ful. I walked over to her and said, 'A beautiful woman like you shouldn't be alone.' She said she wasn't alone, exactly. But she didn't want to be with the guy she was with tonight. I said, 'Well, that can be fixed.' She said not tonight. She was going back to her room—alone. I asked her about tomorrow night. She said yeah. I told her I'd call her at six. I called. She wasn't in. I left a message. She never returned the call. I'd sure like to see her. I'd like to know what she was thinking about."

A man and his wife came over and got an autograph. They left.

"I noticed," said a dinner companion, "that you always stand when women come over to the table."

"Sure," said Namath. "That's the least I can do. I mean, if my mother asked for an autograph, I'd want the guy to stand for her out of respect."

His thoughts drifted to his home town, Beaver Falls, Pennsylvania.

"When I was in high school," he said, "a guy named Pothead nicknamed me Johnny U, 'cause I idolized Johnny Unitas. Those were the days. Did you know I worked one week as a shoeshine boy in a hat-cleaning store? They paid 50 cents a week. A week! I quit after the first week. I knew I was cut out for bigger things, even then." He pushed back his chair and bent over and laughed boyishly.

Joe came up for air, and his close friend and traveling companion, Becher Khouri, said, "I'll check the messages at the front desk, see if the girl called."

For all of the "Broadway Joe" headlines, Namath still seems to choose his friends the way he must have in Beaver Falls—are they loyal? Are they honest? Do they make him laugh? He mentioned a New York friend named Mickey. "He's in a couple small pizza restaurants with his father," said Namath. "I've known Mickey for several years, and I didn't know until recently that he never went past the ninth grade. I can dig that. I went to college, I told him, but I didn't learn much past the ninth grade anyway."

Khouri returns. No message from the blonde. Namath then pours more wine. More people descend for autographs. The intermittent conversation rambles; Namath talks about how much he still admires Unitas and watches him on television whenever he can to steal some of the old master's quarterback tricks. "And he's still got 'em all," said Namath.

He asked about the protestors he had recently read about. "People were picketing in New York about the Irish problem," he said. "I don't understand that. If people want to do something, why don't they just go to Northern Ireland and talk face-to-face with the people there who can do something about it? What good is picketing in New York?"

He lamented the theft of his $10,000 full-length mink coat from his Manhattan apartment. "Funny thing is," he said, "I never wore it. I didn't pay for it. I got it for doing some PR. But I loved it. I may buy another one."

He was laughing again, pouring more wine.

Just then, there was a tap on his shoulder. He turned. "I don't believe it. I don't believe it," he said into his napkin to muffle his surprise. He stood.

"Hello, Diane," said Joe. He pulled up a chair for her. It was the young woman with shoulder-length blonde hair.

Namath sat back down and crossed his legs, leaned back in his seat, smiling quizzically at her. The flicker of the candle lit up his boyish blue eyes and he uttered a barely audible, "wow."

The Top of Their Game

There are others who have succeeded in their fields who have been described as "the best," but none are mentioned any more in that category, from my view, than Muhammad Ali, Michael Jordan, Jack Nicklaus, and the great "Galloping Ghost," Red Grange, are in their fields.

Muhammad Ali: The Ageless Champ

It was about an hour before the Thomas "Hitman" Hearns-"Marvelous Marvin" Hagler middleweight title bout in Las Vegas and I went over to Muhammad Ali, seated at ringside, to ask him if there was a time in the next few weeks when I could visit him in his home in Los Angeles for a feature story. I hesitated to disturb him since he was in conversation with the actress Bo Derek, she of the famous "10" beauty designation, sitting behind him. When he turned back, I made my approach. While it was getting harder to understand him because of symptoms of his Parkinson's disease, he still obviously could be conversant. He recognized me and he agreed to an interview. He gave me his phone number. When I did call him to set up an interview, I had a difficult time understanding him by phone. I began to sweat, but eventually made out his address.

I wrote the story and sent him a copy of it. I asked if he'd like any more copies. He sent back my note but added this: "Send 2 or 3 copies. Muhammad Ali. Thank you." He added a heart with spokes, like sun rays, extended from it. Below is that story.

Age Hasn't Cooled the Fire Inside Ali

April 28, 1985 / Los Angeles, California

The sprawling three-story house was quiet, except for the tinny too-wa, too-wee of birds in a small aviary next to the office room on the first

38

floor. It was early on a recent morning and the cool, shadowed office was dimly lit by two antique candelabras which had a few of their small bulbs burned out. An antique lamp was also lit and with its slightly crooked shade peered over the large black mahogany desk scattered with letters and an Islamic prayer book. Nearby were several open boxes stuffed with mail.

Behind the desk, three large windows opened onto a back yard, half in sunlight, with cypress trees and pruned bushes and a swimming pool. Along another wall in the office, a pair of black men's shoes stood by themselves in the middle of a brown-suede couch. In another corner, a television set, with another on top of it, rested on the Oriental rug that covered most of the floor of the room. On the wall facing the desk was a marble fireplace without a fire.

Suddenly, a torch appeared in the doorway. The fire, burning at the end of a rolled-up newspaper, was followed by a large man in black-stockinged feet who trotted into the room. "Hoo, hoo," he said, as the flame burned closer to his hand, and he tossed the torch into the fire-place. Quickly, the logs in the fireplace crackled with the flame, and Muhammad Ali, the torchbearer, watched them burn. Then he sat down in an armchair in front of his desk and in a moment closed his eyes.

He said something, indistinct, in a gravelly mumble, and the visitor, in a chair facing him, asked Ali if he would repeat it.

"Tired," he said, with a little more effort, his eyes still closed. It was eight o'clock in the morning and Ali had been up since 5:30 saying his daily prayers.

He stretched his legs. He wore a light blue shirt, unbuttoned at the cuffs, which was not tucked into his dark blue slacks. At forty-three, Ali's face is rounder and his body is thicker than when he first won the world heavyweight championship by knocking out Sonny Liston in Miami in February 1964. The 6-foot-3 Ali weighed 215 then and is now about 240 pounds.

In the ensuing years, he would weigh as much as 230 in the ring as he lost and regained the title two more times—an unprecedented feat in the heavyweight division. Ali, who was stopped in a one-sided bout by Larry Holmes while attempting to win the title yet a fourth time, retired five years ago, but he is hardly forgotten.

A few days before, he had been at ringside at the Hagler-Hearns middleweight title fight in Las Vegas, Nevada. Numerous ex-champions were introduced before the bout. Ali was saved for last.

He was asked now how he felt about that moment. He said nothing, and it appeared he was sleeping. Then: "A-li, A-li, A-li," he said, opening his eyes and mimicking the chant that arose among the 16,000 fans when the ring announcer introduced him.

"I had to go like this," he said softly, raising his right index finger to his lips, "to calm the people down.

"A lot of fighters, when they quit no one ever hears of them again. But I've gotten bigger since I quit boxin'. Look at this," he said, nodding to a box in the corner, "people from all over the world writin' me. Thirty-one boxes full of fan mail in four years."

One was from Bangladesh, sent to "Loos Anjeles," and calling Ali "my unknown Uncle." Another from West Germany asked "Mr. Ali" for his autograph. A third was from Drakefield Road in London and sent to the New York Presbyterian Hospital, where Ali had gone late last summer for a checkup. He has been diagnosed as having Parkinson's Syndrome, a nerve disorder.

Ali asked the visitor to open the letter and read it aloud.

"I am very sorry to know of your temporary problem," wrote the Briton, "and wish you most sincerely a rapid recovery. Many of my friends who are fans of yours are thinking the same, that you will in a very short time be back to your old poetic self and come and see us in dear old London . . ."

Do you still write poetry? the visitor asked Ali.

"No," he said, "no more. That was in a different time. Eighteen times callin' the round. 'That's no jive, Cooper will fall in five. Moore in four.'"

The visitor recalled a personal favorite, when Ali predicted how his first fight with Liston would go. it turned out that Liston didn't answer the bell for the seventh round. Did Ali remember the poem?

"Mmmmm," he said. It wasn't sure what he meant by that.

But he began, his voice still very low:

"Ali comes out to meet Liston, And then Liston starts to retreat.

"If he goes back any farther, he'll wind up in a ringside seat."

He paused thoughtfully, then continued.

"And Liston keeps backin' but there's not enough room, "It's a matter of time—There! Ali lowers the boom.

"Ali lands with a right—what a beautiful swing!

"The punch knocks Liston right out of the ring . . ."

Just then the phone rang. "My phone's ringin'," he said. "Hold on." He reached over to his desk. "Yeah, naw, naw," he said sleepily into the phone. "I wouldn't try that for no $5,000, you crazy?" He noded. "Check ya later." And hung up. "Where was I?"

He was reminded that he had just knocked Liston out of the ring.

"Who woulda thought," he continued, "when they came to the fight, "That they'd witness the launchin' of a hu-man satellite.

"Yes, yes, the crowd did not dream when they laid down their money, "That they would see a total eclipse of the Sonny."

Ali's voice was fading again. "I wrote that twenty-two years ago," he said, his words getting lost in a throat. "That was a long time." He is taking voice lessons from Gary Catona, who had come into the room during the recital of the old limerick. Catona is a voice and singing teacher who three weeks ago had come to Los Angeles from Austin, Texas, to try to help Ali speak more clearly.

Ali began to speak more slowly and less distinctly over the last several years. There was much speculation about him suffering a variety of illnesses. During his hospital visit in New York last September, doctors determined that he had Parkinson's Syndrome.

Catona believes that the only problem with Ali's voice is that his vocal muscles are weak, that they lack resonance.

Ali was asked what was wrong with his voice. "I dunno," he said, "somethin.'" "Muhammad never really had strong vocal muscles," said Catona. "He used to scream out his words. His normal speech was never a normal speech."

Ali and his voice teacher schedule a one-hour lesson every day, but Ali travels a lot and they don't always connect. "But he's good when we do it," said Catona. "It's like building body muscles, you've got to work at it. He sings the sounds of the scales. 'Ah! Ah! Ah! Ah!'" Catona sang, his voice rising at each "Ah!"

Catona and Ali had already had the session at the piano in the living room, and beyond this Ali was asked what he's been doing with himself lately.

"People are interested in you," he was told. "You're one of the most popular figures . . ." "Popular niggers?" he interrupted. "Figures," the visitor repeated.

Ali looked at him playfully out of the corner of his eye.

"What am I doin' now, oh, I'm so busy," he said, growing serious now. "I'm busy every day. I've got all this mail to answer—they're startin' fan clubs for me all over the world, in Asia, in Europe, in Ireland, in China, in Paris. But my mission is to establish Islamic evangelists, and to tour the world spreadin' Islam."

He converted from Christianity to the Islamic faith twenty-one years ago, changing his name, as the world knows, from Cassius Clay to Muhammad Ali.

On the shelf above the fireplace stood a *Sports Illustrated* cover from May, 5, 1969, laminated on a wooden plaque. The cover showed the young boxer wearing a crown, with the caption, "Ali-Clay—The Once—and Future?—King."

What's the difference between Cassius Clay and Muhammad Ali? he was asked.

"As much difference as night and day," he said. "Cassius Clay was popular in America and Europe. Muhammad Ali has a billion more fans all over the world. Cassius Clay had no knowledge of his self. He thought Clay was his name, but found out it was a slave name. Clay means 'dirt, with no ingredients.' Cassius—I don't know what that means. But Ali means 'The most high,' and Muhammad means 'worthy of praise and praiseworthy.'

"Cassius Clay had Caucasian images of God on his wall. Muhammad Ali was taught to believe that there should be no image of God. No color. That's a big difference."

He rose and got a large briefcase from under his desk. He withdrew several religious pamphlets with pictures of Jesus Christ. All but one was white. Then he took out a Bible and opened it to Exodus 20:4, and asked the visitor to read it. "Thou shalt not make unto thee any graven image, or any likeness of any thing that is in heaven above . . ."

"Ooohh," said Ali. "Powerful, isn't it. But what are all these. Man, you thought boxin' was powerful. Boxin's little. These pictures teach supremacy. The Bible says there should be no pictures of God, no images, he should be no color. But you see that God is white. Tarzan, King of the Jungle, was a white man. Angel's food cake is white, devil's-food cake is black. Man, ain't that powerful? "Cassius Clay would not have the nerve to talk like this—he'd be afraid of what people might say or think. Ali is fearless, he's hopin', prayin' that you print this. Cassius Clay would not have the courage to refuse to be drafted for the Vietnam war. But Muhammad Ali gave up his title, and maybe he would have to go to jail for five years."

He rose again and this time brought back a plastic box, flipped up the latches, and opened the lid. It was a box of magic paraphernalia.

He took two red foam rubber balls and made them become four right before the visitor's eyes, then turned them into a box of matches, then made them disappear altogether. His eyes widened in mock shock. He still has the fastest hands of any heavyweight in history. It was a very good trick. How did he do it? "It's against the law for magicians to tell their tricks," he said. "It's a tricky world," he said. He next transformed three small unstretchable ropes of varying sizes into the same size.

He made a handkerchief disappear, but, on the second showing, he was too obvious about stuffing it into a fake thumb.

"You should only show that trick once," he said, a little embarrassed.

He redeemed his virtuosity by putting four quarters into the visitor's hand, snapping his fingers, and ordering the quarters to become two dimes and two pennies. The quarters obeyed. He snapped his fingers again and the quarters returned; the pennies and dimes vanished.

"It's magic for kids," he said. "It's my hobby. See how easy they can be deceived? But these aren't childish things. They make you think, don't they?"

It was mentioned that perhaps Ali's best magic trick was transforming the small house he lived in as a boy in Louisville into this 22-room house with expensive antique furniture. He made more than $60 million in ring earnings and endorsements. "But the Government took 70 percent," he said. He says he is financially secure. He doesn't do commercials, for example, because, he said, "I don't need the money."

He lives here in Wilshire with his two children by Veronica Ali, eight-year-old Hana and six-year-old Laila. They employ a live-in housekeeper. His six other children live with his two former wives.

"My wife likes antiques," he said, walking into the living room. He pointed to a tall clock against the wall. "It's 150 years old," he said.

Gary Catona now took his leave, and arranged for a session the following morning. Ali led his visitor for a tour of the house. "I'm not braggin'," he said, "just showin'. I don't like to talk about what I have, because there's so many people hungry, homeless, no food, starvin', sleepin' on the streets."

In the dining room, is a long dark table with twelve tall, carved chairs. On the second floor are the bedrooms. In the kids' rooms, toys and stuffed animals tumbled across the floor. There's an Oriental sitting room, and guest room.

The phone rang. "City morgue," he answered. He spoke briefly and hung up.

They ascended the carpeted staircase to the third floor. On a wall are a pair of red boxing gloves encased in glass. One glove is signed, "To the champion of champions—Sylvester Stallone." On an adjoining wall is a robe with multi-colored sequins that bears the inscription, "The People's Choice." In the corner of the case was a photograph of a man with his arm around Ali. It is Elvis Presley, who gave Ali the robe.

In the adjoining room is a large pool table with a zebra skin lying over it. Trophies and plaques and photographs line the wall and cover the floor.

He was asked about recent efforts to ban boxing.

"Too many blacks are doin' well in it, so white people want to ban it," he said. "But how do I live here without boxin'? How would I ever be able to pay for all this? Look at Hearns and Hagler. Two poor black boys, but now they help their mother and father and sisters and brothers. It's from boxin'.

"There's more deaths in football than boxin'. Nobody wants to ban football. You see car races. 'Whoom, whoom.' Cars hit the wall, burn up. Motor boats hit a bump. Bam! Don't ban that, do they?"

45

Going back down the stairs, the visitor is met by a nearly life-size painting of Ali in the ring wearing white boxing trunks. He is on his toes and his arms are raised in triumph. The signature in the corner of it reads, "LeRoy Neiman, '71."

Did Ali miss fighting? "When the fight's over," he said, "you don't talk about it anymore."

The visitor asked about his health. "I don't feel sick," Ali said. "But I'm always tired."

How did he feel now? "Tired," he said, "tired."

A doctor friend, Martin Ecker of Presbyterian Hospital, has said that if Ali takes his prescribed medication four times a day—the medication is L-Dopa, which in effect peps up the nervous system (the disease does not affect the brain)—then Ali's condition would be improved substantially. The medication does not cure the disease, but it increases alertness.

Ali is inconsistent in taking the medication. He believes it doesn't matter if he takes the medication, because he is in the hands of Allah, and that his fate is sealed. Days go by when he doesn't take the medicine. But when friends urge him to, or when he is going to make a public appearance, then he is more inclined to take his dosage.

Did he feel that after twenty-five years of amateur and professional fights, of countless hours of sparring, that he had taken too many punches?

He stopped on the second-floor landing. He rubbed his face with his hands. "Uh uh," he said, softly. "Look how smooth. I very rarely got hit."

As the visitor turned from Ali and opened the door to go, he heard an odd cricket sound behind his ear.

The champ smiled kindly but coyly. There was either a cricket in the house or something that sounded like a cricket in his hand.

Walking to his car in this quiet, elegant neighborhood, and then driving out past the security guard at the gate, the visitor realized he would not plumb the mystery of the cricket sound in Muhammad Ali's house. It's a tricky world, he recalled, and he would leave it at that.

Joe Elsby Martin, 80, Muhammad Ali's First Boxing Teacher

September 17, 1996

One rainy night in 1954, Joe Elsby Martin, a Louisville, Ky., policeman who ran a local recreation center called the Columbia Gym, saw a skinny twelve-year-old boy with tears in his eyes come into the gym seeking him out.

The boy was distraught because his new red Schwinn bicycle, a Christmas present from his father, had been stolen. He had been told that a policeman named Martin would fill out a police report for him.

"What's your name?" Martin said.

"Cassius Clay," the boy said, adding angrily that he would whip the thief if he could find him.

Martin then asked the young Clay if he could fight, saying, "You better learn to fight before you start fightin.'"

In this way did Martin, who died at his Louisville home on Saturday at the age of eighty, launch the boxing career of Muhammad Ali, an Olympic gold medal champion, a three-time world heavyweight boxing champion and a controversial and often beloved international figure.

In his autobiography *The Greatest: My Own Story*, written with Richard Durham, Ali recalled his meeting with Martin and introduction to boxing.

"I ran downstairs, crying, but the sights and sounds and the smell of the boxing gym excited me so much that I almost forgot about the bike," Ali wrote. "There were about 10 boxers in the gym, some hitting the speed bag, some in the ring, sparring, some jumping rope. I stood there, smelling the sweat and rubbing alcohol, and a feeling of awe came over me. One slim boy shadowboxing in the ring was throwing punches almost too fast for my eyes to follow."

After the lad had written out the report and was about to go, Martin tapped him on the shoulder. "By the way," he said, "we got boxing every night, Monday through Friday, from 6 to 8. Here's an application in case you want to join the gym."

The boy had never worn a pair of boxing gloves, but was excited about trying the sport.

"When I got to the gym," Ali wrote, "I was so eager, I jumped into the ring with some older boxer and began throwing wild punches. In a minute my nose started bleeding. My mouth was hurt. My head was dizzy. Finally someone pulled me out of the ring."

"Get someone to teach you," a slim welterweight told the young Clay.

And that someone was Martin. He had worked for years with amateurs and had been instrumental in integrating Louisville's amateur boxing, combining separate gyms for black and white fighters. While Martin was not a professional boxing trainer, he knew enough of the rudiments of the sport to get the young Clay started.

"He could show me how to place my feet and how to throw a right cross," the fighter later wrote. And while Clay threw wild punches, "something" was driving him. "I kept coming back to the gym."

Martin told him: "I like what you're doing. I like the way you stick to it. I'm going to put you on television. You'll be on the next television fight." At that time, Louisville amateur fighters, some from Martin's gym, appeared on a weekly televised boxing card called *Tomorrow's Champions*.

"Thrilled at the idea of being seen on TV all over Kentucky, I trained the whole week," Ali said. "They matched me with a white fighter, Ronny O'Keefe, and I won my first fight by a split decision.

"All of a sudden I had a new life."

Martin's tutoring helped the young Clay win six Kentucky Golden Gloves titles and two national Amateur Athletic Union titles leading up to the 1960 Olympics in Rome, where Martin was a coach and where the fighter won the heavyweight gold. After Ali turned professional with the backing of some businessmen, Martin continued to train amateurs and remained active with Golden Gloves, serving for a time as the Kentucky representative on the organization's national board.

In all, he held the Kentucky Golden Gloves franchise for almost forty years. In 1977, he was inducted into the Amateur Boxing Hall of Fame.

A police officer for thirty-four years, Martin did some auctioneering after retiring from the force. In 1980, Ali appeared in a sparring exhibition to raise money for Martin's campaign for Jefferson County sheriff, but Martin lost in his bid to win the Democratic nomination, the second time he was defeated for that post.

Martin is survived by his wife, Christine; a son, Joe Jr.; and a granddaughter.

Stinging and Floating Come Harder Now For Ali

July 14, 1971 / Chicago, Illinois

A couple of flies did midair imitations of the Ali Shuffle as the original, Muhammad Ali himself, sat in the motel lobby talking with a companion. One fly alighted on the right knee of Ali.

"See that fly?" Mind that fly," said Ali, his conversational tone interrupted by his whisper. His large left hand began to creep out. His eyes were fixed on the fly.

"You gotta know how to do it," he said, barely moving his lips. "The fly is facing me and he can only fly forward. Now, I come forward and turn my hand backhanded. It's like a left jab."

Ali struck. Then he brought his fist in front of the man seated next to him. "Watch this," said Ali. He slowly opened his hand. Ali looked up wide-eyed. "Thought I had him," he said. "My timing's off."

Ali was in Chicago training for his July 26 bout with Jimmy Ellis in Houston. This was shortly after the announcement that the Supreme Court had overturned his conviction for refusing the military draft.

"It's hard to train now," he said. "I got bigger things on my mind, bigger than just beatin' up somebody. Fighting's not the thing any more for me. I see myself fighting for another year, at most. I'll have one more fight with Joe Frazier.

"Then I got obligations to keep. I want to help clean up black people. I want to help respect black women. I want to help the wine-heads in the alleys. I want to help the little black kids in the ghettos. I want to help narcotics programs. I want to serve the honorable Elijah Muhammad, the head of the Black Muslim religion." Ali is a member of that religious organization, of which he is a minister. However, he has been temporarily suspended.

Ali was suspended by Elijah Muhammad because Ali continued as a fighter, a profession supposedly anathema to the religion. But Ali has been a boxer since boyhood in Louisville. And he needs money to pay alimony to his first wife and also to pay the astronomical legal fees which have piled up in the last four years as he fought his draft case and been banned by boxing organizations.

Ali swiped at another fly. Missed. And again. Same result. One more. Nothing.

"Champ, you've missed five times," said the companion.

Ali looked embarrassed. "Five?" he repeated.

"These flies keep flyin' 'round me," he said. "They must know I'm not all I used to be. Twenty-nine years old. They must see the little gray hairs that been growin' in my head lately.

"If Ellis is as quick as these flies, I'm in trouble."

A man approached and asked for Ali's autograph for two small boys. "Their mother has trouble making them clean their room," the man said off-handedly.

Ali wrote, "To Timmy and Ricky. From Muhammad Ali. Clean that room or I will seal your doom." Ali smiled at his spontaneous doggerel, the man laughed and thanked him.

The implied threat to the boys was in keeping with his easy wit, his breezy charm, the bluster that too many people have taken too seriously over the years. His still-smooth face and, now, subdued yet animated ways seem to belie his vicious profession. And when he refused to join the military he asserted that he was a conscientious objector, saying, "I got no quarrel with them Viet Cong," many held that he was being hypocritical. A fighter is a fighter, they held, none too logically, whether in the ring or a rice paddy.

A fly again landed on his knee. Ali suddenly grew still. He slowly reached out to snatch the fly. Jabbed. Had it! "My timing's back!" cried Ali. "See, at least I'm not *too* old."

He dropped the fly to the carpet. The fly didn't move.

"He's staggered," said Ali proudly, bending down. "That's a science, y'know. To stagger the fly and not to kill him. You get him in your fist, but you don't squeeze."

Ali flicked the fly with his finger. "Go on, fly, fly away. I don't want to kill him Let him live, like us."

The fly flew off.

* * *

Ali beat Jimmy Ellis on a technical knockout in the 12th round. Ali continued to have memorable fights including and especially with Joe Frazier, beating him in their last two (of three) fights. Ali retired from the ring in 1981, having won the heavyweight championship four times. He died in 2016, at age seventy-four.

Michael Jordan: First in Flight

It was May 1993, and I had traveled to Cleveland to do a column on Michael Jordan. On a Sunday late morning I went to the Cavaliers' arena where Jordan and the Bulls were working out in preparation for their playoff game the next night. After the workout I spoke with Jordan and asked if he planned to watch the Knicks-Hornets playoff game on television that afternoon. He said he was. I asked if he could use company. He said, "Sure, I'm at the Ritz-Carlton. Come on up." A few hours later I stepped onto the hotel elevator, as did an older couple. They spoke a foreign language which I believed to be Hebrew. It happened that we both got off at the same floor. I thought I recognized the man.

"Excuse me," I said to the man, "but aren't you Abba Eban?"

"Yes, I am," he replied.

"I just wanted to tell you how moving and eloquent your remarks at the United Nations were during the Israeli-Arab Six-Day War." Eban had been the Israeli ambassador to the U.N. at that time, in 1967.

"Thank you."

I introduced myself as a sports columnist for *The New York Times*, he introduced me to his wife, and then I said, "Out of curiosity, Mr. Ambassador, what are you doing in Cleveland, of all places?"

He mentioned that a famous Cleveland rabbi was retiring and he had been asked to speak in honor of the rabbi.

He said, "And what are you doing here?"

I said that I was here to see Michael Jordan, who is staying in a room down the hall.

Mrs. Eban asked her husband, "Who's Michael Jordan?"

There was no glimmer of recognition in the ambassador's eyes. And as a consummate politician he said to me, "You tell her."

I said that Michael Jordan was a great basketball player and was here for a playoff game the following evening.

They both nodded, and parted.

I went down the hall and knocked on Jordan's door. He answered in sweats.

"Michael, you won't believe what just happened," I said.

"What happened?" he said.

"I just met the only man in America who doesn't know who you are."

"Who's that?" he said.

"Abba Eban," I said.

"Abba Eban? Who's Abba Eban?"

"He was the great Israeli diplomat."

"And he doesn't know who I am?"

"That's right."

"Good," said Jordan, "he won't ask me for tickets."

Within a year, Michael Jordan would retire from basketball, and try his hand at baseball. I visited him when he was in the minor leagues and saw the transition from the ultra-confident basketball player and the confused and uncertain baseball player.

He retained, however, his car's North Carolina license plate (he grew up there), with the state's motto, "First in Flight," in honor of the Wright brothers' initial experiments with the first airplane at the turn of the twentieth century. It seemed also an appropriate designation for Jordan, who appeared on the basketball court to fly through the air.

I also covered his return to basketball and wrote a column on his first appearance at Madison Square Garden, which was published on the front page of the next morning's *Times*, above the fold. Jordan was that nationally significant.

Jordan Hits Garden at Cruising Speed: 55

March 29, 1995

People were poring over the record books to find out when anyone had done in Madison Square Garden what Michael Jordan had done last night against the Knicks. Like most points in a half, or most points in a game, or most points in. . . . They were looking in the wrong place.

You don't find what Jordan did in the game in the record books. You check memories, like the time in the Garden that Ol' Blue Eyes had the joint swinging, or the Stones had it rocking, or Gunther Gebel-Williams tamed his lions and mesmerized the crowd, or the first Ali-Frazier fight.

The hype for this game was similar to that for the previous four Jordan had played in since he returned 10 days ago from his prodigal stint as a minor league fly chaser in the White Sox organization. That is, Michael Miracle is back. Over all, though, he had been simply a miracle waiting to happen.

Last night, it happened.

The World's Greatest Hoopster scored 55 points, including a jump shot to put the Bulls ahead by two with 25 seconds left in the fourth quarter. And then, with the game tied, and with 3.1 seconds left, he went up for the shot that everyone knew he'd take and, with Knicks lunging after him, he passed to Bill Wennington under the basket for the stuff that won it for the Bulls, 113–111.

The game opened about as spectacularly as it ended. Jordan hit a jump shot from the left to start the scoring. The next time down he hit a jump shot from the top of the key. He missed his next shot and then flew down the baseline and laid in the ball. He hit six of his first seven shots before Phil Jackson, the Bulls' coach, removed his shooting star, presumably for a rest. But perhaps he was taking pity on

John Starks and Anthony Bonner and Derek Harper and Greg Anthony who, individually and en masse, were taking futile turns trying to guard Jordan.

Jordan returned and wound up with 20 points in the first quarter. At this rate, he would score 80 for the game. Inevitably, he cooled down. He only scored 15 in the next period—including one delicious double-pump shot off Patrick Ewing—dropping the pro rata to 70 points for the game.

And thus he wound up one of the most preposterous first halves in the history of the Garden. Jordan hit on 14 of 19 shots, including your occasional 3-pointer.

It was reminiscent of the first Ali-Frazier fight in which Muhammad Ali, so charismatic, with his red tassel white shoes and his dancing skills, dominated the spectators' attention. In the excitement, however, Joe Frazier was winning the fight. Similarly, at the half, the Bulls were losing, 56–50.

But it was everything and more that the capacity crowd of 19,763 could have hoped for.

In Jordan's four previous games since his return to basketball, he had fairly lackluster games, for him, other than the last one, against Atlanta, in which he hit a jumper at the final buzzer for a 99–98 victory. He seemed not quite his old self, even somewhat nervous, since he hadn't played a National Basketball Association game since June 1993, when the Bulls beat Phoenix for their third straight NBA title.

His opener 10 days ago in Indianapolis saw him miss 21 of 28 shots. He appeared nervous, as he did last Friday night in his home opener in the new United Center in Chicago. When he was introduced to the crowd of 20,000, there followed a crashing, blinding, sound-and-light show that one might have expected for something else, like Moses receiving the Ten Commandments.

Both teams sought to make statements last night, the Knicks that they could whip the Bulls with Jordan, the Bulls that they were monsters once again.

And Jordan was eager to return as the great scorer he was when he left the game—he had averaged 32 points a game, the highest in history. But if there was a fault to his game last night, it was that he was looking for only one open man—Mr. Miracle. His first assist came with 50 seconds left in the game. He didn't get his second until—well, until it was time to win the game.

"When I was playing baseball, I still felt I could play this game," Jordan said with a smile in the interview room afterward. "I'm starting to get a little hang of it again."

In fact, for fans who came to see something memorable, a performance for the ages, they wound up in the right place. They hardly noticed that he had chilled from his hot start, and finished with only 55 points. For those scouring the record book, if they must, it was the most ever scored by an opponent in the new Garden. The previous mark was 50, by—who else?—Michael Jordan.

* * *

In the fall of 1993, Jordan retired from basketball—the retirement would be short-lived, less than a year and a half.

A Humbled Jordan Learns New Truths

April 11, 1994 / Birmingham, Alabama

Every morning when he wakes up, Michael Jordan was saying, he sees the face of his dead father, James. Every morning, as he did this morning when he rose from bed in his hotel room here, he has a conversation with his father, his greatest supporter, his regular companion, his dearest and most trusted friend.

"I talk to him more in the subconscious than actual words," said Jordan today, in front of his locker in the Birmingham Barons' Class AA clubhouse. "'Keep doing what you're doing,' he'd tell me," said Jordan. "'Keep trying to make it happen. You can't be afraid to fail. Don't give a damn about the media.' Then he'd say something funny—or recall something about when I was a boy, when we'd be in the backyard playing catch together like we did all the time.

"It takes your mind away from what's happening. Lifts the load a little bit."

The memory and the pain of his father's murder are still very much alive in Michael. It has been less than a year since James Jordan was murdered last July, at age fifty-six after having pulled his car to the side of the road one night to take a nap in North Carolina. The police say his killers were two young men who chose at random to rob him.

The days since then have often been wrenching for Jordan, who retired from his exalted state as the world's greatest basketball player and decided to pursue a career as a baseball player. And while he still says his baseball experiment is fun, these days lately for Michael Jordan have not been strictly a fantasy camp. They have been difficult.

"For the last nine years," he said, "I lived in a situation where I had the world at my feet. Now I'm just another minor leaguer in the clubhouse here trying to make it to the major leagues."

He is a thirty-one-year-old rookie right fielder for the Barons of the respectable Southern League, considered a "prospects league," and his debut has been less than auspicious.

"It's been embarrassing, it's been frustrating—it can make you mad," he said. "I don't remember the last time I had all those feelings at once. And I've been working too hard at this to make myself look like a fool."

In his first two games for the Barons, Air Jordan had hit little more than air, striking out five times in seven tries, along with a pop-out and groundout.

There has been much speculation about why Michael Jordan would walk away from basketball to subject himself to this new game, one he hasn't played since he was seventeen years old, and had played in high school and the Babe Ruth league.

"It began as my father's idea," said Jordan, in the season of 1990 when the Bulls were seeking their first National Basketball Association title. "We had seen Bo Jackson and Deion Sanders try two sports and my father had said that he felt I could have made it in baseball, too. He said, 'You've got the skills.' He thought I had proved everything I could in basketball, and that I might want to give baseball a shot. I told him, 'No, I haven't done everything. I haven't won a championship.' Then I won it, and we talked about baseball on occasion, and then we won two more championships. And then he was killed."

On the night last October when Jordan announced to Jerry Reinsdorf, the owner of both the White Sox and Bulls, that he was going to quit basketball, they were sitting in Reinsdorf's box watching the White Sox-Toronto playoff game. Eddie Einhorn, a partner of Reinsdorf on the White Sox, was home recuperating from an illness when he got a phone call from Reinsdorf that night. Reinsdorf told him what had happened and then added, "And guess what he wants to do next. Play baseball!"

In December, Jordan was hitting in the basement batting cage at Comiskey Park. This spring, Reinsdorf allowed him to play with the White Sox in Sarasota, Florida, and then permitted Jordan to try to realize his dream—and "the dream of my father, both our dreams"—by starting in Class AA ball.

"My father used to say that it's never too late to do anything you wanted to do," said Jordan. "And he said, 'You never know what you can accomplish until you try.'"

So Jordan is here trying, lifting the weights, shagging the fly balls, coming early to the park for extra batting practice, listening while another outfielder, Kerry Valrie, shows him how to throw from "the top," or over the head, and Jordan then practicing over and over by throwing an imaginary ball.

This morning, he sat among players who are as much as twelve years younger than he is. Black-and-silver uniforms hang in his locker with the No. 45, which he wore in high school, and not the No. 23 he made famous in Chicago. He had several bats stacked there, with the names of Steve Sax, Shawn Abner, and Sammy Sosa on them. He is still looking for a comfortable bat, the Michael Jordan model.

"It's been humbling," he said. And you could see that in his eyes. Gone is that confident sparkle they had at playoff time against Magic's Lakers, or Bird's Celtics, or Ewing's Knicks.

"I just lost confidence at the plate yesterday," he said about his three strikeouts on Saturday. "I didn't feel comfortable. I don't remember the last time I felt that way in an athletic situation. You come to realize that you're no better than the next guy in here."

Doing Penance

The other day in Chicago, Einhorn offered a theory on Jordan's baseball pursuit.

"This is the most amateur form of psychology, but I wonder if Michael in some way is not trying to do penance for the murder of his father," said Einhorn. "I wonder if he's not seeking to suffer—to be with his father in this way."

"Seems to be true, doesn't it?" said Jordan, removing his designer bib overalls and reaching to put on his Barons uniform. "I mean, I have been suffering with the way I've been hitting—or not hitting."

He smiled wanly. "But I don't really want to subject myself to suffering. I can't see putting myself through suffering. I'd like to think I'm a strong enough person to deal with the consequences and the realities. That's not my personality. If I could do that—the suffering—to get my father back, I'd do it. But there's no way."

His eyes grew moist at the thought. "He was always such a positive force in my life," said Jordan. "He used to talk about the time my Little League team was going for the World Series and we were playing in Georgia and there was an offer that if anyone hit a homer they'd get a free steak. I hadn't had a streak in quite a while, and my father said, 'If you hit a homer, I'll buy you another steak.' It was a big ball field, and in the fourth inning I hit that sucker over the center-field fence with two on to tie the game, 3–3. We lost it anyway, 4–3, but I've never experienced anything in sports like hitting one out of the park."

He was reminded about the time his father, bald like Michael, was told that he has the same haircut as his son. "Same barber," said James Jordan. "That," said Michael, "was my father."

The effects of his father's death remain with Jordan in other ways. He has purchased a couple of guns that he keeps in his home in Highland Park, Illinois. He says he always looks out of the rearview mirror of his car and drives down streets he wouldn't normally take. "You never know, someone might be following you. I'm very aware of that. It's second nature now."

And his offer to lease a luxury bus for the Barons' road games had another motive beyond just giving his 6-foot-6 frame more leg room. "I don't want to have a bus break down at one o'clock at night in the South," he said. "You don't know who's going to be following you. I don't want to be caught in a predicament like that. I think about what happened to my dad."

The people in the organization see progress. "When I first saw him hitting in the winter," said Mike Lum, Chicago's minor league batting instructor, "it was all upper body. He was dead from the waist down. I think that's been a big change." But Jordan still has not demonstrated power in a game, though in the Cubs-White Sox exhibition game in

Wrigley Field last Thursday he hit a sharp double down the third-base line. "He's got to learn to hit before he hits with power," said Lum. "He's got to master the fundamentals."

Jordan has had so much advice that, he said, "I've got a headache." Before today's game, he said, "I was thinking too much. It's just got to flow."

Respectable on Defense

He has played adequately in the field, catching all the flies hit to him and playing a carom off the "Western Supermarkets" sign in right field with grace and making a strong throw to second base that held the runner to a single. "My defense has kept me respectable," he said.

The players in the clubhouse, at first in awe of this personage, have come to treat him like a teammate. "And I can learn from his work ethic," said Mike Robertson, a three-year minor league outfielder. "He's good to be around."

One fellow who wasn't so happy was Charles Poe, who was sent down to Class A to make room for Jordan. Poe had said that he resented Jordan's having taken his position.

"I talked to Charlie about that," said Jordan. "The coaches told me that he was going to be sent down anyway, that he wasn't ready for Double A. But I said to Charlie, 'Sometimes in life, things don't go your way. You just have to use that as energy to move forward. Never give up.'

"I don't think he really meant to come down on me. But he has to learn that as much as he loves the game—as much as I love the game—it's a business. Charlie's a good kid. He had a tough life, growing up in South Central Los Angeles.

"I told him, 'Charlie, you and I are in the same boat. We're hoping to make it to the big leagues. If it's meant to be, we will. I had some bad days in basketball, and things improved. We just got to hang in, no matter what.'"

Jordan said he had planned to play all season, all 142 games, make all the bus rides—some as many as 10 and 12 hours long—and then see what happens. As for the NBA, the only reminder is a sticker on his locker that someone had put up. It reads: "Barkley for Gov."

Charles Barkley, an Alabama native, has spoken of his desire to run for governor of the state. "I told Charles," said Jordan, "that if that ever happened, you be like Huey Long in the movie 'Blaze,' a total dictator. I told him to stick to TV commercials."

Jordan laughed, then grabbed a couple of bats and went out to the batting cage to try again, and again. After that, he trotted out to right field, a position his father's baseball hero, Roberto Clemente, played. Perhaps it is only coincidence.

Jordan Tries, So Don't Be 'Stoopid'

September 2, 1991

Michael Jordan, probably deep in a summer bunker somewhere on this globe, has been attacked recently, not by bogeys, but by a couple of former athletes.

In a recent *Sports Illustrated* article, Hank Aaron, who was to baseball what Michael Jordan is to basketball, said that Jordan hasn't done enough for the black community.

Jim Brown, who was to football what Michael Jordan is to basketball, also said in a radio interview a short while ago that Jordan hasn't done enough for the black community.

Each implies that Michael Jordan has been too eager to take the money from White Corporate America, and run.

Each says that Michael Jordan could provide a greater inspiration to disadvantaged blacks by speaking out more, being more visible in the black communities.

Sharp criticism of a high-profile high-flyer like Jordan is not uncommon. The largest targets must dodge the most arrows. But when big-game hunters like Aaron and Brown are stalking you, it could mean not only that there is trouble, but that there is substance in their quivers, too.

In this case, however, both are wrongheaded.

Jordan, currently out of the country, was quoted in defense of himself in an article recently in the *Chicago Sun-Times*:

"I think that kind of criticism is totally unfair. I've been trying to have people view me more as a good person than a good black man. I know I'm black. I was born black and I'll die black. That goes without saying. But because I want every kid to be viewed as a person rather than as a member of a certain race does not mean that I'm not black enough.

"I've done a lot of things in the black community. If I'm guilty of anything, I'm guilty of not seeking publicity or keeping a record of everybody I've ever helped. I don't want any publicity for it anyway."

Tim Hallam, the public relations director for the Chicago Bulls, said: "You can't believe the tremendous number of requests he gets, from sick kids, from hospitals, from schools and community centers, and you can't believe how much stuff he does. Stuff nobody knows about."

There are numerous confirmed stories like these: Jordan spending time with a terminally ill white boy, bald from chemotherapy, and signing his Bulls jacket, and the boy later being buried in the jacket, as he had wished. Jordan meeting a little black girl in a wheelchair who was so nervous to meet her hero under the stands that she shook and cried while her parents were snapping a photograph.

"Wipe your eyes, honey," Jordan said, "we can't have tears in the picture." Her parents later wrote Jordan a letter thanking him and telling him it was one of the few times in recent months that their daughter had smiled.

If interested, one might discover the more public Jordan, in which his foundation has given money to black charities that include the United Negro College Fund and the Midwest Association for Sickle Cell Anemia.

He has provided more than a dozen college scholarships to needy black students. And he has lent his name to numerous causes, including one in which his picture was shown on billboards in Chicago and other cities with, "Don't Be Stoopid, Stay in School," written five times like a blackboard exercise.

But for Michael Jordan to be helpful to the community, why shouldn't he be as important to white kids as to black kids?

Why shouldn't he visit handicapped white kids as well as black?—his basic obligations, for now, are to do a good job as a basketball player and to be a good citizen. If he wants to be a social leader like Dr. Martin Luther King Jr. or a humanitarian like Albert Schweitzer or a philanthropist like Walter Annenberg, that's even better.

What we see in Michael Jordan is first a man who has an honest job, a man of great talent, surely, but who by very hard work has honed and enlarged his skills.

What we see in Michael Jordan, at this point, is someone who, unlike some other prominent athletes, has never been arrested, never had a drug problem, never had a street corner scuffle, never thrown a woman off a motel balcony, shows signs in his diction of a college education (or at least an awareness of expression), and in his positive demeanor of having listened to his parents.

Michael Jordan says he wants to be known as "a good person." While he's hardly perfect, he seems well along in achieving his goal. That alone is enough for whites and blacks and any other colors to admire, respect and learn from.

So let Michael Jordan enjoy his summer vacation, if hacking your way through woods and streams in pursuit of a little white ball is your idea of enjoyment.

* * *

Jordan retired as a basketball player for the final time in 2003, at age forty.

Jack Nicklaus: The Golden Bear Extraordinaire

On that sun-sweetened spring-time April afternoon at the final hole of the 1965 Masters tournament at the legendary if not sainted Augusta National Golf Course, the blond, thickly built, 5-foot-10, twenty-five-year-old Jack Nicklaus emerged from the hilly fairway. In white fedora with black band, light shirt, dark pants, two-toned shoes, he was preparing to putt out for his second Masters title. This was the last of his stunning four-day course journey—and would end with a tournament record of 271, seventeen strokes under par and with a record-tying 64 in the third round. He accomplished this remarkable performance amid holes named for their flora and fauna including Pink Dogwood, Flowering Peach, Flowering Crab Apple, Chinese Fir and Magnolia, Nandina, Azalea, and at eighteen, finally, Holly.

The bleachered crowd, in shirtsleeves, shorts and masked in sunglasses, roared as he sank the short putt on the final 18th hole, nine strokes in front of Gary Player and his then consummate rival Arnold Palmer, who tied for second.

Shortly after, at the trophy presentation, the equally legendary if not also sainted golfer and co-August a National course designer Bobby Jones handed the hardware to the broadly smiling Nicklaus. "Young man," said Jones, "you play a game that I am unfamiliar with."

It is true that Nicklaus helped transform the game with his power—often hitting short-irons into most of the par four holes and mid-irons into many of the par fives—but he had leavened it with finesse. Jones, who famously in 1930, in newsboy cap and knickers, won the Grand Slam of Golf—that is, the four majors in one year, the Masters, the US Open, the Open Championship (then known as the British Open) and the PGA championship—and he did it as an amateur (he would retire from tour golf in 1930 at age twenty-six, a year older than Nicklaus was now, and pursue a legal profession in Atlanta). Jones, in his era, was to golf what Babe Ruth was to baseball, Jack Dempsey to boxing, Red Grange to football, and even Man O'War to horse racing.

Five years later, in 1970 (and a year before his death at age sixty-nine), I called Jones at his law office and asked him about that startling quote, how Nicklaus played a game of golf that in its remarkable skill was distinctly foreign to him.

"Oh," said Jones, "I was just layin' on a compliment. You know how you do those things."

In other words, the old Southern gentleman was simply being Dixie gracious. It's my experience that athletes of an older generation, while paying some lip service of admiration and respect to the newer stars, still maintain, privately or publicly, their superiority. (I'm reminded of something Joe Louis said to Muhammad Ali, who was bragging about himself. "You know I used to have a bum-of-the-month club"—for a period, Louis knocked out one contender after another in swift succession. Ali said, "I heard about that." Louis said, "You woulda been one of them bums." And when I asked Oscar Robertson how Michael Jordan would have done in his day, Robertson said, "He could have scored 20 points a game." I said, "But Oscar, you averaged around 30 points a game." He said, "I know. I handled the ball more.")

In fact, Nicklaus, nicknamed "The Golden Bear" for his blondness, broadness and gilt-edged success, may well have played a game that Jones had never seen before, reaching pinnacles where he stood alone, beginning with his record 18 major championships—Tiger Woods is second at 15. And Nicklaus performed the spectacular feat of winning the Masters for the sixth time, in 1986, at age forty-six, becoming the tournament's oldest winner (in 1975, when he won his 14th major, in the PGA tournament, he broke Bobby Jones's record of

13 major wins). Nicklaus finished second in majors 19 times, third in nine others. He finished his career with 117 professional wins. Never another like him.

And Nicklaus rose to his golf greatness by first having to deal with his prime rival the effervescent and ever-popular Arnold Palmer. There was Palmer being followed by throngs that were called Arnie's Army. There he was hitching up his pants, tossing aside the cigarette that had dangled from his mouth in Humphrey Bogart style, and then addressing the ball on the fairway and whacking it with his unorthodox swing, almost as though he was about to strangle himself. But straight to the green the ball whizzed. Nicklaus, meanwhile, methodical (he said he came across as "too cold and grim and Teutonic"), hit the ball farther and sometimes straighter.

The rivalry that took them primarily through the 1960s began in 1960 in the US Open at the Cherry Hills Country Club in Cherry Hills, Colorado. Nicklaus, then an Ohio State student and the defending US Amateur champion at age twenty, finished second by two strokes to a hard-charging Palmer's "go for broke" style in which he became heralded for taking outrageous chances to come back in the last handful of holes to win tournaments thrilled the galleries—at Cherry Hills he erased a seven-stroke deficit in the final round. Palmer, a Masters winner, was ten years older than Nicklaus. Ben Hogan, who played the last 36 holes of that tournament with Nicklaus, said, "If the kid knew what he was doing he should have won by 10 strokes."

Nicklaus obviously was a quick study. Two years later, now having turned professional, he defeated Palmer in the US Open at Oakmont Country Club in Oakmont, Pennsylvania. by three strokes in an 18-hole playoff. "Now that the big guy is out of the cage," Palmer said afterward, "everybody better run for cover."

In 1963 Nicklaus won the Masters and in 1964 finished second in Augusta, six strokes behind Palmer. It was Palmer's last major win.

Nicklaus also had to combat a weight problem, and the abuse he endured from fans, not least of which were soldiers in Arnie's Army. "Fat Jack," he was called, as though he were the evil villain of a rasslin' show. Some even put up signs in front of sand traps which read, "Put it here, Jack."

But soon he not only lost weight, going from around 210 pounds to 185, and, no longer the plump pretender, he gained the respect and admiration of the galleries. And though he would never have the nation by its heartstrings the way Palmer had, still cries from the gallery like "Get 'em, Jack" became more frequent, as he piled up tournament win after tournament. Indeed, the big guy was out of the cage.

* * *

In 1986, few gave Nicklaus a chance to win the Masters at his advanced athletic age of forty-six—some referring to him as "The Olden Bear." The outsized talent and compelling drive for excellence had not escaped him, and he shot a blistering 30 on the back nine on the final day. I witnessed some of that intensity a mere eight months later when he joined three of his sons in a tournament in Boca Raton, Florida, near Nicklaus's home in North Palm Beach. I covered that event.

Rare Foursome: Nicklaus and Sons

December 12, 1986

The Bear and his cubs huddled this morning under broad green-and-white and red-and-white umbrellas to ward off the rain that was just starting. After a moment, Ursa Major said to his Ursa Minors, "Let's go, guys!"

This was no ordinary growl of bears, this was Jack Nicklaus, known widely as the Golden Bear, and a trio of his brood: Jack Nicklaus Jr., age twenty-five; Steve Nicklaus, twenty-three; and Gary Nicklaus, seventeen. They left the practice green together, armed to the teeth with wedges, putters, drivers, and 2-irons.

They were about to charge the Broken Sound Golf Club course in the $600,000 pro-am Chrysler Team Championship here, in the first of a four-day PGA Tour event.

As they approached the first tee, the first time the four of them have played together in a tournament, someone in the crowd called, "Where's Daddy?"

And Jack Jr. looked around. His father wasn't there. He was back on the practice green.

Nicklaus pere had looked at his watch, seen there were still seven minutes to tee time and turned to his caddy. "John," he said, "I'm gonna take a few more chips." And the old man, the old bear, the old champion went back to doing what he had done so often, getting in just as many practice shots as he possibly could . . .

As for what it's like playing with his father, Gary had said, "I play with him all the time. It's like playing with anyone else, I guess." It began to rain harder as the Nicklaus entourage gathered around the first green. The trees were dripping rain, the grass under the feet of the gallery was getting squishy and the slickers of the players crackled as they moved.

Steve was lining up his putt: "Fiddle around for a minute," said his father, under the umbrella held by his caddy, "so you don't have to putt in this." "That," he added with a smile, "is strategy."

Jack Jr. is a professional, two years out of the University of North Carolina . . . Steve and Gary are amateurs. Steve was a wide receiver on a football scholarship at Florida State and was known to his pals as "Arnie." ("Didn't bother me," he said. "Why should it?")

The Nicklauses finished the round seven under, six strokes behind the leaders. Jack said that his boys were relatively quiet on the course.

"But that'll change soon," he said. "Pretty soon they'll be telling me, 'Relax, dad, don't worry so much.'"

He said that they might even turn down his advice and play a putt left instead of right. "But that's good," he said. "You want them to have minds of their own. I never tell them to do very much concerning their lives. I suggest, I'll introduce them to things—yes, like golf—but it's up to them to do with it what they want."

His "suggestions" come in various forms. About Steve he said the young man plans to return to school. "He said," Nicklaus now crossed his fingers, "that he was going to pick up some books." And, Jack, who was an honorable mention all-state Ohio high school basketball player, told Gary, a high-school basketball standout, "the pump fake, the pump fake!"

"Were you nervous today?" Jack was asked after the foursome's round at Broken Sound.

"Sure," he said. "I had three kids out there. You want to make sure they're behaving themselves.'" (His wife, Barbara, also had a twenty-one-year-old daughter, Nan, and a thirteen-year-old son, Michael.)

Nicklaus paused. "And I guess my boys were nervous, too. They were concerned about keeping the old man in line."

* * *

The emotional and unconventional case of the disabled professional golfer Casey Martin would reach the hallowed halls of the United States Supreme Court, opposed by the PGA, the sports ruling body. And Jack Nicklaus would contribute his view as, to be sure, an expert witness.

Casey Martin in 1998 had sued the tour to use a cart when Klippel-Trenaunay-Weber Syndrome kept blood vessels in his right leg from working properly. The case would wind its way through the courts and end up at the United States Supreme Court, where it was decided on May 30, 2001.

Tiger Woods, Arnold Palmer, and Nicklaus had testified that a cart should not be used in tournaments. "I am concerned for Casey Martin; however, I very much believe that to play the sport, you have to have the physical part of it, too," Nicklaus said. "If I were allowed to use a cart, I would be able to compete much better on the regular tour, simply because my hip just wears out on me . . . I have a lot of sympathy for Casey. Unfortunately, I am going to have to go the other way."

Martin did win his case in Federal District Court but the USGA appealed. I happened to be at an event in Washington, DC and met Justice Antonin Scalia, having been introduced to him as a sports columnist for *The New York Times*. We had about a 15-minute conversation, just the two of us, that ranged from *The New York Times* (the staunchly conservative jurist said he didn't read it—but his wife, Maureen, gets a separate subscription to *The New York Times Sunday Book Review* section) to a jacket I was wearing ("I'd like to get one like that") to the Casey Martin case to which he had heard arguments before the Court. Of course, he said, he couldn't comment on his views before the decision was announced but he did offer this: "There is a rule book, you understand."

I told him that, with all due respect, I took a different view and that I'd written about it in the *Times*. I told him I'd be happy to send the column to him. He seemed vaguely interested. And indeed I sent it to him.

Fairness and Riding a Golf Cart

February 1, 1998

I was all for Casey Martin's losing his case and not being allowed to ride a cart in PGA tournaments—until 1964.

I was all for Martin, who has circulatory problems in his right leg that hinder his walking, to be defeated in his lawsuit against the PGA in his trial that begins tomorrow in Eugene, Oregon—until that dramatic, scorching 98-degree last day in the United States Open at the Congressional Country Club in Washington in 1964.

The most stirring golf story of fortitude and stamina is generally told about Ken Venturi's victory in the Open in 1964. As Arthur Daley wrote in this newspaper about that event: "The slim little guy in the white linen cap looked wilted and worn. In the blistering heat . . . he walked with the leaden steps of an old man, the strength sapped from him. He had virtually collapsed after the morning round and a physician accompanied him on the final tour of the course, watching with anxiety.

"Some inner force kept driving Ken Venturi onward until he had reached his date with destiny."

The greatest argument, espoused recently by such golfing deities as Arnold Palmer and Jack Nicklaus, against Martin's using a golf cart in tournaments is that stamina is a major part of golf; sometimes a golfer has to walk as many as five miles and up and down hills.

Venturi had struggled mightily to complete the day's final rounds, which were then a single-day 36-hole conclusion.

The following year, the PGA decided to break that test of stamina into two days of 18 holes each. It did so because television wished it, for commercial purposes. "The stamina has been removed," Daley wrote in 1965. "Only the skill remains."

While Palmer and Nicklaus disagree—and, apparently, Venturi does, too, since he will be testifying for the PGA with the other two—the Congressional began to put a different slant on things.

In recent years, some equipment changes in golf have also made a difference in the play. The Big Berthas, for example, the metal clubs that have added some 30 yards to many players' drives. It has made players of all sizes hit longer without cranking up, and expending the kind of energy they needed when using hickory-shaft clubs, or even the graphite cudgel. And it contributes to lesser players hitting straighter.

The PGA Championship was also changed, from match play to medal play, because of the demands of television.

An argument is that all these changes were across the board, and all players were equal because they were playing the same number of holes on the same days, and they could use whatever clubs they wanted to use.

In turning down the PGA's request to dismiss the lawsuit, and sending it to court for trial, Tom Coffin, the Federal magistrate, said that the PGA Tour is a public entity and that under the Federal Americans With Disabilities Act it must provide reasonable accommodations for someone with a permanent disability. Golf courses during tournaments, he said, are "places of public accommodations" as defined by the disabilities act.

Coffin added: "What is the PGA Tour? It is an organization formed to provide and operate tournaments for the economic benefit of its members. It is part of the entertainment industry, just as all professional sports are."

His reasoning here isn't compelling. After all, when talking about professional golfers, one speaks of self-employed businessmen, not amateur performers. And what is most important is the level playing field—even if it is one, in this instance, with hillocks and valleys. But that doesn't go to the heart of the issue, which is this: Does use of a cart change the nature of the game of golf?

No one is certain. But some presume, and heavyweight golfers like Nicklaus and Palmer must be respected, that the physically disadvantaged Martin would have a golfing advantage.

Others presume that Martin would have a golfing disadvantage, because walking loosens up the body for the next shot, instead of riding in a carriage that stiffens the limbs.

But rule changes have transformed most sports. Tennis is not the same since the oversized racquet. Baseball is not the same since the designated hitter and artificial grass. Football is not the same since receivers can wear gloves.

Yes, yes, say the critics, but it's fair for everyone. One player using a cart is a different story.

With that the case, then, as Marie Antoinette might have said, let them all ride in carts if they wish.

As for the PGA Tour executives upholding the bastion of tradition in the Royal and Ancient Game, it should exclude Casey Martin only when the true test of stamina—36 holes on the final day of competition—is returned.

Which will be never, because the PGA takes its marching orders— a felicitous phrase, no?—from television.

* * *

Shortly before the Supreme Court adjourned for the summer of 2001, it handed down a 7–2 decision which "rejected the Tour's argument that making an exception for Martin, with his degenerative condition in his right leg, would fundamentally alter the nature of championship golf."

Justice John Paul Stevens, an avid amateur golfer, wrote for the court: "From early on, the essences of the game has been shot making . . . and the walking rule was at best peripheral and not an indispensable feature of golf at any level. Thus it might be waived in individual cases without working a fundamental alteration."

Justice Scalia (along with Justice Clarence Thomas) dissented, and replied that, as he told me, "The rules are the rules," and added sardonically, that the court had undertaken the "solemn duty" to "decide What Is Golf." He added that the majority had acted with "a benevolent compassion that the law does not place it within our power to impose."

It might be added that Justice Scalia, while opposing Justice Stevens' stated opinion, never responded to mine, either.

Following the Court's decision, Casey Martin was quoted in *Golf Digest* about a conversation he had with Nicklaus's son Gary while the two played a practice round: "We were friends and had played a lot together. Gary said, 'Just so you know, the tour put a lot of pressure on my dad to testify, and I don't think he felt great about doing it.' Well, OK. But when I had some physical problems a year later, Jack phoned me. He wanted to know how I was doing and asked if he could do anything for me."

* * *

One of my favorite writers, and one of the funniest writers that ever penned a line (he did not use a typewriter), was the novelist and short-story writer P. G. Wodehouse. I interviewed him at his home in Remsenbug, Long Island, in 1969. The tall, baldish eighty-eight-year-old Wodehouse, who grew up playing golf in his native England, credited his golf game with much of his writing success. "I think it is rather a good thing to be a poor golfer," he told me. "You get comic ideas."

One of his characters, for example, "The Oldest Member" of the golf club, comments on "love" and "golf." "Love is an emotion which your true golfer should always treat with suspicion. Do not misunderstand me. I am not saying that love is a bad thing, only that it is an unknown quantity. I have known cases where marriage improved a man's game and other cases where it seemed to put him right off his stroke . . .

"There are higher, nobler things than love. A woman is only a woman, but a hefty drive is a slosh."

He paused to light his pipe. "How I loved the game," he continued. "I have sometimes wondered if we of the riffraff don't get more pleasure out of it than the top-notchers. For an untouchable like myself, two perfect drives in a round would wipe out all memory of sliced approach

75

shots and foozled putts, whereas if Jack Nicklaus does a 64, he goes home morosely that if he had not just missed that eagle on the seventh, he would have had a 63."

Red Grange: One Remarkable Galloping Ghost

The fame of Harold (Red) Grange, nicknamed "The Galloping Ghost," spread so quickly that it seemed that not only his hair but his reputation burned brightly. In his first game as a sophomore running back for the University of Illinois, against Nebraska, he ran 35 yards for a touchdown in the first quarter, 65 yards for another score in the second, and 12 yards for a third touchdown in the final period. He continued in this pace. In his junior year, against undefeated Michigan, he took the opening kickoff 95 yards for a touchdown. On the Illini's first play from scrimmage, he broke through for a 67-yard touchdown. He followed that with touchdown runs of 54 yards and then 44 yards. Before a crowd of 66,609 in Memorial Stadium in Champaign, Illinois, as *The New York Times* reported, "Grange astounded everyone present, including the larger football world, by rushing for 265 yards and 4 touchdowns in the first 12 minutes of the game. He later scored again on a 13-yard run and also threw a 20-yard touchdown pass in the fourth quarter, as Illinois won 39–14. He was a three-time first-team All-American.

When he turned pro in 1925, signing a huge contract with the Chicago Bears, he single-handedly (single-leggedly?) elevated the poorly attended National Football League, then only five years in existence, into national prominence. Though hampered by injuries through most of his nine-year pro career, and retiring in 1935 at age thirty-one, he was good enough when healthy to twice make first-team all-pro and was elected eventually into the Pro Football Hall of Fame (along with having been inducted into the College Football Hall of Fame).

He was in his time and for decades after the most famous football player on the planet. He made the cover of *Time* magazine in 1925, made Hollywood serials playing himself as "The Galloping Ghost," and in Arthur Miller's play, *Death of a Salesman*, which premiered on Broadway in 1949, fifteen years after Grange had played his last game, the protagonist Willy Loman says about his son, Biff, a high school football star, that "They'll be calling him another Red Grange." In 2008, ESPN ranked Grange the best college football player of all time, and in 1969, on the 100th anniversary of college football, the Football Writers Association of America selected its all-time All-American team and Grange was the only unanimous choice.

The Ghost Galloped Into History

January 30, 1991

"All Grange can do is run," Fielding Yost, the football coach of Michigan, was quoted as saying.

"All Galli-Curci can do is sing," said Bob Zuppke, the football coach of Illinois.

Harold (Red) Grange, that marvelous man and the subject of that long-ago exchange, died Monday morning in Lake Wales, Florida, at the age of eighty-seven. It was the morning after the Giants had beaten the Bills in the Super Bowl in Tampa, some 75 miles west of where Red Grange died.

In an indirect but significant way, Red Grange helped invent the Super Bowl, something he would have taken no credit for. First, because he was genuinely self-effacing, and secondly because, as he once told me, he had little interest in football anymore. "I've played and seen so much football," he said, "that I've been footballed up to my eyeballs."

There is an old, grainy black-and-white film clip I have of Red Grange running. It was shot on a rainy, miserable, muddy Saturday in October of 1925 when Grange ran for Illinois against Penn, one of the nation's best teams then. Wearing a helmet without bars, the haberdashery in those days, Red Grange is running in the thickness and ooze. But he runs with extraordinary grace and swiftness and change of pace and power.

He runs as if the other players are playing in the rain and mud, and he, except for the mud dripping from his uniform and the mud flying from his cleats, is running on a dry field.

In that game at Franklin Field in Philadelphia, Grange scored three touchdowns and gained 363 yards as Illinois won, 24–2. He did stuff like that a lot, and, in that age of the blooming of ballyhoo, earned the label, The Galloping Ghost.

One of the sportswriters at that Penn game was Damon Runyon. "This man Red Grange of Illinois," wrote Runyon in his newspaper account, "is three or four men and a horse rolled into one for football purposes.

"He is Jack Dempsey, Babe Ruth, Al Jolson, Paavo Nurmi, and Man o' War."

Grange's fame endured. He was one of the sports heroes of the Roaring Twenties that included people like Ruth and Dempsey and Bobby Jones and Bill Tilden and Johnny Weissmuller. And Red Grange was the last of them.

Grange left college to turn pro when pro football was so little regarded in comparison to the wildly popular college game that its crowds were small and the stories of the games were often buried in the sports sections.

One man changed all that, Red Grange. He signed with the Chicago Bears for $100,000 in 1925—an incredible sum then—and people flocked to the stadiums to see him run. A Red Grange industry emerged.

There were Red Grange caps and T-shirts, and people bought radios because they couldn't wait until the next day to read what Grange did. He went to Hollywood and made films, including serial cliff-hangers and a feature, *The Galloping Ghost*, starring the Ghost himself.

"We were through with World War I and all the boys were back and radio was just coming in and there was prosperity and the country and writers were looking to make big names of people," Grange recalled. "They needed someone in football and I guess I was the one they picked. I was happy that I was, too."

A number of years ago I asked him how he liked the modern players. "Some are wonderful," he said. He mentioned Larry Csonka and Dick Butkus, in particular. "But Bronko Nagurski was the best football player I ever saw," he said. "He played both ways like all of us did— and he played linebacker as good as Butkus and fullback as good as Csonka."

Grange retired from football in 1935, was a charter member of the Pro Football Hall of Fame, lost most of his money during the Depression, got back on his feet by selling insurance—"I'm very proud of that because I did it alone," he said. "In football you have ten guys blocking for you"—and later was a sports broadcaster.

The old great runner lived the latter years of his life in a comfortable home in Indian Lake, Florida, with his wife, Margaret (called "Muggs"), and their two dachshunds. The Galloping Ghost was still broad-chested, still had that gentle smile that I remembered from pictures, and still had his hair, though the red had turned white.

His trophies and scrapbooks were closeted somewhere, or given away. He said his neighbors knew he played football "a long time ago for some Midwestern college, and I let it go at that." He seemed more excited by the pair of sand-hill cranes that had alighted on his front lawn. "They're panhandlers," said Grange. "They like to come around here because they know we'll feed them."

At one point he gazed at joggers puffing past his house. "I think they're crazy," he said, with a touch of irony. "If you have a car, why run?"

About his football days, Grange said: "I never knew how I ran; I just ran. They built my accomplishments way out of proportion. There are a lot of doctors and teachers and engineers who could do their thing better than I could."

I asked him whether his wife called him Harold or Red. "Neither," he said. "She calls me honey."

A Trio of Nearly Unbeatable Record Holders

One day I received a phone call and voice at the other end didn't immediately identify himself.

"Don't you know who this is?" the caller asked.

"The voice is familiar, but I can't say I recognize it," I said.

"Give you a hint, I'm tall, dark, and handsome," he said.

"Hmm," I said thoughtfully. After a brief pause, I said, "I give, who are you?"

"It's me, Wilt," Chamberlain said.

"Wilt! If you had just said tall and dark, I might have gotten it. The handsome threw me off."

A great laughter came through the telephone wire. Wilt always could take a joke, sometimes even at his own expense.

Wilt Chamberlain owns so many National Basketball Association records that it seems he should have one book devoted solely to those records. One, most rebounds in a game, 55, was achieved against of all opposing centers, the Boston Celtic great Bill Russell (who had 19 rebounds, and the Celtics still won the game 132–129). Perhaps Chamberlain's most famous record, though, regards the night he scored 100 points in a game. That record still stands, a third of a century later.

Similarly, Ted Williams's batting average of .406 in 1941 has not been surpassed. That's better than three-quarters of a century.

Gale Sayers scored six touchdowns in one game, equaling a record by the Cleveland Browns' Dub Jones. A few runners in the National Football League have scored five touchdowns in a game, but none have crossed the goal line seven times. And Sayers did it as a rookie, yet!

The Night Chamberlain Scored 100

March 1, 1987

He was so large and so strong and his feats were so outlandish that he wouldn't be nicknamed for anything so mundane as a mere world, or planet, or star. He was named for an entire constellation. He was the Big Dipper.

When someone without an ounce of creativity tried to tag him with Wilt the Stilt, he scorned it—the rhyme too obvious, the symbolism too limiting. Big Dipper, however, was acceptable.

Wilton Norman Chamberlain would be to basketball what Paul Bunyan was to logging, Hercules to stables, and King Kong to assorted skyscrapers.

Chamberlain once recalled driving across Arizona or New Mexico and pulling his car momentarily to the side of the road, when he was attacked by a mountain lion. He said the mountain lion jumped on his shoulder, and he grabbed it by the tail and flung it into the bushes.

"Well, I wasn't there," Cal Ramsey, the former Knick announcer, once said, "but Wilt says it happened, and I'm not about to say it didn't. Besides, he showed me these huge scratch marks on one shoulder. I don't know any other way he could have gotten them."

When Frank McGuire became Chamberlain's coach with the Philadelphia Warriors before the 1961–62 season, he called all his players individually into his office to chat with them. "When Wilt came in," said McGuire, "I asked him how long he'd like to play. He said, 'Forever.' I almost fell off my chair. I said, 'No, Wilt, in a game.' He said, 'I don't ever have to come out of a game.' And he didn't."

That season, Chamberlain averaged 50.4 points and 48.5 minutes per game, in a 48-minute game (the overlapping percentage point in minutes played was caused by overtimes).

In his first season in the National Basketball Association, with the Warriors, the 7-foot-1, 275-pound Chamberlain, the swift Chamberlain (he had been an outstanding high school quarter-miler in Philadelphia), the agile Chamberlain (he had been a superb high-jumper for the University of Kansas), the unbounded Chamberlain (he would one day seek and come close to fighting for the heavyweight championship against Muhammad Ali), and now this rookie Chamberlain broke the record for most points averaged in an NBA season, 37.6. He broke that record the next season, with 38.4. In his third season, he averaged a Babe the Blue Ox figure of 50.4 points a game. This was 1961–62, and in a triple-overtime game against the Lakers early in the season, he broke Elgin Baylor's single-game scoring record with 78 points. Baylor had scored 71 a year earlier.

"One day," Al Attles, a teammate, told a friend in mid-February, "Wilt's going to score a hundred points. Wait and see."

Neither Attles nor the friend had to wait long. On March 2, 1962—twenty-five years ago tomorrow—Chamberlain scored 100 points. (The closest anyone has ever come to that, other than Wilt himself, of course, was David Thompson in 1978, with a paltry 73 points).

Chamberlain, then twenty-five years old, established the mark against the Knicks, in the Hershey Arena in Hershey, Pennsylvania, and did it, in the mold of the fabled, despite having had no sleep the night before.

Chamberlain was too huge for just one city, and so he played for Philadelphia but lived in New York, on Central Park West.

"He was always on time, and never missed a practice, or a bus, or was late for a game," said McGuire.

On the night before the night of the game in Hershey, Pennsylvania—a site at which the Warriors would play a handful of "home games"—Chamberlain was out on a late date in New York and never did get to sleep.

When he walked into the dressing room in Hershey, McGuire came over and showed Chamberlain two New York newspapers with quotes from some Knicks about how they were going to "run me ragged," Chamberlain recalled, because, the players said, they "know" he is pretty slow and doesn't have stamina.

"Coach McGuire knows that's ridiculous, but he doesn't know I haven't had any sleep yet," said Chamberlain, "so he just grins slyly and says, 'Let's run 'em tonight, Wilt.'"

"We ran, all right—and ran and ran and ran."

Chamberlain now lives in the exclusive area of Bel Air in Los Angeles, in a $1.5 million mansion he had built about fifteen years ago. Now fifty years old, he seems to have aged little. Occasionally, there is still a report that some NBA team wants to sign him for part of a season. He laughs about this, and graciously declines. When last seen in Manhattan, over the summer, Chamberlain was still a well-chiseled specimen, with a slim waist and biceps the size of, well, not quite watermelons, but cantaloupes, anyway. He is still busy in sports, and is an avid volleyball player, and retains ambitions of playing for the 1988 United States Olympic team.

But now he was looking back instead of forward, back to that Friday night twenty-five years ago in Hershey. It was a rather small arena, seating 7,200, and a crowd of 4,124 showed up.

"It's amazing," Chamberlain recalled in a telephone interview recently, "but I'll bet I've had 25,000 come up to me and say they saw the game. What's more amazing is, most of them say they saw it at Madison Square Garden. That's some feat. Can you imagine how good their eyes were?"

One person who was not at the game was Phil Jordan, the Knicks' starting center, who was ill. Eddie Donovan, the coach of the last-place Knicks, started his second-string center, Darrall Imhoff. It was Imhoff's assignment to guard Chamberlain -with, of course, help from the forwards when possible, as was the case with all the centers in the NBA who played Wilt. "You're all I've got tonight," Donovan told Imhoff. "Try not to foul out."

Imhoff tried, but didn't succeed. "He was getting down the court so fast I couldn't keep up with him," recalled Imhoff, who played a total of 20 minutes and fouled out in the fourth quarter. "We tried collapsing three guys around him, but it didn't help."

Chamberlain recalled that he hit his first six jump shots from the outside, and at the end of the first quarter the Warriors were ahead, 42–26. Chamberlain had 23 points, including 9-straight free throws.

"Remember, I was a notoriously bad free-throw shooter in games," said Chamberlain. "But now I thought I might break a record, but it was for consecutive free throws. Breaking the single-game record for total points didn't enter my head—not even at the half."

At halftime, Chamberlain had 41 points, on 14 of 26 from the field, and 13 of 14 from the free-throw line.

"I'd often come into the dressing room at halftime with 30 or 35 points," said Chamberlain. "So 41 was not a particularly big deal."

Everything was going in for him from the foul line and from the field: his fade-away jumper off the backboard, his jump shot from in front of the basket, his finger-roll, and, of course, his periodic dunks.

He recalled that there were few dunks, although Richie Guerin, the Knick guard who scored 39 points that night, remembers that there were more than a few.

No one will ever be certain. It was a simpler age, an age in which sports were considerably less inundated with technology than they are today, and not all games were televised. This one, unfortunately, was not. So all we have are the memories of eye-witness accounts, some of which differ in small detail.

In the third quarter, Chamberlain scored another 28 points, and now had 69. "It looked like I had a good chance to break my record of 78," he said. "I didn't even think of 100."

On the Warrior bench McGuire was coaching, as he recalls it, just another game. "But somewhere in the fourth quarter, one of the players woke me up and said, 'Coach, do you realize Wilt has 86 points?' Or some number like that. And I really hadn't been aware of it."

David Zinkoff, the public address announcer at the Warrior home games, started calling out how many points Chamberlain had every time he scored in the fourth quarter. And the fans began screaming, "Give it to Wilt, give it to Wilt." And the Philadelphia players were. "We did for two reasons," said Attles. "One was, our style of play as designed by Coach McGuire was to get the ball as close to the basket as possible for a shot, and that meant getting it to Wilt in the low post. The other was, we wanted Wilt to break the record. We all liked Wilt a lot. He's got a reputation by some as being kind of tough, or whatever. But he's really a wonderful guy. We were happy to get him the ball."

Earlier in the season, McGuire recalled, he had informed the team of his philosophy to get the ball to Wilt. "And they said fine, no problem," said McGuire. "But they asked me one thing. When the season was over, and their personal statistics might be a little barren, would I go to management at contract time and talk for them. I said, 'Absolutely.'"

Now Wilt had about 90 points with a few minutes to go. McGuire, a New Yorker, said he felt a little sheepish about having Wilt go for the record, "I never want to embarrass anyone on the basketball court," he said, especially a New York team.

The New York team wasn't happy about it either.

"We began to foul their players," recalled Guerin, "and sometimes even foul Wilt. And they began to foul us to get the ball for Wilt because we began to stall. It turned into a travesty. It's not what basketball is supposed to be all about."

Bill Campbell, doing the radio play-by-play, made an audio tape of Chamberlain's final 8 points of the game: Chamberlain made a 12-foot bank shot to give the Warriors a 161–139 lead, and Chamberlain 94

ONE OF A KIND—EVERY ONE OF THEM

points. He made another basket moments later: 96 points. With 1 minutes 27 seconds left, Chamberlain had 98 points. He then stole an inbounds pass and shot for 100, and missed.

"The Knicks are eating up time and the Warriors foul Guerin deliberately," said Campbell. Guerin made two free throws.

Then Zinkoff told the crowd, many of whom had left their seats and were now surrounding the court, "He's going for 100, sit back and relax."

The crowd screamed: "Give it to Wilt! Give it to Wilt!"

The Knicks pressed, and Guy Rodgers threw a long pass to Chamberlain, who shot and missed. A reserve forward, Ted Luckenbill, rebounded the shot, passed it back to Chamberlain, who missed again, and Luckenbill rebounded again, and passed to Joe Ruklick, another reserve, who passed the ball to Chamberlain, who shot again, and scored! Finally!

"What a relief," Chamberlain would recall.

Suddenly the invisible wall that kept the fans on the outside of the rectangle of the court broke, and they came flooding wildly onto the court.

"I remember Wilt was carrying four or five kids on his back," said McGuire. "It was quite a scene."

There were 46 seconds to play, but the game would not be resumed, and the Warriors won, 169–147. "It was just as well," recalled Attles. "That round number of 100 is magical. It wouldn't be quite the same if Wilt came back and scored a total of, say, 103."

In the dressing room afterward, Wilt checked the statistics sheet and noted that he had shot 36-for-63. "My God!" he said. "That's terrible. I never thought I'd take that many shots in a game." He was pleased, though, with his foul-shooting: 28-for-32, the most free throws scored in a regular-season NBA game and one of the best nights from the foul line in his career. (His career foul-shooting percentage was only .511.)

Others had had good games that night, as well, although they were overlooked. Attles, not known as a good shooter, had a perfect shooting night: 8-for-8 from the floor, and 1 for 1 from the foul line.

"For years afterward, I'd kid Wilt that I took the pressure off him so that they couldn't sink back and guard him," Attles said.

"Not true," Chamberlain recalled recently. "He scored so well because no one was guarding him. He was crying so much about no one ever knowing he'd had a great shooting night, that about three years ago I gave him the damn game ball from that night."

It was also a symbol of Chamberlain's appreciation to his teammates. "Without them I could never have broken the record," he said. "They went way beyond the call of duty."

For all of Chamberlain's athletic achievements, that 100-point game stands out in the minds of many.

"Even today when I'm an airplane terminal, or hotel lobby, I hear people saying, 'He's the guy who scored a hundred points,'" Chamberlain said.

They also say something else, according to Chamberlain. "They say, 'Yeah, but his team lost the game.' We didn't, though we did lose the one where I scored 78 points. But I always said, 'Nobody roots for Goliath.' But now, I don't know, maybe people are beginning to appreciate some of the things I did."

On the bus ride back to New York after that night twenty-five years ago tomorrow, Imhoff sat alone in deep thought. Finally, he looked up and shook his head. "I can't have a nightmare tonight," he said. "I just lived through one."

Chamberlain also went back to New York. He remembers driving back with Willie Naulls and a few other Knick players.

"We talked about the record, and they said it might never be broken, and I thought it would—records are always broken," said Chamberlain. "Even though I had just scored a hundred points against these guys, it was a nice ride back. I was extremely tired—remember, I hadn't slept in about a day and a half—but I was still on a high, and it would be hours before I finally got some sleep."

* * *

Wilton Norman Chamberlain died of congestive heart failure on October 12, 1999. He was sixty-three years old. At Chamberlain's death, Bill Russell, his long-time rival on the court and personal friend, said, "The fierceness of our competition bonded us together for eternity."

* * *

The first time I met Ted Williams was in spring training, Pompano Beach, Florida, 1969 when he was manager of the Washington Senators. Nineteen-sixty-eight was the "Year of the Pitcher," in which batting averages plummeted and pitching records soared. The sociologist Marshall McLuhan said that baseball was a dying sport, with interest declining. "Baseball," he wrote, "was doomed." I asked Williams about that. "Everything," he said succinctly, "goes in cycles. Baseball will rebound." Indeed it did.

Ted Williams: The Slugging Professor

March 23, 1985 / Winter Haven, Florida

In his open-air classroom here among the swaying palms and noisy bats, Prof. Theodore Samuel Williams was expounding on the virtues of getting your bellybutton out in front of the ball.

"It's that little magic move at the plate," he was saying recently, beside the batting cage on a field behind Chain O'Lakes Stadium. He wore a Red Sox uniform and a blue windbreaker with little red stockings embossed at the heart and stood on ripple-soled baseball shoes. It was late morning, cool but sunny as he spoke to a couple of young players. "Hips ahead of hands," he said in a deep, ardent baritone, "hips ahead of hands."

And the one-time Splendid Splinter—he is a Splinter no longer—demonstrated with an imaginary bat and an exaggerated thrust of his abdomen. "We're talking about optimum performance, and the optimum is to hit the ball into your pull field with authority. And getting your body into the ball before it reaches the plate—so you're not swinging with all arms—that's the classic swing. But a lot of batters just can't learn it, or won't."

Dr. Williams—and if he isn't a bona fide Ph.D. in slugging, who is?—is author of the authoritative textbook "The Science of Hitting." He also is the last professor or hitter or anyone else to bat .400 in the major leagues (he hit .406 in 1941) and had a scholarly career average of .344. This spring, he is serving the Red Sox as batting instructor with minor league players.

Ted Williams on hitting is Lindbergh on flying, Picasso on painting and Little Richard on Tutti Frutti.

Professor Williams is now sixty-seven years old and drives around the Red Sox complex in a golf cart, stopping now at this field, now at that. And though he says he's "running out of gas," it hardly seems so to the casual visitor, and there are many who come just to see him in the leathery flesh. He arrives before 9 a.m. at the training site and spends a long, full day under the Florida sun observing the young players.

He knows that there are as many theories on hitting as there are stars in the sky. "Like I've heard some where they tell a batter to keep his head down," he said. "No way you can open your body and carry through with your head down that way." He says that he may not be right for all the players, but he urges them to "listen—you can always throw away what you don't want, and keep what works for you." And, like the good teacher, he listens, too. An image returns of him in the clubhouse, sitting on a storage trunk and nodding in understanding while a minor-leaguer quietly talks to him.

In the batting cage now was the third baseman Steve Lyons, a 6-foot-3, 190-pound left-handed batter who bears a physical resemblance to the young Ted Williams. Lyons, after four seasons in the minor leagues, has a chance to make the parent club.

Williams watched him swing. "He's improvin' good," said Williams, "improvin' good. Has good power and good contact."

Last season, Lyons's batting average jumped to .268 in Triple A ball, 22 points higher than the previous year in Double A. He credits some of that improvement to Williams.

"He's not quick to criticize or change you immediately," Lyons said. "He watches, and then when he talks, people listen. He tries to be positive in his approach. He'll say, 'You've got a good swing, but there's not enough action into the ball. Cock your bat back farther.'"

When Williams was young, he sought advice. Before his rookie year with the Red Sox in 1939, he met Rogers Hornsby and asked, "What do I have to do to be a good hitter?" Hornsby said, "Get a good ball to hit."

"That's not as easy as it sounds," said Williams. "If the pitcher throws a good pitch, low and outside or high and inside—in the strike zone but not in the batter's groove—you let it go with less than two strikes. With two strikes, you move up a little bit on the knob of the bat. But too many hitters aren't hitters from the head up, and never become as good as they can be."

Sometimes the best advice is no advice at all. "When I was comin' up," said Williams, "Lefty O'Doul said to me, 'Don't let anybody change you.' And when I saw Carl Yastrzemski, I thought pretty much the same thing. He had a big swing, and I thought he should cut down his swing just a little. But I never came right out and said it. I'd say, 'Gotta be quicker, a little quicker.' And I think it took him longer than it should've to get his average up. Look at his record. He batted under three hundred his first two years in the big leagues. Then he hit .321. Same guy, same swing, same everything. But he got a little quicker, got a little quicker."

It was Paul Waner who told Williams about getting the bellybutton out in front of the ball.

"And I saw the best hitters doing it. Cronin did it, and Greenberg did it, and York and DiMaggio," he said. Of current-day players, Pete Rose and Rod Carew hit that way. "Reggie Jackson doesn't, but he's so strong that he can get away with that arm action. Now, Al Oliver isn't the classic hitter—a swishy, inside-out hitter—but he's gonna get 3,000 hits because he makes such good contact.

"Guys like Mantle and Mays—great, classic hitters—could have been even better if they had thought more at the plate. They struck out too much—and they'll tell you that, too. You got to concede a little to the pitcher, even the greatest hitters have to. Look at DiMaggio, he struck out only a half or a third as many times as he walked. It meant he was looking for his pitch—he was in control, not the pitcher."

Williams no longer teaches by example, and said that the last time he stood in the batter's box was in last year's old-timer's game in Fenway Park.

"I hit two little ground balls to the pitcher," he said. "I was so anxious up there, I couldn't wait for the ball, and hit them at the end of the bat."

Was he embarrassed? "Was I?" said the professor. "I didn't want to run to first base."

* * *

Ted Williams, retired from baseball after managing the Texas Rangers in the 1972 season, but continued in his other passion, fly fishing (he is in both the baseball and international fishermen's Halls of Fame). Williams died on July 5, 2002, at age eighty-three.

Gale Sayers: "*Brian's Song* Reprise"

November 2, 1988

It began as a humdrum affair, this annual dinner put on by the Professional Football Writers. This was on a night in May of 1970 at the old Americana, if memory serves. This writer finished the meal, witnessed a few annual awards presented, heard a few speeches and, naturally, began a discreet move toward the exit.

Gale Sayers, the swift running back for the Chicago Bears, then rose on the dais to accept the award for the most courageous football player of the year, having come back in 1969 from knee surgery the previous season and led the National Football League in rushing.

I stood at the door for a moment as Sayers began to speak. He seemed serious, and he dispensed with the unusual banter. He began talking about his teammate, and his backup at halfback, Brian Piccolo.

He talked about their friendship, and about how he, a black man, and Piccolo, who was white, roomed together on the road, highly unusual in those days, and not common today, some twenty years later.

Then he said something else, and to recall it exactly I returned to Sayers's 1970 autobiography, *I Am Third*, written with Al Silverman.

"He has the heart of a giant," Sayers said of Piccolo, "and that rare form of courage that allows him to kid himself and his opponent, cancer. He has the mental attitude that makes me proud to have a friend who spells out the word courage twenty-four hours a day for his life."

People in the banquet hall turned to each other and asked, "Did he say cancer?" Most people had been unaware of how seriously ill Piccolo was.

Also, Sayers had a tendency then to speak quickly, and sometimes in his shyness and in his rush to get the words out they got a little muffled in his throat.

But Sayers had indeed said "cancer," and for the first time, it was out in the public about Piccolo.

"You flatter me by giving me this award," added Sayers, "but I tell you here and now that I accept it for Brian Piccolo. Brian Piccolo is the man of courage who should receive this . . . award. I love Brian Piccolo and I'd like all of you to love him, too. Tonight, when you hit your knees, please ask God to love him. . ."

It was all kind of unbelievable, and the "knees" and "God" and "love" were bunched together, but the sense of it was clear, and I had goose bumps, rooted there at the door.

Piccolo died a few weeks later. The relationship between the two men—and that scene that I witnessed—has been celebrated in a film, *Brian's Song* (Sayers is played by Billy Dee Williams, Piccolo by James Caan), that has been shown regularly on television since the early 1970's.

"I've been retired for eighteen years, and I only played 68 games in six seasons," said Sayers, "and a lot of people remember me as a football player, but most people, especially those under twenty-five, remember me from the movie. People bring it up everywhere I go." Yesterday, Gale Sayers was in town. He is forty-five years old and, in gray business suit, still trim at his playing weight of 205. He was here promoting a charity sponsored by Old Spice and called the Gale Sayers Humanitarian Citation. It goes to the rookie in the National Football League who most actively supports his charity through community good works.

There has never been a rookie, however, quite like Sayers. He broke a record in 1965 for touchdowns in a season (22), and tied one for touchdowns in one game (6), and he led the league in scoring. He would be All-Pro five times before a second knee injury brought his career to an end.

"Before Brian died at twenty-six," said Sayers yesterday, "there were only three things in the world that were important to me. They were football, football and football. After that, I realized how selfish I was. I felt I needed to adjust my life, to look around me, at my family, my friends—and my future."

In the fall of 1970, Sayers became chairman of the Cancer Society in Chicago, and he has continued to participate in that organization.

Even before this, though, Sayers had taken seriously the advice given him by George Halas, the owner of the Bears, and Buddy Young, a representative of the NFL. They had said that it was important for him to prepare to play football, but it was also important for him to prepare to quit.

After his spectacular rookie season, in fact, he went to school to learn to be a stockbroker. The following year he received his license. He did that a few years, tried broadcasting, then missed football and wanted to return, not as a player or coach, but in the front office.

There were no blacks in the front office of the NFL, and there are very few today. Also, there remain no black head football coaches, despite 50 percent of the players being black.

Sayers returned to his alma mater, Kansas, earned a master's degree and was an assistant athletic director for four years, and then went to Southern Illinois as athletic director for five years.

Now he was ready, he had paid his dues. He wrote to every one of the 28 NFL teams seeking a position in the front office. Some answered, some didn't. The nicest reply, he said, was "No."

Sayers gave up thoughts of the front office in football—he says he is only a casual watcher of games these days—and is owner of a computer company with offices in Skokie, Ill., and Phoenix.

He says he is not bitter, that one day a black man will break the barriers of the NFL, but he says it won't be him.

He says he has other concerns now, and that, just as he discovered eighteen years ago, those three elements that were once paramount to him, football, football and football, no longer are.

* * *

It was in the early 1970s when I ran into Gale Sayers and his then wife Linda. I told them that I had recently interviewed Edward Villella, premier dancer of the New York City ballet, and with him being a sports fan, asked who of the outstanding athletes he had observed would have made a great ballet dancer. He said without hesitation, Gale Sayers, for his great graceful ability to move his body to avoid tacklers. Linda Sayers gave a smile. "What was funny?" I asked. "Gale," she replied, "can't dance." Sayers disputed her. "Yes, I can," he said, "a little." In 2013, Sayers was diagnosed with dementia, a result—most likely—of concussions he had suffered during his playing days.

Young, and Stardom Awaits

The remarkable professional careers of LeBron James, Sidney Crosby, Martina Navratilova, Tiger Woods, and Derek Jeter hardly need recital here. All indications were headed in that vastly upward direction when they were in their teens, or shortly out of them.

LeBron James: At 16, and Leaves No Doubt

July 9, 2001 / Teaneck, New Jersey

A stellar array of basketball cognoscenti that included scouts from almost every NBA team and college coaches—pads and pencils at the ready, projected mental insights awhirl—flocked yesterday to see some 220 of the best high school players in the world showcased at Fairleigh Dickinson's Rothman Athletic Center. One player in particular, however, caught much of their attention.

He is a sixteen-year-old from St. Vincent-St. Mary High School in Akron, Ohio, who will be a junior in the fall. Many of the gathered connoisseurs believed that the lad, LeBron James, a 6-foot-7, 210-pound point guard, shooting guard and small forward—sometimes he plays as if he is all three in one, a kind of hoops Swiss Army knife—would have been taken in the first round of the most recent NBA draft, possibly a lottery pick.

Hey, it was one thing for three of the first four picks in the draft to be high school seniors, for the first time ever, and four of the first eight—but a high school sophomore potentially going pro? "And next year," said Sonny Vaccaro, founder and director of the Adidas ABCD four-day camp, which began yesterday, "LeBron could surely go in the lottery. He'll be bigger, stronger and smarter."

OK, still, a high school junior making the jump? Got to be kidding? No?

Tom Konchalski, who evaluates high school players for his respected H.S.B.I. Report, said: "LeBron isn't an extraterrestrial athlete, but he has a tremendous feel for the game. He sees situations two passes ahead of the play. He's been compared to Vince Carter and Tracy McGrady. But I think he has a better feel for the game than they do."

He meant than they did when they were James's age, right? "No, I mean right now," Konchalski said. "I doubt seriously if he's going to college."

So LeBron James, in a yellow uniform and wearing No. 155, his hair tufted out and his pants baggy, began one of the four games going on at once, after the first round of four games had been completed. There were marvelous players on the courts, including 6-foot-6 Lenny Cooke of Old Tappan, New Jersey, and 6-foot-8 Carmelo Anthony of Baltimore, but none except James made first team All-America last season as chosen by *USA Today*, the first underclassman named to the first team in the eighteen years that such authoritative selections have been made.

He tried his first shot, a 3-pointer from the top of the key, and it swished. His next shot was a 3-pointer from the corner. Swish. There was a fast-break dunk, a clever pass for a basket, a missed jump shot, then he snared a rebound and stuffed it with both hands behind his head.

"Wow," one of the other players in the stands said. "Wow," said nearly everyone else.

James's mother, Gloria, watched her only child play. She is an enthusiastic fan of LeBron.

"What I want for LeBron is his happiness," said Gloria, who has worked in accounting and sales but is now unemployed. "He loves basketball. But I would like to see him graduate with his class from high school, at least. But we'll make a decision when the time comes. He's a level-headed boy. He's never given me a lick of problems. He's manner-able and respectful."

LeBron James, a solid B student, said that he wasn't sure what he planned to do. "College is important," he said, "you can't play basketball all your life. You should prepare for something else, too." To be safe, his mother said she was taking out an insurance policy on him.

Kwame Brown, the No. 1 pick by the Washington Wizards last month, received a $12 million contract for three years. "That's a lot of money," James said. "But we've struggled this long, a couple more years won't make that much difference."

Billy Donovan, head coach at Florida, had signed Brown to attend his university. "And he wanted to go to college," Donovan said. "But he made a decision that he thought was best for him, and his family. I can't fault him for that."

Ernie Grunfeld, general manager of the Milwaukee Bucks, was in attendance, primarily, he said, because his 6-foot-6 son, Danny, who will be a senior, was playing—he's a good player but not a pro prospect, yet. "I wish all the kids would go to college first," Grunfeld said. "But I also don't think you should prevent someone from trying to earn a living. I just hope the kids who do skip college have the emotional and physical maturity to succeed."

Among the players, 6-foot-7 Demetris Nichols from Barrington, Rhode Island, who will be a junior, dreams about an NBA future, like many of his peers, but is also realistic. "We talk more about college than the pros," he said. He also thought there was substance in the talk that Kobe Bryant gave to the group Saturday night. Bryant, the Lakers' star, jumped from high school to the pros. "Kobe said: 'Go to college. You have something to fall back on. If you break a leg, then where are you?'" Nichols said.

But Kobe—who, like Brown, is an alumnus of this camp—didn't go to college. "He's good," Nichols replied, with emphasis. He added that he has to be careful: "Everybody wants a piece of you. If somebody tells me I should go pro, I'm going to make sure he knows basketball."

From appearances, that could be somebody like LeBron James, counsel also to himself.

* * *

When LeBron James graduated high school and declared for the National Basketball Association draft, it was the same year, 2003, that freshman Carmelo Anthony had led Syracuse University to the NCAA championship. I was interviewing Jerry West, then the general manager of the Memphis Grizzlies, and said I thought it was a tossup who to choose in the draft because both James and Anthony were so good, and maybe the scale was weighted to Anthony for his college success. West looked at me like I was crazy. "There is no question," he said. "James goes first." And while Anthony has had a very good professional career, James's was clearly superior, leading both the Miami Heat and the Cleveland Cavaliers to NBA titles, achievements Anthony has never matched.

Sidney Crosby: The Next One Is Here

October 5, 2005 / Pittsburgh, Pennsylvania

Before arriving in training camp on Sept. 13, most of the Penguins players had never seen Sidney Crosby.

They did know that Crosby, a center from Cole Harbour, Nova Scotia, was the first pick in the National Hockey League Draft on July 30. He was being hailed as the "Next One," in homage to Wayne Gretzky, the Great One, and as the new face of the league after it went dark for 16 months because of a lockout that wiped out last season.

Yet Craig Patrick, the executive vice president and general manager of the Penguins, had never seen Crosby play in the flesh before the draft.

"My scouting staff had seen him, and I had seen video clips, but they don't show everything, like positioning, like heart," Patrick said. "I was curious, too."

Mario Lemieux, the captain of the Penguins as well as their chairman and chief executive, said: "It's one thing to have talent. It's another to develop that talent. I wondered, What kind of work ethic does he have?"

Patrick said that he had seen enough videotape to appreciate the eighteen-year-old Crosby's skill at handling the puck, his vision on the ice in seeing and setting up teammates for goals, and his dexterity and strength on skates. "What concerned me," Patrick said, "was, Can someone this young handle the pressure, all this attention, all these expectations?"

In less than a month after drafting Crosby, the Penguins sold more tickets than the 475,080 they did for the 2003–04 season, in which they averaged 11,877 fans a game and had the lowest attendance in the league. The Penguins, who finished last in the Atlantic Division in the previous three seasons, drew news media coverage as never before to their first day of training camp in Wilkes-Barre, Pennsylvania. Everyone had come to see Crosby, a courteous, brown-eyed, boyish-looking player with dark, cow-licked hair cropped short. At 5-foot-11 and 193 pounds, he is put together bountifully, but does not have the prodigious build expected of someone counted on to be the team's savior.

"Like everyone else, our guys were curious about Sidney, in all this heightened fever," Coach Ed Olczyk said. "So was I. We all knew he had torn up the junior hockey leagues the last several years. But we all wanted to see what he could do here, now."

Indeed, Crosby was the player of the year last season in the top-caliber Canadian Hockey League, and with career scoring totals in the league second only to Gretzky and Lemieux, whom the Penguins drafted first over all in 1984.

"We got our first real look at him in his first preseason game, against Boston," Olczyk said of the September 21 game in Wilkes-Barre. "He had looked good in training-camp scrimmages, but this was his first real game against an NHL opponent."

And so, strapping on his skates, and donning his shoulder pads and elbow pads and hip pads and knee pads and shin pads and gloves and helmet as well as his Penguins jersey, No. 87, for his birth date, 8/7/87, Sidney Crosby, with stick in hand and with what appeared to be little trepidation, skimmed onto the ice.

"There was one play in which he split the defense on a shot from the middle of the ice in that game," Olczyk said. "It was so quick, like the two defenders were standing still."

The puck caromed off the goalie's glove, and Mark Recchi, one of a handful of veteran free agents signed by the Penguins to ease the transition for Crosby, slapped it in for a score. "All the players gave each other quick glances when Sid made that play," Olczyk said. "They knew they had seen something special."

Patrick has been impressed with Crosby's poise, on and off the ice. "He has a maturity that you don't expect from someone so young," he said. "But he's been in the limelight since he's been thirteen years old. So I guess he's accustomed to dealing with it. And he works very hard on the ice, in the weight room. He's eager to learn."

In the locker room after practice Tuesday, Crosby said that he was not about to compare himself to Gretzky or Lemieux.

"What they accomplished, they did over a long period of time," he said. "Right now, my goal is simply to help the team, to be a really good all-around player, not just scorer."

102

If Crosby does, he will be deserving of his $850,000 salary for each of the next three years; he can earn up to $4 million with performance bonuses.

Crosby's father, Troy, was a top amateur hockey player. "His advice to me? Never take anything for granted," Crosby said.

Crosby will make his regular-season debut on the road as the Penguins open against the Devils on Wednesday, Lemieux's fortieth birthday.

There has been a learning curve for Crosby. At the first home pre-season game, on Tuesday against the Columbus Blue Jackets, he received a standing ovation from the crowd of about 8,000 at Mellon Arena when he entered the game, but he played relatively quietly.

"It wasn't the best he's done in preseason, but I thought he did a couple of really good things," Olczyk said. "If you were really watching, he made two or three really good plays that just didn't get finished."

Crosby, who said he had butterflies before his first preseason game, had his own analysis: "I needed to mix it up a little more. I was too passive. I had shots and maybe passed up a few chances when I should have shot."

He had one assist in the 7–2 victory over Columbus, while Lemieux had one goal and three assists. Crosby saw what mastery it takes to succeed in the league.

"He's an unbelievable player," Crosby said of Lemieux, whose family he is living with this season. "It was fun just to watch him out there. He knows where to be on the ice, and he finishes his chances."

As for Crosby, Columbus Coach Gerard Gallant, said: "He's a presence on the ice. He's a dynamic kid to watch. He sees the ice so well. He'll be an impact player, definitely, and for years to come."

* * *

Crosby had an outstanding rookie season but truly made his mark in his second season, leading the NHL in scoring with 120 points to become the only teenager to win a scoring title in any major North American sports league, and was named the league's Most Valuable Player. In 2009, he led the Penguins to the Stanley Cup title and, at age twenty-one, was the youngest captain in NHL history to win the Cup. He subsequently was also named one of the 100 greatest players in NHL history.

The Americanization of Martina

December 26, 1975

In the leather-thick and darkly wooded-wrought Oak Room of the Plaza Hotel in Manhattan, Martina Navratilova sliced into her $14.94 prime rib of beef au jus, and pronounced it too rare. The nineteen-year-old Czechoslovak tennis standout, who defected last September to the United States, sent the meat back.

Another piece appeared, and disappeared. Still undercooked.

No one, apparently, is going to make Martina Navratilova swallow anything that is too red, political, or edible.

A Communist nation could not intimidate her, nor could the world's best women tennis players, nor did the glitter and strangeness of a new homeland; and neither could elegant surroundings and a serving-man dressed like a penguin.

Waiting for an encore from the kitchen, Martina sipped apple juice. No liquor. No hors d'oeuvre. No bread. She battles a weight problem. She appears fit but admits to being over 160 pounds, while the best playing weight for her 5-foot-7 1/2-inch frame, she says, is 147 pounds.

Arriving in the United States for the first time three years ago to play in tournaments, she swooned over American ice cream and cheesecake and Big Macs. As well as the face of America.

"People here smile," she said. "In my country, they are sad. It is dreary. There is no freedom. Freedom is everything."

She applied herself to learning the English language, and now speaks with virtually no accent nor does she grope for words. She says she had been planning to defect for more than a year.

"The sports club in Czechoslovakia kept putting more and more restrictions on me," she said. "They said I would not be able to leave Czechoslovakia so freely. They did not like that I was so friendly with American girls, like Chris Evert. They thought I was becoming too American."

Martina paused, eyed the French bread, then crossed her arms on her tan sweater and floral blouse. She turned her high-cheeckboned face toward her dinner companion and went on.

"Once I was a big hero in Czechoslovakia," she said. "Now they say I'm a bad girl. They don't even carry my results in the newspapers anymore."

The results have been spectacular. In fact, Evert is the only woman tennis player remaining whom the lusty southpaw Navratilova does not whip regularly.

Martina will join Evert, Virginia Wade and Evonne Goolagong in competition for the second annual L'Eggs World Series of Women's Tennis January 10–11 in Austin, Texas. If Martina wins the $50,000 first prize she can keep all money—after taxes, just as with the $300,000 over the next few years she will be receiving from the Cleveland Nets of World Team Tennis.

This year, she has won $180,000. Before defecting she was forced to give 20 percent to the Czech sports club. In 1974, she won $35,000 and forked all of it over because she was under 18.

Martina now lives in Beverly Hills with her agent and his family, but soon will be moving to Palm Springs where she will be a highly paid tennis pro, and condominium owner.

She has, it seems adjusted easily to the rhythms of American life, from shopping in Hollywood boutiques to speeding on freeways in her new Mercedes 450SL, to wearing a gold necklace with a diamond insert shaped in the numeral 1, symbolic of her drive toward upper mobility in tennis.

Besides these trappings of the nouveau riche, she can become impatient at a reporter's questions and also holds the view that "If you are poor in America it is only because you do not work hard enough." However, she acknowledges that she meets few poor people in her country-club milieu.

Martina mails money to her parents and twelve-year-old sister in Revance, 15 miles outside of Prague. In the last two years, she has contributed $35,000 to the household, and plans to continue to do so, enough to allow her father, a financial adviser, to retire, if he wishes.

"There are men there who resent me," said Martina, "because they don't understand how I will make in one year maybe a hundred times more than they will in their lifetimes."

She says she misses her family and her dog, a German shepherd named Babetta. Martina calls home every week. The cost is $75 for, customarily, a half hour of crackled chat.

"My parents are happy that I am happy," she says. "But when my dad begins to speak about how we used to save our little money to go to tournaments together, and also how he and I would walk in the forests and picked mushrooms, I begin to cry.

"I know the country will let me back in if I ever decided to return. The question is, would they let me back out?"

There have been no reprisals against her family, "but there are still some things I cannot talk about," she said. "If, for example, I think President Ford is stupid, I can say it. But if I think Brezhnev is stupid, I cannot say it."

Martina was interrupted when a third serving of beef showed up. Now, she seriously brushed back her fine, short brown hair. Then she cut a piece of the meat. The waiter—waited.

"This," pronounced Martina Navratilova, after a chew or two, "is the way I like it."

* * *

It was obvious from that dinner that Martina knew what she wanted, and knew how to get it—which was to become one of the greatest women tennis players ever. She wound up winning 18 Grand Slam singles titles and 31 major doubles championships. Most impressive, perhaps, was that she was the year-end singles No. 1 seven times, including a record five consecutive years.

Tiger Woods: A History Lesson from Joe Louis

April 22, 1997

Tiger Woods brings up the aspects of legacy—of the golfers, and athletes of color who had preceded him, and who struggled against discrimination. Immediately after winning the Masters, and in an interview while at the Bulls-Knicks game on Saturday, he spoke of Charlie Sifford and Lee Elder and Ted Rhodes in golf, and of Jackie Robinson in baseball.

Some wonder if the twenty-one-year-old hadn't been programmed by the image-makers at Nike or Titleist—who are paying him a combined $60 million to be their billboard—to say this, in light of acidic public response brought on by some black ballplayers, such as Vince Coleman and Frank Thomas, who, more or less, said that they had no time for and little interest in history, black or white or beige.

Woods, however, seems genuine. He was apparently a legitimate candidate to get a degree at Stanford, the university he attended for two years, until it became clear that he'd be a dunce to pass up, as it were, the green.

As Woods and the nation pay homage to Robinson on the 50th anniversary of his breaking the color barrier in modern major league baseball, it is of historical pertinence that Robinson, also a product of a West Coast university, UCLA, had a definite model as he battled the many-headed monster of bigotry.

Joe Louis, Robinson once wrote, had "been an inspiration to all of us. Joe made it easy for me and the other fellows now in baseball. I'm sure his example had a lot to do with my breaking into big-league ball. I imagine that Mr. Rickey said to himself when considering the idea: 'Joe Louis has proven that a Negro can take honors and remain dignified. If we get one like that in baseball, the job won't be hard.'"

Louis, the great heavyweight champion, had become in the 1930s a national hero, to whites as well as blacks, by virtue of his fists and his demeanor. When he knocked out Max Schmeling, Hitler's Ubermensch, in the first round in 1938, he was hailed as emblematic of a powerful America. And while he was unlettered, he was knowing. Irwin Rosee, a publicist close to Louis, recalls the time another black man objected to Louis's decision to enlist in the Army in 1942. "It's a white man's Army, Joe, it ain't a black man's Army," the man said. Louis looked at him, and explained his decision: "Lots of things wrong with America, but Hitler ain't going to fix them."

When Robinson joined the Army, it was Louis, a sergeant but with State Department connections, who succeeded in getting him and other blacks into Officer Candidate School. When Robinson had a racial incident in the school, Louis interceded on his behalf again. When Lieutenant Robinson was at Fort Hood, Texas, and refused to move to the back of a military bus, he said he was following what Louis and Sugar Ray

Robinson had done, which had helped mandate open seating on military vehicles. Robinson's protest, however, resulted in a court martial; he was acquitted of all charges, and eventually was honorably discharged.

In the early '70s, I had a conversation with Louis, and mentioned his influence on Branch Rickey. "I never knew Branch Rickey," Louis said, "and I didn't know that about Jackie and him that way. But Jackie was my hero. He don't bite his tongue for nothing. I just don't have the guts, you might call it, to say what he says. And don't talk as good either, that's for sure. But he talks the way he feels. He call a spade a spade. You need a lot of different types of people to make the world better.

"I think Paul Robeson did more for the Negroes than anyone else, even though someone like King did a lot. Robeson went to Russia in '36 and he said this place is better for the Negro than in America, more opportunity, better treatment. What happened was the American politician got mad and said it was a lie. Ralph Bunche is a result of that. They gave him a chance after that."

When Robinson went before a House Un-American Activities Committee in 1949, he denounced American racial policies but also was critical of Robeson, the one-time athlete and deep-voiced singer and actor, and said he was not going to "throw away" his hopes and dreams for America "for a siren song sung in bass."

Robinson would later say that his rebuke of Robeson was one of the gravest mistakes of his life. But Robinson lived and learned. So, it is anticipated, will Tiger Woods.

* * *

After huge success on the golf course, falling short only to Jack Nicklaus in Grand Slam tournaments won (18 to 15), and just one win from Sam Snead's record 82 PGA tour victories, but suffering physical problems (including major back surgeries), and after embarrassing failures in his personal life (particularly regarding adulterous affairs), Woods apparently had matured, and when he won the 2019 Masters (his fifth), at the ripe age of forty-three, he seemed to have much of America rooting for him.

So Many Hits, So Much Time for Jeter

August 30, 1999

It was a beautiful, butterscotch day, Yankee Stadium was bathed in sunlight and Derek Jeter, who seems to move in perpetual sunshine, was at bat. Jeter cocked his bat in his customary stance, the bat held in such a high, unorthodox manner that it appears he is sprouting an antenna from his helmet. It was the third inning, runners on first and third, none out and the Yankees were behind, 2–0, to Seattle pitcher Paul Abbott. Abbott, a right-hander, threw, and Jeter, a right-handed hitter, whipped the bat around with the speed of a mongoose attacking a lizard, and lined a single to right field, the 762nd base hit of his major league career.

The myriad statistics that baseball elicits can give one a headache, but a particular number that Jeter is fashioning is remarkable. It places him in a category with the greatest hitters in baseball history. With his two singles yesterday in the Yankees' 11–5 victory over the Mariners, he has more hits in the first four full years of his career, 751 (he had 12 in 1995), than hitters like Ted Williams (749 in his first four seasons), Cal Ripken (745), Lou Gehrig (736), Ty Cobb (729), Pete Rose (723), and Henry Aaron (718) had. If Derek Sanderson Jeter continues at his present, league-leading pace of hits (175)—he is batting .348, third in the American League to Nomar Garciaparra's .350 and Bernie Williams's .349—Jeter projects to collect 220 hits this season and 796 for his first four full years. He will have passed Stan Musial (792) and Joe DiMaggio (791).

"If," said Jeter, seated at his locker before yesterday's game. "Man, if's a big word. Baseball's a game of failure. Obviously you fail more than you succeed."

His track record as well as his persona portray anything but the concept of failure. At age twenty-five, he appears the most level-headed of athletes. He is approachable and, as Yankee management has learned, coachable. "He's not one of these young guys who thinks he's got it all figured out," the Yankee coach Jose Cardenal said.

In the other clubhouse, Jamie Moyer, a Seattle pitcher, said Jeter had made "huge adjustments at the plate."

"When he first came up," said Moyer, "it was obvious he had talent, but he also had some glaring holes. For one thing, you could pitch him up and in, get him out on his front foot—that is, get him to shift onto his front foot before he swung. You did that with change of speed, and it took a lot of sting out of his bat."

But, added Moyer, Jeter adapted. "That hole no longer exists."

It doesn't exist because Jeter spends good chunks of his time at his craft. While his reputation of dating stars like Mariah Carey may be earned, it has not proved a debilitating distraction to his occupational chores.

Over last winter, he regularly appeared on the Yankees' Tampa spring-training grounds to work on driving inside pitches to left field, instead of fighting them off and slicing them to right. He didn't find this kind of diligence extraordinary. "I live in Tampa," he said, with a shrug. "I work on my game all the time."

Don Zimmer, the Yankees' dugout coach, who has been in professional baseball for fifty-one years, said that unlike some superb hitters, like Rose and Wade Boggs, Jeter hits with power, and to all fields. "How do you think he hits balls over the right-field fence—tapping them?" Zimmer said. "He's got a big swing, and for him to have so many hits is phenomenal."

Jeter is also a good-size shortstop, at 6-foot-3, 195 pounds, bigger and with greater range and richer than Johnny Pesky, whom Zimmer remembers as having a terrific major league start. Pesky was a Red Sox shortstop in the 1940s, and had 779 hits in his first four seasons. Pesky got 208 hits in his second season with Boston, in 1946, and batted .335. He dropped slightly in 1947, getting 207 hits with a .324 batting average.

"But they made him take a cut in pay after that season," Zimmer said. "He was a coach for me when I managed the Red Sox, and Johnny told me he's never forgotten that he went from something like $7,000 a year to $6,000."

Jeter, to underscore a difference in eras, went from $750,000 in his third year to $5 million this year, after arbitration. But he says there are no hard feelings about that between him and George Steinbrenner, the team's principal owner. "But he gets upset when Michigan beats Ohio State in football," said Jeter, who is from Michigan while Steinbrenner is from Ohio, "and I do get on him about that."

Jeter, who grew up a Yankee fan in Kalamazoo, said that his favorite player was Dave Winfield, who was not one of Steinbrenner's favorites. "I thought Winfield was the greatest all-round athlete there was," Jeter said. And as far as Winfield's being Mr. May, as Steinbrenner had disparaged him, Jeter said, "He must have got a lot of hits in May then, to get 3,000 for his career."

As for his career numbers, Jeter said: "I just want to be consistent and play as long as I'm having fun. I hope to have a lot of great years left. After all, I'm still the youngest guy on this team."

Looking around the clubhouse of the defending World Series champion Yankees, it turned out he was right. Only twenty-five. Just a babe. Which gives rise to yet another agreeable, if plump, historical baseball image.

* * *

A 14-time American League All-Star Game selection, Jeter played 20 years in the major leagues, all with the Yankees, leading them to five World Series championships. He holds numerous club records, including most hits, 3,465, ranking him sixth in major-league career hits and first among shortstops.

A Historic Sullivan High School Baseball Game

March 2017

The most Remarkable? Improbable? Amazing? Stupendous? Thrilling? Quirky?—all of the latter?—sports event in Sullivan High School history, a history that dates back to 1933, occurred on the afternoon of June 10, 1957, on a dusty, sunbaked baseball field in Winnemac Park, alongside Foster Avenue, when the Sullivan Tigers faced the Lane Tech Indians. Okay, there may have been other Sullivan sports events close but none, it says here, could top this one. Not only was I an eye-witness, I was also a participant, of sorts.

The Sullivan Tigers were having one of our better baseball seasons when we met up with Lane. At the time, my senior year, we—I was stationed at first base—were in third place in the competitive Chicago Public High School North Section behind Lane Tech and Taft, prep powerhouses that eventually played for the City championship at season's end.

Lane, the defending (1956) Illinois state champs, had its star right-handed pitcher, Jim Woods, on the mound against us. He and his team were undefeated coming into our game that '57 season. Woody, as the newspapers called this senior phenom, was mowing down batters at a remarkable rate. He had picked up where he left off the season before—in, for example, the semifinals of the state championships, he beat Belleville while striking out 18 of the possible 21 outs (high-school games are seven innings). The red-headed Woody was also a prodigious hitter, batting .444 with power in his senior year. A *Chicago Sun-Times* article compared him to another Lane Tech standout, the former Cubs all-star Phil Cavarretta. Woods was 6 foot tall, about 170 pounds—not imposing—but he was simply gifted.

So gifted, in fact, that three weeks after we both had graduated from our nearby high schools, the Cubs signed him and he went straight from Lane Tech to Wrigley Field, a matter of two miles by bus, but a world away from that high-school sandlot where we batted against him. Woods was seventeen years old and in the major leagues! He wore number 15 on the back of his Cubs uniform and, wide-eyed as he would later recall to a reporter, soon shared turns into the batting practice cage with, among others, future Hall of Famer Ernie Banks. Billy Williams, the Cubs' future Hall of Fame outfielder who had been a minor-league teammate of Woods, recalled that "Woody had a great arm." This came as no surprise to we who had batted against him.

Indeed. But here is where it gets, well, weird, though, from a Sullivan standpoint, wonderful.

Some time ago I came into possession of the Lane Tech Daily, the school newspaper, from Friday, June 14, 1957. Leading off the sports page, the first paragraph read: "Jim Woods, who has never pitched a no-hitter in his high-school baseball career, was near perfect Monday, when he allowed Sullivan only one hit, a blooper, in the very first inning (but) Sullivan white-washed the Indians 1–0 at Winnemac Park."

"When Woods fanned the first two men to face him in the game it looked like another win racked up for Gentleman Jim. The next batter (All-city center fielder) Bob Sanders, grounded slowly towards (second baseman) Bob Becker. Becker fielded the ball smoothly, but made a wide throw past first to put a man on second. Roger Grahf followed with a bloop single, the only hit off Woods in the game, to drive in what proved to be the winning run. Jim was near-perfect through the remainder of the game,

Woods pitched from the same mound 60-feet-6-inches away from the batter's box as everyone else, but to me he seemed unfairly close, his ball whizzing in, or breaking sharply. I was, naturally one of Woods's strikeout victims (batting fifth, I also ground out to shortstop and walked once).

Roger Grahf, our sophomore right-hander, pitched brilliantly. He allowed eight hits, including a double by Woods, but got out of that jam, and one other—he gave up two hits in the first inning, and it looked dire for us, so early in the game, but Roger left the base runners stranded. To sum up this greatest game (my assumption) in Sullivan sports history: Sullivan, with an enrollment of some 600 boys versus Lane with about 6,000 boys, beat the defending state champions and the state's star pitcher who, though we didn't know it at the time, was virtually a major-leaguer! We managed one hit in the first inning—the only hit we got in the game—and scored one run off of it, the only run *either* team scored in the game. Sullivan 1, Lane 0. Fantastic!

We finished the season third in the section, with a 9–5 record. When Woods signed with the Cubs, he did so as a third baseman, since it was felt that he was more valuable as an everyday player than as a pitcher. Nineteen-fifty-seven was his only season with the Cubs. He played in only two games with them, both as a pinch-runner—once against Stan Musial's St. Louis Cardinals (and was picked off third in a rundown, and I could imagine how nervous he must have been)— and was sent to the minors for "more seasoning." He had just turned eighteen that September, his baseball future looked bright. In 1960, still in the minors, he was traded to the Philadelphia Phillies (with veteran major-leaguers Alvin Dark, infielder, and John Buzhardt, pitcher, for future Hall-of-Fame outfielder Richie Ashburn).

In Triple A with Indianapolis Woods made the International League all-star team, and was brought up to the Phillies, playing in 34 games in 1960 and 1961. He hit three homers and crushed a double off Sandy Koufax as a pinch-hitter. He was, however, sent back to the minors, and drifted there for a while, down to Double A, signed by the Cincinnati Reds organization, but was soon out of baseball, at age twenty-four. His lifetime Major-League batting average was .207. The Major Leagues, to be sure, is a tough place in which to succeed, even for the gifted. Years later Stan Hochman, an astute baseball writer for the *Philadelphia Daily News* who had covered the Phillies when Woods played for them, told me that Woods was "overmatched" in the big leagues. Oddly, Woods never tried to pitch in professional baseball, believing, apparently, that hitting would be his ticket to stardom.

Like a lot of the guys who played with and against Jim Woods, I followed him in the papers in those days to see how he fared, and while he didn't fare all that well, he was still our connection—our proud connection—to the big leagues.

Addendum: The other Sullivan starters were Barry Stein, second base; Stu Menaker, shortstop; Gary Stutland, right field; Bruce Brammer, left field; Cal Feirstein shared catching duties with Jim Rudnick and Larry (Zeke) Zini was another starting pitcher.

Older, but Few Better

Some of the most unusual, gifted and intriguing people I had the good fortune and pleasure to interview were found in a variety of sports—from hockey to boxing to discus throwing—in either the latter part of their playing days, or in retirement. The list below even includes a horse, Citation, though his trainer did the talking for him.

Bill Shoemaker: One Great Jockey

The most unusual horse race I ever covered, so to speak, was the 1986 Kentucky Derby run in the twin-spired Churchill Downs in Louisville but I experienced it in a midtown Manhattan hotel room two years later and the jockey that rode Ferdinand to victory did it while propped up in bed. It was Bill Shoemaker who rode the three-year-old stallion to the finish line in the Run for the Roses. I always admired jockeys, for their athleticism as well as their bravery—there is a long and tragic list of jockeys being killed and/or crippled in racing accidents on the track—and Shoemaker, though sustaining numerous injuries in spills on the track, was at the top of the list. He returned from hospital from head, back and leg injuries to become the leading jockey of his time, and for twenty-nine years held the record for total professional jockey victories, 8,883, when he retired after forty-two years in the saddle. He had won 11 Triple Crown races—four Kentucky Derbies, two Preaknesses and five Belmont Stakes. The fact that he sustained his worst injury when away from the racetrack, in a paralyzing car accident, is tragic irony. But first about that win in the '86 Derby.

117

The Shoe Was Sittin' Chilly

April 9, 1988

The most remarkable hands in the history of sports may belong to a man who wears a size 1 1/2 shoe.

The hands belong, in fact, to a man called Shoe: Bill Shoemaker, who is 4-foot-10, weighs about "5 pounds," as the folks in his trade call it ("They usually throw way the 100," he says), is fifty-six years old, graying, and still one of the nation's finest athletes.

The hands have, since Shoemaker's first race at Golden Gate Fields on March 19, 1949, in which he came in second on Waxahachie in a small claiming race, guided and urged, sometimes gently, sometimes, if needed, sternly, a thousand or so pounds of horse through thick and thin, through mud and over grass, from starting gate to finish line, on race courses across the country.

They are the hands of a jockey who has won 8,748 races, more than any rider in history, and has earned more than $100 million in prizes.

This afternoon those hands will be conducting Lively One, a three-year-old dark brown colt and a Kentucky Derby hopeful, who is the morning-line favorite at 2-1 in the Santa Anita Derby, an important test for the colt.

Lively One has won three of his first six races, and is being compared with Ferdinand, another California horse, and the one Shoemaker stunningly raced to victory in the 1986 Kentucky Derby.

Lively One is trained by Charlie Whittingham, who had trained Ferdinand—it was the old trainer's first trip to the Derby in twenty-six years, and his only Derby victory—and it was Shoemaker's fourth Derby victory, and his first in twenty-one years, and he felt fortunate to be given a mount at all.

"At my age," he had said, "I never thought I'd get another shot."

Lively One, like Ferdinand, started racing relatively late, and last February won his first stakes race, the Santa Catalina.

In Lively One's last race, three weeks ago in the San Felipe Handicap, he finished fourth, after a bumpy ride, and bled. For today's race, he will receive Lasix, an anti-bleeding medication.

In his newly issued autobiography, *Shoemaker*, published by Doubleday and written with Barney Nagler, the superb columnist for the *Daily Racing Form*, the jockey spoke of the importance of hands, and said that a rider with good hands "sends a message to his horse through the reins." He said, "A horse knows kind hands from rough, insensitive hands."

Shoemaker, in a Manhattan hotel room recently, now took hold of an imaginary mount as he sat up in bed. His small feet were not in boots and not in the irons, but crossed at the ankles and in black socks. His silks were a white-monogrammed shirt, a dark tie, and gray suit slacks.

The hands are "kinda wide," as he described them, and not small, "about a size 7 glove," and looked strong when curled around a fistful of reins, real or otherwise.

"You can't take too much hold of a horse," he was saying, his hands, with the light from the lamp shining on them, developing a riding rhythm in bed. "Most horses don't like it, and some have run off with jocks. I learned to kind of gallop along with them. You want them to relax and take hold of the bit, and not spit it out. I've never been much of a whip jockey, so I have to rely on my hands, on finessing the horse—more so as I've gotten older -and keep the touch light, like putting in golf."

He recalled that one day in his riding youth Eddie Arcaro—"one of the best hand riders ever"—had taken him aside and told him that near the finish line he was pulling too hard on the reins, when a nose at the wire would make a difference between winning and finishing second. "It's a little push, but in motion with the horse's body and head," said Arcaro.

They watched films of both of them riding, and, Shoemaker recalled, "what he was doing and what I was doing became very clear. It was so small, just a little fraction, but what a difference!"

It was that one fine line between doing something just right, that most deft of brush strokes, or just missing.

HE talked about the handling of various horses, from Forego, who could be somewhat fractious and needed a no-nonsense pair of hands behind him, to Spectacular Bid. "You'd take Spectacular Bid back with just two fingers," said Shoemaker, crooking the index finger of each hand, daintily.

Shoemaker recalled the 1957 Kentucky Derby, in which he mistook the finish line, his hands pulling up Gallant Man, only to have Iron Liege and Bill Hartack sweep past. Shoemaker immediately admitted the mistake, instead of blaming the horse or the track, and his honesty impressed many.

"It was a blow, and it took me some time to get over that," he said. "I was getting a little conceited until then, and that made a better person of me."

It's hardly a surprise that one of his finest moments in racing, he says, came in the Derby two years ago, his 24th Kentucky Derby.

"We were running last in the first turn," said Shoemaker, leaning back against a pillow, his hands grasping the figment of Ferdinand. "I had a nice little hold of him and he was running well. He was pricking up his ears. I decided I wasn't going to chase the other horses and use my horse up early. Let the other horses run out. Some say it's patience, some say it's sittin' chilly."

Then, turning into the backstretch, Shoemaker began "picking up the other horses."

He leaned forward from the bed board, eyes narrowing, and "ducked here, and slowed up a little there, and got through holes on the inside, and then got to the rail and took the lead and made for home in the stretch. And this time," he said, with a smile, "I didn't mistake the finish wire."

Now his hands pulled up on the reins of memory, a winner again, and he sat back in bed and placed his hands in his lap.

It had been some ride, all thirty-nine years of it.

* * *

The first time I met Bill Shoemaker—he was then commonly called Willie, though I'd later learn that he preferred Bill—was shortly after I arrived in New York to work for NEA in the fall of 1967.

I was in the jockeys' room following a stakes race he had just won. The title of the piece I wrote was "DAMASCUS OR A PLATER—WILLIE'S OUT TO WIN":

Willie Shoemaker was in a hurry. He had neither the time nor desire to savor the victory in the $100,000 Woodward at Aqueduct. He had more work to do.

He stood in the jockeys' lounging room, quickly tucking in the black silk shirt with red dots and patiently answering reporters' questions. He was changing silks between the seventh and eight races, between a stakes race and a cheap claiming race.

Only fresh specks of mud on his face, and on his white, tight breeches and black boots that he would not change, revealed he had just been riding.

"Damascus," he said, a thin, shy smile slitting his small, almost pinched face, "is as good a horse as I've ever ridden."

And Billy Lee Shoemaker, born thirty-six years ago in Fabens, Texas, has ridden his share. He has been a jockey for half his lifetime, and has been up on nearly 6,000 winners.

("Somebody," a jockey once said, "should give Shoemaker a saliva test instead of a horse.")

Shoemaker tugged on a new arm band for the eighth race. A jowly, middle-aged man poked his head in the door. "Hey, Willie," he called. It was Harry Sibert, Shoemaker's manager. Willie walked over. Sibert bent low and kissed the 4-foot-11, 98-pound jockey on the cheek.

"Beautiful ride," he said. "Bee-yoo-tee-ful." Willie smiled, his narrow, blue-gray eyes almost closing. Sibert and Shoemaker have teamed since Willie quit picking cotton as a boy in Texas and also gave up hopes of becoming flyweight boxing champion.

("He's the most cold-blooded kid I'd ever known," Sibert had said. "He'll win a big one and while everybody else is going wild, he'll start talking about something else.")

"I gotta get goin'," Willie said to reporters, snapping on the attached bow tie. "I'm up in the next race."

The 10-length victory of Damascus over Buckpasser and Dr. Fager, all highly regarded thoroughbreds, was already a thing of the past for Shoemaker. He lives in the present. And the eighth race, a claiming race, was the present.

("Riding is a deal," Shoemaker has said, "where you come to work and get tack and do the best job you can and keep your mouth shut about it.")

Willie had whisked into the jockeys' quarters after rushing through the Woodward winner's circle routine of pictures and handshakes. As familiar as he is with it, he still seemed uneasy. Like a boy with wetted-down hair and wearing a suit at a birthday party. Willie had other things to do.

He had come swiftly into the dressing room. He had slipped out of the white silks with red dots and into the black one, switched cloths on his helmet, grabbed his tack—whip and his goggles—and weighed in.

His neat, graying hair carefully in place, he pulled on his helmet. With quick, determined strides he went out the door and toward the track.

It had been a busy and profitable day for Billy Lee Shoemaker, one-time cotton picker. But it wasn't over. He had one more race, a cheap claiming race, that he hoped to win."

* * *

Twenty-four years after that first time when I met Bill Shoemaker came the dreadful news, which I addressed in my *Times* column:

Horses Had Wings for Shoemaker

April 23, 1991

In the spring of 1949, Sammy Renick, who had gone from riding horses to riding the airwaves as a racing telecaster in New York, received a phone call from his former jockey agent, Harry Silbert.

"Sam," said Silbert, calling from San Francisco, "I have the best jockey prospect I've ever seen. He's a fifteen-year-old kid from Texas, about 5 feet tall and weighs 90 pounds. Horses fly for him in the morning. You should see him in the workouts. He's got great moves, and he's very bright. His name is Willie Shoemaker, and you're going to hear a lot about him."

Renick recalled that conversation the other day: "That's just what Harry said. And it was right around then that Shoe won his first race, in his third start, at Golden Gate Fields."

Shoemaker and Silbert remained a team for forty years, until the agent's death. And through Silbert, Renick and Shoemaker became friends.

Renick closely followed the forty-one-year career of Shoemaker, who rode 8,833 winners for a career record. Shoemaker won the Kentucky Derby four times, the Belmont five times and the Preakness twice.

123

He also won about $10 million as his share of purses before retiring from riding last year and becoming a trainer. No other rider has combined his ability, his longevity and his gentlemanliness. Then, on a Tuesday morning two weeks ago, Renick heard on the radio the news about Shoemaker: The car he was driving on a southern California highway had plunged off a 50-foot embankment and flipped over. Shoemaker, fifty-nine years old, was now in a hospital and paralyzed from the neck down.

"And the news hasn't gotten any better," Renick said. "Shoe's not in good shape. It looks like his condition is permanent. And they bore a hole in his pipes so he can breathe. It's so sad, so awfully sad."

Renick, who is seventy-six, then spoke about Shoemaker the horse rider and said that he had good riding hands, great balance on a horse and a knack for communicating with them.

"He was known as a come-from-behind rider, and I was sitting with Shoe once in '21' and he told me how he got his style," Renick said. "When he was an apprentice, he was on a horse that was riding badly and was three or four lengths behind the last horse. Usually a rider will go to the whip and cluck at the horse, but Shoe happened to just sort of steady him. And all of a sudden, this horse took hold of the bit—that's how a horse tells the rider he's ready to run—and he took off. Shoe said, 'Well, I realized I didn't have to rush horses out of the gate. Let 'em get their stride and find their rhythm.'"

But even the best falter. One of the most famous errors in racing occurred in the 1957 Kentucky Derby when Shoemaker, aboard Gallant Man, misjudged the finish line and stood up in the irons as Iron Liege swept past them to win. "But it was easy to make that kind of mistake if you didn't ride regularly at Churchill Downs, as Shoe didn't," Renick said. But Shoemaker made no excuses and felt terrible, especially for Ralph Lowe, the horse's owner and his friend.

"Lowe was a wealthy oilman from Texas, and after the race he invited Shoe to visit him at his home," Renick said. "When Shoe got off the plane, Lowe showed him a new Chrysler. The front seat had been fixed for a driver of Shoe's size. 'Get in,' said Lowe, 'it's yours.'"

In turn, Shoemaker endowed an annual trophy for sportsmanship in Lowe's name, keeping alive the memory of Shoemaker's deepest embarrassment. Shoemaker felt a responsibility to his profession, and was a distinguished president of the Jockeys' Guild for fourteen years, until last year, and active in battles with establishment that included pay increases and safety issues.

Renick said Shoemaker loved his new work and recently won his biggest race as a trainer, when Fire the Groom won the $200,000 Santa Anita Breeder's Cup Stakes. Shoemaker was shown a video replay in his hospital room. "He can't talk but I was told he blinked his eyes to show his pleasure," Renick said.

Shortly after the car accident a blood test revealed that Shoemaker had been driving under the influence of alcohol, and had possibly fallen asleep at the wheel. "He had played golf and a friend of ours said he'd had a few beers," Renick said. "I don't know, maybe he had a few drinks. Shoe drank, but I never knew him to drink more than most of the rest of us."

Renick said how terribly hard Shoemaker's wife, Cindy, and twelve-year-old daughter, Amanda, were taking his injury. "He had bought Amanda a horse and taught her to ride, and she's good," Renick said. "I had told Shoe, 'Well, she's got the breeding.'" Renick paused. "I pray for Shoe every night," he said now. "I just pray."

* * *

Shoemaker was paralyzed from the neck down and needed to use a wheel-chair for the rest of his life. He and Cindy Barnes Shoemaker (his third wife) divorced in 1994, after sixteen years of marriage. "Shoe" trained horses with modest success while immobilized until he couldn't do it any longer and, after six years, gave that up in 1997. Shoemaker's first win as a jockey was when he was seventeen years old, on April 20, 1949, and his last was in January 20, 1991, at fifty-nine. As recited earlier, for twenty-nine years Shoemaker held the record for total professional jockey victories, with 8,883, until it was topped by Laffit Pincay Jr. in 1999 (and later passed by Russell Baze in 2006). In 1958, Shoemaker was inducted into the National Museum of Racing and Hall of Fame in Saratoga Springs, New York. On October 12, 2003, Bill Shoemaker died in his sleep at his home in San Marino, California. He was seventy-two years old.

* * *

I'm not sure that I would call the horses that were ridden to fame and fortune athletes, as many people do, but those who worked with them— the jocks, the trainers, the grooms, the owners, some fans—seemed to believe that the best had the heart and stamina and good sense of great athletes. For me, my hearing of Citation the winner of the Triple Crown in 1948, when I was eight years old, remains paramount since it was one of my earliest memories of horse racing. I remember the adults around me marveling at Citation's grand achievement. Many years later, when a columnist for NEA, I was delighted to meet, as it were, the legendary Citation in his lush retirement.

Citation: Still a Ladies' Man

May 8, 1969 / Lexington, Kentucky

The spring is gone now in Citation's legs. He walks with much of his former grace and majesty but, increasingly, with more pain. And he seems

126

to need that little extra oomph provided by the slow, easy swing of his sumptuous black tail.

In his paddock, he walks a few yards and stops and lowers his neck and nibbles a fare of grass. His handsome bay coat shines in the warm Kentucky sunlight.

"Ci has got the rheumatism in the legs," said the horse's groom, Hugh Fields, watching and leaning against the white picket fence at Calumet Farm. "He sets his legs down like a cat with sacks on his feet. That's from an old sayin'—walkin' like a cat with sacks on his feet."

Hugh Fields, a ruddy fellow, tugged his brown cap so it nearly touched his steel-rimmed glasses and he smiled, thinking of Citation. He has been Citation's groom since 1951, when the horse retired from racing after becoming the first thoroughbred to win $1 million in purses and, in 1948, was the eighth and last Triple Crown winner.

"Ci's twenty-four years old now," said Fields. "That's about, oh, eighty years old in human life. He's beginning to break some now—you know, show his age. Got some gray hairs in that black mane, his back swayed, and he's put on 200–250 pounds since he went into stud. Up to about 1,300 now. He's in top health, though, perfect health I'd call it, 'cept for his legs which been givin' him trouble lately.

"But he's still a ham for posin'. When folks with cameras come 'round, his neck sets up and his ears perk and his back straightens."

For a celebrity of Citation's stature and bankroll, Calumet Farm seems an altogether fitting place to while away the waning days. The cuisine is ripe green (though some say it is tinged with blue). White fences tumble over hills as far as the eye can see. Pink and white dogwood trees are in blossom. Sycamore, pine, and oak trees are slipping into green coats. Jonquils and tulips and red sage and blue ageratum are blooming in the sweet springtime. Here and there, colts and fillies frolic.

Yet it is not all a life of leisure for the famous senior citizen. From February to June each year, Citation must perform daily chores, if they may be termed that. Twice a day during the period Citation the stud is asked to "cover" mares.

"I think Ci's enjoying retirement," said Fields. "He's still a ladies' man, naturally. He's one of the best covering horses in the country. His stud fee's gone down, though. Three yers ago it went from $5,000 to $3,500. Some folks think a horse his age won't get a strong foal. But I don't think so.

"His get never did come up to anything equal to himself. He got some useful horses, but not sensational, like Silver Spoon and Guadalcanal and Fabius. But you race a horse like the way they raced and they take the stamina outa him.

"But there's no doubt about it that he ain't the greatest horse that ever lived. Would run anywhere anytime on any track. You know what Eddie Arcaro said? He said ridin' Ci was like drivin' a Cadillac.

"But once a week now he'll gallop 'round the paddock here, but it ain't easy what with the rheumatism in his legs. He likes to roll around, too. Oh, he sure does. Sometimes he'll get mud and dust caked on him an inch deep and it'll take me an hour to clean it off.

"But there'll come a time soon when Ci will lay down and won't be able to get up. He's in perfect health, but he still could die tomorrow. Most horses live only to eighteen or twenty. Course Ci might live to thirty, like Man O'War done.

"Bull Lea, that was Ci's daddy, he lived to twenty-nine. And a few times a month in those last years he'd lay down and couldn't get up, his legs was so weak. A wrecker would come in with a steel cable and motor and we'd roll Bull Lea onto a girt and hoist him up till he stood and got his senses. Then he'd just walk away.

"Ci still eats good and sleeps good. You can hear him snorin' and groanin' and nickerin' here to Louisville. He's intelligent and level-headed like he used to be. He ain't vicious like some stallions—but he will try to bite you if he don't know you. And he'll listen to you if you talk to him right.

"And sometimes, sometimes when some of us are listenin' on the radio to a race and the people get to hollerin', Ci will raise up his head and stand straight and listen. He still thinks he's at the track, I reckon."

Citation died one year later.

Smarty Jones: Belmont Disappointment Hasn't Slowed the Mail

July 8, 2004

The letters continue to pour in, even a month after the surprising and, to many, heartbreaking Belmont Stakes. The correspondence still fills up shopping bags on the floor beside the cluttered desk of the trainer John Servis in his cramped office in Barn 11 at Philadelphia Park.

From a fan in Stockton, California: "Dear Smarty Jones, I am thrilled to know you are training for your next challenge in life. I was not disappointed when you did not win the Triple Crown even though I wanted you to win. It amazes me how you run and reminded me of Secretariat and Seabiscuit. And some other famous horses who run so fast. Well, Smarty, please be careful when you run and go for the WINNING number. YOU are a Precious and Great Horse. May the Lord watch over you when you train and run."

A fan in Granite Springs, New York, wrote to Servis to say that there was "a very special place in my 'hunt room'" for a photograph of Smarty. "Smarty Jones will be pleased," the fan wrote.

From a letter writer in Pasadena, Maryland: "Dear Mr. Servis, I wish you the best and look forward to seeing Smarty in future races. I wish him love and luck also! Anyone can see he has a lot of heart. Go Smarty!"

Servis, looking up from the letters and brushing back the black baseball cap on his head, called the outpouring unreal.

"I get these letters and calls every day," he said. "People don't want it to end. The story captured everybody so much, and everybody in this business said it was the best thing to happen to horse racing in some time. I mean, even people who knew nothing about racing were rooting for Smarty."

It was the story of a small horse who was underrated from the beginning, who was stabled at a small and unglamorous track but nonetheless began to win race after race, coming on the heels of the best-selling book and hit movie about that other come-from-nowhere horse, Seabiscuit. And after winning the Kentucky Derby and the Preakness this spring—making it eight victories in eight attempts—Smarty Jones was a stunning 1–5 favorite to win the Belmont Stakes at Belmont Park.

He led for most of it, until, in the home stretch of the mile-and-a-half race, Birdstone pulled even and, well, such headlines as this told the rest of the tale: "Birdstone Upsets Smarty Jones/ Horse suffers first loss, fails to become 1st Triple Crown winner in twenty-six years."

Birdstone was a 36–1 shot, while Smarty Jones became the 48th horse, and third straight, to win two of the three Triple Crown races.

"Lost by one length," Servis said. "What's so difficult to take is, he ran hard. You can't fault a horse when he runs hard. But I saw at the halfway pole that he was going to have trouble. He wasn't running easy, not settled like he usually is. I think that if he ran that race with the same horses on the same track 10 more times, he'd win 10 times. And, yeah, the disappointment hasn't gone away. It's kind of like a scar."

If he could change anything in the race, he said, he would have had his jockey, Stewart Elliott, go outside in the last third of the race, which might have been easier than going to the inside.

"But all good jockeys would have gone inside to save ground," said Servis. "And Stewart did it right. It just didn't work out. You know this in hindsight."

Immediately after the race, some incredible things happened. The winner's jockey and trainer, for instance, virtually apologized.

"I'm happy, but I'm sad," said Edgar Prado, who rode Birdstone to victory.

"Unbelievable," Servis said. "Those were the first words out of his mouth."

When Servis congratulated Nick Zito, Birdstone's trainer, he found Zito happy, but in a sense, sad, too. "He said he was sorry," Servis said. "I said: 'You raced to win. You did a good job. You deserved it.'"

What next for Smarty Jones? He has three races scheduled: the Philadelphia Derby on Labor Day at Philadelphia Park, Smarty's home turf; the Pegasus Handicap at the Meadowlands in the first week in October; and the Breeders' Cup Classic at Lone Star Park in Grand Prairie, Tex., on October 30.

"I want two things for Smarty at this point," Servis said. "One is to be horse of the year, and if he wins the Breeders' Cup, he'd have to be a shoo-in for it. And the other is to be the leading money-winner of all time."

Servis picked up The Daily Racing Form, thumbed to a page and found how much Smarty has earned so far: $7,563,535.

"The winning purse for the Breeders' Cup Classic is $2.4 million," Servis said. "Cigar is the leading money winner right now at a shade under $10 million. So if Smarty wins at Lone Star, he'll pass Cigar."

Servis then rose and left his office and walked down the 60 or so feet to the stall where Smarty Jones, a deep-chestnut three-year-old with a small white mark on his forehead, ankles bandaged, was standing quietly in a small blue tub of ice water.

"The ice cools him off," said Bill Foster, the barn foreman, petting the nose of the star of the stable. "He just jogged a mile. The ice is just a precaution. You can see he enjoys it."

Two weeks ago, Patricia and Roy Chapman, who own Smarty Jones, sold the breeding rights to the horse to Three Chimneys Farm in Kentucky. The Chapmans will retain a 50 percent interest in the horse, and they have indicated that they would like to see him run next year as a 4-year-old before heading to the breeding shed. Servis said it was his impression that Three Chimneys would make the final call on 2005 and would keep Smarty Jones on the racetrack if it seemed feasible.

Servis said Smarty was tired after losing the Belmont. "He was blowing pretty good after the race," he said. "And he left a handful of feed—he never does that."

Another contained a small teddy bear for Smarty. Another, from a schoolgirl in Beresford, South Dakota, was addressed to the Smarty Jones Team, and contained a haiku titled "Horse Racing"

Their grace, beauty soar
Their hoofs thunder down the track
Crowds cheer: Smarty Jones.

* * *

Due to chronic bruising of the ankle bones Smarty Jones never raced again after the Belmont Stakes. His record stood at eight wins and one second-place finish in nine starts.

Gordie Howe: "Mr. Hockey" and a Puckful of Offshoots

There may never have been anyone, in any sport anywhere, quite like Gordie Howe. And there may never be. He broke into the National Hockey League with the Detroit Red Wings at age eighteen, in 1946 and essentially ended his five-decade career in 1980 with the NHL Hartford Whalers at age fifty-two and ten days, becoming the oldest person ever to play that sport on a professional level—he had previously been the oldest player to ever play in the NHL.

Howe had actually retired in 1971 from the Red Wings, at age forty-three, with the record book weighted heavily in his favor with scoring marks, assists marks, games and seasons played, regular-season records and playoff records, had his uniform number, "9," retired by the team and was soon inducted into the Hockey Hall of Fame in Toronto. But he got itchy for two reasons, apparently, and came back two years later to play for the Houston Aeros of the World Hockey Association.

The two reasons: One, the 6-foot, 205-pound, as muscular as any heavyweight contender, Howe, at his career right-wing position, could still compete at a high level and indeed became in the WHA, as he had been in the NHL (he made 23 NHL All-Star teams, was six times NHL Most Valuable Player and was named WHA's MVP in his first season with the Aeros), a scoring champ and leader—bruising leader, to be sure—of championship teams. Reason two: he would be, astoundingly enough, playing with two of his teenage sons, left winger Mark Howe, eighteen, and defenseman Marty Howe, nineteen—both destined to become league all-stars, along with their father.

Howe continued to live up to his reputation, and became the namesake of the "Gordie Howe hat trick": a goal and an assist and a fight in the same game. Opponents had learned to avoid Howe on the ice in no small measure to his ability to check the guys in the other jerseys so resoundingly that they seemed to bounce off the boards like so many beach balls. He had registered "Mr. Hockey," a name that had become nearly synonymous with "Gordie Howe," a legal trademark.

In 1998, *The Hockey News* released its list of Top 100 NHL Players of All Time and placed Howe third overall, behind Wayne Gretzky and Bobby Orr. Perusing the list, both Gretzky and Orr were quoted as regarding Howe as the greatest player of all time.

As a boy growing up in Chicago in the late 1940s and early '50s, my father took me to several Black Hawks games. I was more charmed by the flashy spectacle of these players skating with such skill in their colorful uniforms on the pearl-white ice and handling the puck with such dexterity that the periodic fights did not dim my pleasure of the games, as they would in later years. I may well have seen Gordie Howe in his earliest playing days in the NHL, but I was more interested in the local players and getting their autographs before the game as they skated leisurely about, players such as Doug Bentley, the Conacher Brothers (Jim and Roy), the "Bill" All-Stars Bill Gadsby and Bill Mosienko, and the twirling-like-a-top goalie, Al Rollins, who in a short time would be seeking to block speeding slap shots in thick knee and shin pads and while armed with lobster-like gloves.

The next time I went to an NHL game was years later, in late 1968, when I was a twenty-eight-year-old sports columnist for the national Scripps-Howard feature syndicate Newspaper Enterprise Association. While my interest in the game had veered in other directions, I was moved to see Gordie Howe play in Madison Square Garden for what might be the last time. He was still a great story. I knew he remained a truly tough player, but when I spoke with him in the Red Wings locker room before the game, I wasn't prepared for his quirky sense of humor.

He was now an elder statesman in the game, the aging superstar, and every year there would be questions on when he might retire. He sat on a stool, dressed for the game and was amenable to a young sportswriter's questions. I remember mentioning to him that the great baseball player Stan Musial, even near the end of his long career in his early forties, still got butterflies before a game.

"Do you still get butterflies as well before a game?" I asked him.

"No," said Howe with a straight face, "I drink insecticide."

I think I followed that with a truly clichéd question, asking him about another player who was said to be very hard-nosed.

"I can't say," said Howe. "I never felt his nose."

I realized that I was over my head, though with a modicum of pleasure because of the joshing but gentle way he handled the questions.

Gordie Howe Isn't Ready to Put Career on Ice

December 24, 1968

For one frozen second only, there was a pang of remorse for the large man with graying temples and long, strong drawn face. He did not seem to belong. With an outside chance to steal the puck near center ice, he dived, missed, sprawled headlong, and now knelt on one knee as the New York Rangers scored, yelping with glee.

Gordie Howe of the Detroit Red Wings, forty years old and twenty-three years in the National Hockey League, blinked the sweat out of his gray eyes. With a huge red glove he wiped the wet, matted, thinning strands of hair from his forehead and face. Hunched with head hanging, he rose and skated slowly, gracefully to the bench.

Only seconds remained in the game. The Red Wings were far ahead, 5–2. They had scored all five goals in the first period, and Howe had two goals and two assists. It pointed up something, for now, about that one frozen second. It was an illusion. Howe still belongs.

The buzzer sounded ending the game. As the players trooped off the ice, Howe was heard to quietly say to a teammate, "I'm glad that's over. Time to relax again."

Teeth were missing from the wide, cheek-creased smile as Howe joked with teammates and reporters in the snug locker room. As he talked, he unfolded a small paper wrapping that held a set of six teeth. He laughed easily and clamped in the teeth.

There is an aura of the confident star about Howe, but none of the prima donna.

When a reporter asked a silly question, "How did you feel about the first period?" Howe softly replied, "Terrible . . . What kind of a question is that? How do you think I felt?" He shook his head in a benign reprimand and threw a light, playful jab at the reporter's shoulder.

When Howe recently received a wreath of red-and-white carnations placed to spell "700," symbolic of his scoring the record 700th goal of his NHL career, he said, "That's lovely, but I'm allergic to flowers."

A year ago the Red Wings played the Canadian National team in an exhibition in Winnipeg. Howe got into a high-sticking tussle with a local star (Howe was born and raised in neighboring Saskatchewan). Howe was booed. The pair were sent to the penalty box. Since the game was almost over, they would go to the locker room. First, though, Howe skated to the Nationals' bench and went down the line shaking hands of youngsters who had grown up idolizing the great Gordie Howe. The players were thrilled, and the fans, who had come mainly to see Howe, switched octaves and cheered lustily.

Now in the Garden, Howe tugged off the heavy padded red pants. His white long johns were sweat-stained as though strawberry soda had been spilled. There have been times, too, when they were stained with blood dripping from his face. But Howe rarely fights any more. The younger players are usually in awe and the older players know he can still punch a nose into sections.

His great strength, which comes from a large chest and forearms like logs and deep sloping but powerful shoulders that allow him to hold back two hanging opponents as he stick-handles the puck with one hand, is, along with an acute understanding of the game and how to position himself in it, primarily responsible for his unparalleled success. Outstanding body balance and an amazingly accurate shot have also contributed much to establishing and holding most of the NHL career records for scoring and longevity.

"How much longer can he play?" Not an original question but one asked wherever he goes. "As long as I stay healthy," he said, "I'll stay in the game. I have a two-year contract. I'll finish that. Maybe there'll be another two-year contract after. See how I feel."

Athletes, traditionally, have always been loath to relinquish the roar of the crowd for the crackle of the fireplace. Often, it is out of fear of giving up the only thing they know and starting a new life.

"If an athlete is honest," said Howe, "he'll admit the fear is real. All athletes are terribly conscious of it. Especially hockey players. They are a different breed. Only 10 percent or so have ever gone to college. I only went to the eighth grade. My whole life has been hockey. A month ago I got involved in the insurance business. Bruce Norris, the owner of the Red Wings, got me in it. Said it would be good for when I'm through playing. But education is simply training of the mind."

And, in a substantial way, twenty-three years in the NHL has been, to be sure, an education in itself.

* * *

I didn't see Howe again until five years later when I was in Houston for NEA to see him play with his boys on the Aeros in the year-old World Hockey Association.

How Aerodynamic Can One Family Get?

January 28, 1974

"Only his cowlick, created by a full head of steam, reveals any effort as Gordie Howe moves gracefully, purposefully in his habitat. His

137

well-groomed pepper-and-salt hair, his white-and-blue uniform, his shimmering skates seem in this, his twenty-ninth year since he began as a professional hockey player to have made him indissoluble with the smoky-white icework.

"He is like some incredibly preserved fossil discovery. He has come out of two-year retirement to play for the Houston Aeros in the World Hockey Association.

"What was the lure for this forty-six-year-old body which has been upholstered in his career with 500 stitches and a record 786 National Hockey League goals?

More, even, was the chance to have fun again at hockey—his life. He said he would not have retired from the Detroit Red Wings had he not been debilitated by team dissension emanating from the front office, which took the joy out of the game for him. He was then given a front-office job in which, he felt, he was forced to be a nonfunctional barnacle in the executive woodwork.

A contract offer of $1 million spread over five years, and $400,000 for each of his sons spread over four years, plus public relations work for his wife Colleen, helped turn his head southward.

So the Howes came to Houston where hockey—and almost everything else except possibly barbecue—was second to high-school football.

Well, the Aeros in the young WHA have recently risen into first place: Gordie is the team's leading scorer and attendance this season is over 6,000 a game, nearly 2,000 better than in the Howe-less 1972–73 season. And fans here make more joyous noise than what's heard in the local zoo's Big Cat House during mating season.

Howe says he still gets a thrill out of playing. For one thing, he can get excited for a championship race, and he gets enormous delight in playing with his sons. He mentioned the recent night when Marty, the defenseman, scored the first goal of his pro career, on a drop pass from his father.

"At first," said Howe, "I thought it was Mark who scored it. But then I circled around and saw Marty, a big grinning Marty, and I knew."

Howe could empathize easily. He says he remembers vividly his first goal in a regular-season NHL game. "It was on old Turk Broda, in the second period of my first game." Broda was the star goalie for the Maple Leafs. "Right after the game," continued Howe, "I wrote at least ten letters home."

Howe said he can play almost as much as he ever could—25 to 30 minutes a game. The arthritis in his right hand has subsided after a two-year rest, and his legs, though feeling heavier at times, seem to be carrying his well-tended body comfortably.

"I do get sore after games," he said, "but not aching. Sure I get tired, but if you put out effort you should get tired. I got tired when I was seventeen."

One of the few concessions his sons make for dad (they call him "Gordie" or "Gord" on the ice) is that on the day of a game, when sister Kathy, fourteen, has to be picked up by car from her high school, Marty or Mark will say "Dad, stay resting on the couch. I'll get Kathy." On the ice, Howe still will hold off an opponent by jamming a big, blue claw-like glove in his face. He can still rattle the rink glass with a shattering body check. And he still gets his face stick-slashed, and then sewn up like a quilt.

"Finally, one is forced to wonder: Does a father of grown kids, a gray-haired Hall of Fame patriarch feel silly still playing a rough-and-tumble game?

"Only if I were wearing tennis shoes on the ice—and then," he said, "I'd feel silly."

* * *

Howe played with Houston until the WHA merged with the NHL in 1979, and Howe and his sons played for the Hartford Whalers of the

NHL. On February 29, 1980, at age fifty-one (!) Howe scored his 800th NHL goal, and had 1,071 goals in his professional career. Both his sons also had extensive careers in the NHL, and both made All-Star teams.

Gordie retired finally after the 1980 season, at age fifty-two. He did come back for one star-turn in one shift with the Detroit Vipers of the International League, at sixty-nine, extending his record of consecutive decades played to six.

On March 28, 2016, three days before his eighty-eighth birthday, Howe appeared at a Red Wings-Buffalo Sabres game at Joe Louis Arena in Detroit, where he was presented with a cake as the crowd sang "Happy Birthday" to him.

Nearly three months later, on June 10, 2016, Gordie Howe died.

Al Oerter: A Discus Spans the Ages

June 17, 1982

Scene: Olympic Stadium, Mexico City. Evening. October 15, 1968. A thunderstorm. Action: Al Oerter, a 6-foot-4 discus thrower, blue USA jacket soaking wet, hair matted, ascends the winner's stand. A soggy official slips the gold medal Oerter has just won around his size extra extra large neck. National anthem. American flag is raised to the highest pole on the rim of the flood-lighted stadium.

Oerter has won his fourth gold medal in four consecutive Olympic Games, covering a period of twelve years. No Olympic athlete has ever matched Oerter's combination of achievement and longevity.

Now the elements spare nothing in dramatizing the moment: the rain pours, the thunder claps, lightning flashes. And on this moving, historic occasion, Al Oerter would recall that he had but one thought— to get out of the rain.

Al Oerter's greatest strength, it seems clear, is not in his abundant muscles, but in his sense of proportion.

He retired after the 1968 Olympics, at age thirty-two, to tend to his family—he has two daughters—and vegetable garden on West Islip, Long Island, and his business. He is a data communications manager for Grumman Data Systems in Bethpage. It was time, he decided, to put aside childish things. He was barely aware of the 1972 Olympic competition, but he watched the 1976 Games and he felt something funny, something familiar. It was that old competitive adrenalin pumping madly.

"I stopped fooling myself and admitted that I missed it and loved it and wanted to try it again," he said. After eight years he went out to try to throw the discus again, lost his balance, fell and broke his ankle. Yet he persisted. In the Olympic Trials in Eugene, Oregon, in 1980, Oerter came in fourth. But with the United States boycott of the Olympic Games in Moscow, which he strongly supported, the "lure," as he terms it, of international Olympic competition was lost for him.

Oerter is still winging the discus. This weekend he will compete in the United States Nationals in Knoxville, Tennessee. He is aiming for the 1984 Games in Los Angeles, when he will be nearly forty-eight years old—middle-aged for the common man, antediluvian for an athlete.

He is throwing the discus farther than ever. His best throw was 216 feet 5 inches; his best Olympic heave was 212-6, in Mexico City. "I think I'm a better athlete than I've ever been," he said. He was in Manhattan in the studio of Cappy Productions recently, where a preview of the last in its PBS series, *Numero Uno*, had been shown. Oerter is represented as the outstanding American athlete on an international level. The half-hour program will be shown in New York City on Sunday, July 4, at 7:30 p.m.

"I'm stronger now," he continued. "I'm up to 285 pounds. When I was in Melbourne for my first Olympics in 1956, I weighed 235. It used to be thought that if you did a lot of weight lifting, your muscles would bunch up, you wouldn't be loose. We know now that that's not entirely true.

"And my technique has changed—I've learned to throw with more of my body. "I think those two elements offset the age factor. I continue to improve. Otherwise, the only other major change is that I'm heavy into Ben-Gay."

Oerter has been noted for not only his great talent, but for his poise, his ability to relax under pressure, and the capacity to drive his opponents bananas. He entered every Olympic competition as an underdog, being neither the American champion nor the world-record holder.

In Rome in 1960, he approached a tough Czechoslovak thrower and asked how Poland was. "Zonk! The guy was walking around like King Kong," recalled Oerter, "Now he was shrunk to size."

In 1968, Jay Silvester, the American and Olympic favorite, showed Oerter a good-luck telegram from Utah. "It's signed by almost everybody in my hometown of Orem," said Silvester. "All 400 of them."

"Four hundred?" said Oerter. "Can't be much of a town." Zonk. Such techniques are byproducts of hard-earned experience. Oerter received his first such lesson at Melbourne, as a nineteen-year-old rookie in 1956.

Practicing with the favorite and world-record holder, Fortune Gordien, Oerter began to hurry his throws because he was aware of Gordien pacing about.

"I got so shook up I finally threw one backwards," said Oerter. "It was an accident, but it whistled right past his ear and slammed into the net. It could have taken his head off. He was shaking. He didn't hurry me anymore after that."

Archie Moore: The Secrets of the Mongoose

November 24, 1987

Archie Moore, born Archibald Lee Wright, a.k.a. The Old Mongoose, was seated at breakfast yesterday at the Downtown Athletic Club and was reminded of a line that was attributed to him years ago.

Moore had been asked, "Does your wife mind kissing you with that beard?"

"No," he replied, "she's happy to go through a forest to get to the picnic."

Archie Moore scrunched his eyes and laughed.

"Were you quoted accurately?" he was asked.

"Well," said The Old Mongoose, "that's the way it was. Hmmm. Yes, indeed." He laughed again.

Moore, the one-time world light heavyweight champion, was in town to receive the Rocky Marciano Award, presented last night, for being "a champion in the ring . . . a champion in life." It coincided with an article in the current issue of *Ring* magazine in which Moore, champ from 1952 to 1962, is rated the best in history in his division.

At breakfast, Moore was wearing a blue suit and blue tie and a gray mustache and a natty sprig of gray hair under his lower lip. In his eye was that characteristic look, at once penetrating and twinkling.

"I used my eyes to catch those punches," Moore said. "Had my eye in a lot of places at once. Like right now. While I'm talkin' I can see out of the corner who gets off the elevator, or without turnin' my head if someone over on the side is comin' through the window." Moore was called The Old Mongoose because he had been in the fight game for so long, and, more, because he was so clever.

"It's said that a mongoose is the only animal a snake can't catch," someone said.

"That's right," Moore said, and, as a confidential aside, added, "except when he's sick."

"You look like a million," said Gil Clancy, the fight manager, stopping by briefly.

"I'm lookin' pretty good," the champ conceded.

It's true. He looks like a very healthy mongoose indeed.

The record book says he was born on December 13, 1913, and won the title from Joey Maxim in 1952, four days after Moore's thirty-ninth birthday. He'd been fighting professionally for nearly seventeen years until that point, finally getting a champ to stop ducking him and give him a chance at the title.

Moore's last fight was in 1963, when he was somewhere around fifty. He finished with the record for most knockouts in a career, either 129 or 145, depending on the record book used.

It was a long and arduous journey out of the St. Louis ghetto, beginning with his first bout, a second-round knockout of Poco Kid, on January 31, 1936, in Hot Springs, Arkansas, for a purse of $10. "And they haven't paid me yet," said Moore. No matter. "Boxing," he said, "was the dearest thing to me."

If Moore wasn't the oldest to ever win a world boxing title—and the oldest to hold it, ten years later—he is certainly one of the oldest.

"I lasted because I learned to keep my head out of the way of blows," he said. "I could take a punch, but it's better to evade them, I always say. Constant punching can cause severe implications.

"So I'm feelin' just fine today. I'm seventy-eight years old."

Seventy-eight? "Archie, the record book says you'll be seventy-four."

"Hmmm," he said. "So it does." One puncher he couldn't evade was Marciano, who knocked him out in the ninth round, in 1955. Marciano was then thirty-two, from ten to fourteen years younger than Moore. It was Marciano's last bout.

Was it simply a coincidence that Marciano retired after fighting Moore?

"Well," said The Old Mongoose, "I think he knew he had been in a fight with me. You know, Rocky used to look awkward because he swung and missed with the left, but he usually did that to get leverage for the right. It's an old trick, an old trick." He recalled Sugar Ray Robinson. "He used to call me Otch. He was a beautiful fighter. But he could be savage. Randy Turpin was handlin' Ray pretty good one night and caught Ray upside the eye. Blood spurted all over the place. Ray came back and dropped Turpin with vicious punches. He had him layin' over the ropes like a laundry shirt."

Was Robinson, as many contend, pound for pound the best fighter ever?

"I won't admit that," said Moore, with a smile. "But he was smart. He never wanted to fight me. That shows how much good sense Ray had."

Through the years, Moore has worked with young people, showing them the right way to throw a punch, as well as explaining to them the right way to live. "Like in the ring, you have to be in condition to have technique and strength and willpower and courage to go in the face of odds," he said. "And that means no drugs and no drink."

Before Moore received a plaque at lunch, four college boxers were introduced to him.

"Line up!" he ordered. The college kids, a bit bewildered, stood in a row.

"Now I'll teach you to throw the jab." On the third syllable of "position," he said, "you snap into your stance."

He barked the command like a drill sergeant. On the third syllable, they snapped into it.

"No!" He slapped a pupil's fist, nudged an elbow, righted a shoulder. "Like this!" He demonstrated, in buttoned-up suit jacket.

"Now, smash your man's nose! Boom!" He commanded again: "Po-zish-UN!"

And: "Extend your fist! Snatch it back! Out! Recoil! Out! Recoil!" He jabbed. They jabbed. "Out! Out! Out! Out! OK, as you were!"

He stopped. He stared. "That was your first lesson in how to jab, whatever you say. Class dismissed!"

Then The Old Mongoose walked off, shoulders squared, and slyly winked to a friend.

The LaMotta Nuptials

April 20, 1985

Neither of the Las Vegas dailies, nor, for that matter, *The New York Times*, reported in their society news sections the wedding of Jacob (Jake) LaMotta, sixty-three years old, erstwhile pugilist, and, Theresa Miller, younger than the bridegroom and decidedly prettier.

Perhaps it was determined in some editorial conclave that to cover one of Jake's nuptials is to cover them all, for this was the sixth time he's tied the knot. But to Jake, each, of course, is unique. His first wife divorced him, he says, "because I clashed with the drapes." Another one, Vicki, complained about not having enough clothes. "I didn't believe her," LaMotta says, "until I saw her pose nude in *Playboy* magazine."

The betrothal of LaMotta, the former world middleweight champion, to Miss Miller, this was her second trip to the altar, took place last Saturday night in Las Vegas at Maxim Hotel and Casino in a room stuffed with a wide assortment of beefy people with odd-shaped and familiar noses: They included such ex-champions as Gene Fullmer, Carmen Basilio, Willie Pep, Joey Maxim, Billy Conn, Jose Torres and, the best man, Sugar Ray Robinson, plus a potpourri of contenders, trainers and matchmakers, all of whom were in Las Vegas to attend the Hagler-Hearns world middleweight title fight two nights later.

For LaMotta, having Robinson as the best man was a sweet and perfect touch. "I fought Sugar six times," he said. "I only beat him once. This is my sixth marriage and I ain't won one yet. So I figure I'm due."

Both the groom and the best man wore tuxedos with white corsages in their lapels. The bride was radiant in a white dress with mother-of-pearl-and-lace design, and a garland of baby's breath in her auburn hair. The wedding party assembled under a white lattice arch in the corner of the room as District Judge Joe Pavlikowski of Clark County presided over the ceremony.

Despite the loud, happy chatter of the guests, the judge began a recital of the vows. "Quiet, please," a man shouted. "Quiet." When that didn't work, the man stuck two fingers in his mouth and whistled. That got their attention.

The judge continued. He asked Jake and Theresa if they would love and obey. They said they would, and Jake kissed the bride.

"Wait a minute," said the judge. "Not yet."

Jake looked up, and Theresa smiled. The judge coughed.

In another corner of the room, a phone rang.

Jake looked around brightly. "What round is it?" he asked.

The room broke up. Theresa, laughing, said, "I've changed my mind!" Then she hugged Jake, who smiled proudly at his bon mot.

"We've got to finish," said the judge. The room settled down somewhat. "With love and affection," continued the judge, speaking quicker now. In short order, he pronounced them "Mr. and Mrs. Jake LaMotta."

Applause and cheers went up, and the couple kissed again, this time officially.

"Jake's ugly as mortal sin," observed Billy Conn. "He's a nice guy, though."

Shortly after, Jake and Carmen Basilio argued about who was uglier.

The issue wasn't resolved. Steve Rossi, the comedian, who was performing at the hotel, was the master of ceremonies at the wedding. He brought the fighters onto the stage, where they talked and laughed and feinted and hit one another with friendly jabs and hooks.

When all the fighters were on stage, Rossi said, "Let's all go eat before the platform collapses."

Teddy Brenner, the matchmaker, asked Joey Maxim, "Who was the only white guy to beat Jersey Joe Walcott and Floyd Patterson?" Maxim said he didn't know. "You, ya big lug," said Brenner. They both laughed. The story gleefully made the rounds, varying a little with each telling, until finally, "and so he asked Joey, 'Who was the only white guy to beat Louis and Ali?'"

Someone asked Fullmer how many times he had fought Robinson.

"Three-and-a-half," he said. "The second fight, I asked my manager, how come they stopped it? He said, "cause the referee counted to 11.'"

Basilio said he had recently retired as a physical education instructor at Le Moyne College in Syracuse. Someone asked if he had a degree.

He smiled and brushed the ashes from his cigarette off the sports jacket of the person he was talking to. "I got a degree from H. N.," he said. "The school of hard knocks."

Billy Conn, who lives in Pittsburgh, was telling about the time that his brother Jackie, a noncomformist, visited Conn on a Thanksgiving Day. "We were having the Mellons over and I told Jackie that we wanted everything to run smoothly, so here's fifty bucks and go buy a turkey for yourself. But he kept the fifty bucks and took the two turkeys we had in the stove."

What did the Conns and the Mellons eat that night?

"We didn't eat," he said, "we drank whiskey all night. Oh, Jackie was a character. Jackie's dead now."

Roger Donoghue, once a promising middleweight from Yonkers, and now a successful liquor salesman, was recalling the television-fight days of the early 1950s. Basilio came over and handed Roger a small camera and asked him to take a picture of him and his wife.

"I got hit in the head a lot," said Roger, looking at the camera, "but I'll try."

The doors of the room were opened and the clanging of slot machines was heard from the adjoining casino. People wandered in and out of the wedding party.

Jake was explaining, "You wanna go through life with someone, and she's a great kid, a great kid."

"This one," said Theresa, "is going to last until we die."

Now, Jake and his bride stepped onto the dance floor. A trio, headed by a piano player wearing a black cowboy hat, played "The Nearness of You."

Joey Maxim removed the cigar from his mouth as he watched Jake dance with his new bride. "Ain't that nice?" he said.

"Hey, buddy," said a man who walked in from the casino, "you know where a fella can get two tickets for the fight?"

A Most Unlikely Duo: Bear Bryant and Ann Landers

December 11, 1982

Several times over the years, Paul W. (Bear) Bryant, an academician at the University of Alabama, has penned letters to Ann Landers. They are not the conventional ones she gets that seek advice for the lovelorn.

The old football coach, with a faced lined like a walnut, is still tough at age sixty-nine, but he does not seem lorn of love. When he writes Ann, America's equivalent of the Oracle of Delphi, it is generally to compliment her on a column. He says he has read "jillions of 'em" to his football players. He says he appreciates her moral stance and her sense of humor.

Ann Landers replies quickly, not only because she is the most dedicated of respondents, but, she says, she was flattered by the Bear's attention.

Even though she has never been able to learn football—"I just can't hack it," she says, "I keep looking for the ball while everyone else is cheering"—she is aware that the Bear has won more games than any other coach in college football history.

Once she dropped him a note of thanks and said if he were ever in Chicago, where she lives, to please call, she'd love to meet him.

Last August, she received an unexpected telephone call. "It was from the Bear," she said. "He didn't growl, as I thought he might, he purred like a pussycat." He was calling from Tuscaloosa and requested a column she had done twelve years ago. The column, which he reads every fall to his freshmen football players, had been misplaced and, he said, he didn't know where in the world it was.

The column is entitled "Dead at 17." It's a hypothetical account of a boy who takes the family car, drives carelessly, has a wreck and then sees himself declared dead and buried.

"It's a story that really gets to ya," said Bryant. "And Ann very graciously said she'd rerun it." Bryant, in New York this week for the National Football Foundation and Hall of Fame dinner, had been discussing his morning reading habits.

"I get the newspaper," he said, "and glance at the front page, then read Ann Landers, and then go to the stock market and sports." One may not expect Bear Bryant to be reading the letters of La Rochefoucauld or Montesquieu at breakfast. But not epistles beginning, "Dear Ann," either.

"I'll take advice from anyone, if I think it's good," said Bryant. "And anyone who's been in business as long as she has, has to be good."

The same might surely be said of Bryant himself. His record of 322 coaching victories is unsurpassed. Bryant has been a college football coach for thirty-eight years, and Ann Landers has been writing her column for twenty-eight years.

Her advice regarding football, she says, has been limited to the many letters from mothers that begin, "I don't want my boy to play football because I'm afraid he'll get hurt."

"The mother is usually up against her son and his macho father, who didn't make it in football himself," said Ann Landers. "I know that football players are wearing a lot more stuff on them than they used to, but it's still a dangerous game. But life is dangerous, too. It's a tough call. I tell a mother that if football is truly important to her son, then she's probably going to have to let him play. There comes a point when children have to be let off the leash, and they've got to be allowed to take their lumps. Then they can make their own decision on whether to continue."

As for football coaches, she is impressed with Bear Bryant. "He must be a very sensitive, warm person to care so much about the kids who pass through his life," she said. "I have a feeling he cares more about them than he does his record of being the coach with all those wins."

The Bear has always been known as a demanding coach, standing atop his spiral-staircased tower and, with a megaphone, leading practice. He has made headlines for his suspensions, such as that of Joe Willie Namath, a quarterback and maverick who enjoyed the good life and went around campus in sunglasses—even at night—and drove a beat-up car with a missing door.

Another former player, Bob Gain, also went from playing for Bryant to starring in professional football for the Cleveland Browns. "I love Coach Bryant now for the things I once hated him for," said Gain.

Bryant had been so tough at times that when his team lost he blamed overworking them. This season the Crimson Tide had only a 7–4 record, one of their poorest in years, and lost their last three games. For Bryant, it seemed that football was no longer, as he once said, "hog heaven."

Bryant had said that perhaps the university might want to think about a new, younger head coach. "But I haven't heard anything from them," said Bryant. It is unlikely that a change will be made.

"I'm not going to put my finger on every little thing we did wrong this season," said Bryant, "but we've got good people and good players and we shouldn't have lost what we did. I take the responsibility for doing a poor job.

"It's harder now to keep up the enthusiasm and stamina for 11 or 12 games. If I had a three-game season, I'd still be a helluva coach. But you get tired of the problems all the time, and the recruiting—which is the worst thing about college football."

If he were to write a letter to Ann Landers asking for advice, what would he say? He replied, "Dear Ann: Help. Bear." And how would Ann Landers respond? "I'd say, 'Hang in there, Bear. They need you. Don't let a bum season discourage you. You've still got plenty to give.'"

* * *

After this column ran, I received a note from Ann Landers—real name, Eppie Lederer—and she said she "loved running into her name on the sports page." We developed a correspondence and a friendship. One time, she used an item in a column of hers that was meant to show that even great people fail at times: "Babe Ruth struck out 1,330 times—a major league record." She got a letter saying that Reggie Jackson, not Ruth, was the leader in strikeouts. She scripted a note to me on the margin of that letter: "Is this true? I haven't had any other mail about it. Help. R.S.V.P. Eppie." Alas, I responded, it is true: "Reggie had whiffed 2,597 times."

Nolan Ryan on Satchel Paige's "Social Ramble"

March 9, 1992 / Port Charlotte, Florida

The only time Nolan Ryan met Satchel Paige was in the mid-1970s in Los Angeles, and the old pitcher—now the late old pitcher—gave the younger man a piece of advice. "One of the best pitches is the bow-tie pitch," Paige said.

Ryan looked at Paige, then about seventy years old. Ryan was close to thirty and already an experienced big-league pitcher, but he was puzzled. "What's a bow-tie pitch, Satch?" he asked.

"That's when you throw it right here," said Paige, drawing a line with his hand across his Adam's apple. "Where they wear their bow tie."

This was sound advice, Ryan believed, and he has not been above using the bow-tie pitch to keep batters off the plate and make them reluctant to dig in. Of course, Ryan's pitches remain bullet-fast, which also makes the batter wary, whether he's concerned about a baseball plunked on his bow tie or not.

Last season, Ryan's twenty-fourth in the major leagues, he was still one of baseball's best pitchers. Among other achievements, he was third in the American league in strikeouts—adding to his career strikeout record, which stands at 5,511—and he flung his seventh no-hitter, three more than anyone else in history. Now, at forty-five, an age when most old ballplayers are home clipping coupons or out hooking drives, Ryan looks forward to yet another remarkable year on the mound.

While his hair is thinning, and there are the little crow's feet about the eyes, the rest of him looks pretty fit. "And my arm? My arm is just fine," he said the other day in the clubhouse here at the Texas Rangers' spring training camp.

Can he top the seniors' mark of Satchel Paige, who pitched in the majors when he was forty-seven years old?

"I don't know, but then no one really knows how old Satchel was," Ryan said. "He might have been fifty-seven. At least I have a birth certificate. And I have people who could verify it, though not as many as there used to be."

Ryan isn't certain why he has had such staying power—especially throwing as hard as he does at the age he is—but he believes genetics probably has something to do with it, as well as diet, exercise and attitude. Ryan said he had once read Satchel Paige's rules for keeping young and thought at the time that they were "applicable" to him.

In the interest of public service and the field of geriatrics, enduring concerns of this column, Ryan was asked to comment on Paige's six famous points to promote health and longevity:

Paige: "1. Avoid Fried Meats, which angry up the blood."

Ryan: "I think from a cardiovascular standpoint, Satchel's right. I stay away from fried foods now, even though I grew up in Texas where a frying pan was always sitting on the stove. Nowadays I have my food broiled. I stay away from fatty foods, and chocolate cakes and chocolate pies, which I used to love. But I don't know anything about angrying up the blood."

Paige: "2. If your stomach disputes you, lie down and pacify it with cool thoughts."

Ryan: "I take naps when I can, and I always try to get seven or eight hours' sleep a night. You want to keep relaxed. I tried to teach my kids that. They've been around the clubhouse since they were little bitty tykes. And they've seen a lot. They've seen players get into fights, they've heard cussing, they've seen managers go crazy. I told them: 'That's not how we act. There are a lot of different type people in the world. But we're not like that.'

"Also, don't let things upset you that you can't control. And try to make any difficult situation better. Last season, for example, we brought up a rookie catcher, Ivan Rodriguez, and he caught me in his second game. We weren't in rhythm, because that takes time. But I set my mind beforehand not to get upset, and to work with him. So I shook him off until he called the pitch I wanted, and it didn't throw off my concentration."

Paige: "3. Keep the juices flowing by jangling around gently as you move."

Ryan: "My assessment of that is, basically, stay loose by stretching. At this age, you tend to stiffen up when sitting in one place for too long." What about jangling? "Sure, if you know how to jangle. I'm not sure I do."

Paige: "4. Go very light on the vices, such as carrying on in society. The social ramble ain't restful."

Ryan: "Very true. You can do a lot of things with the body, but do everything in moderation." How does Ryan characterize "social ramble?" "Bar hopping, staying out late in a joint or something. Overindulging. Listen to your body. Sometimes the rumble is because of the ramble."

Paige: "5. Avoid running at all times."

Ryan: "Here I disagree with Satchel. I think a pitcher needs to run to build up stamina and to strengthen the legs, the hips, the knees, the lower back. But I don't run for distance anymore, and maybe I run 40 percent of what I used to. The recovery rate to bounce back gets longer. If this keeps up, there's a good chance that when I'm forty-seven I won't be able to run at all. So Satchel might be right again."

Paige: "6. Don't look back. Something might be gaining on you."

Ryan: "I take Satchel to mean that you can't start worrying now. You know there's always some kids behind you. Let them worry about it."

Then Ryan went over and climbed on the stationary bicycle. And one was reminded that Satchel Paige's exercise machine was also stationary. It was a rocking chair.

Tom Seaver: From the Hill to the Hall

August 2, 1992

"Honey, where'd you hide the baseballs?" Tom Seaver called to his wife, Nancy, from his small office in his home. "I want to put them back up on the shelves."

"The baseballs?" she called from another part of the house. "They're in the shopping bags. In the hallway."

This was in the early afternoon on the week before George Thomas Seaver was to be inducted into the Baseball Hall of Fame in Cooperstown, New York, and he was moving about his office putting up some pictures that had only recently been taken down by the carpenters, and seeking to return the baseballs, each of which had some special meaning to him, back on the wall ledges.

Seaver, still husky, still youthful at forty-seven, and still in the public eye as a broadcaster for the Yankees, wore a turquoise shirt with sleeves rolled up, tan corduroy jeans, worn sneakers and a pair of pruning shears that were hooked onto his belt. He had been out in the yard until it had begun to rain, a rain that now drummed darkly on his window.

This was in the renovated barn on seven acres of well-tended land in Greenwich, where the Seavers have lived for more than twenty years, or ever since he began to establish himself as the Franchise, as Tom Terrific, as, simply, the best pitcher the Mets ever had. Over a twenty-year major league career, from 1967 to 1986, with four teams, including also the Reds, the White Sox and the Red Sox, Seaver won 311 games; struck out 3,640 batters, which was the third best in history; threw 61 shutouts, the seventh best ever, and won three Cy Young Awards.

And now he was trying to restore his life at home to some semblance of order while workers hammered and clattered and moved furniture. Friends and family would be coming soon—friends and family who were "all part of the whole picture," as Seaver termed it—and then all would accompany him for the induction ceremonies that are being held this afternoon in Cooperstown. And so there was some fixing and expanding to be done to accommodate the guests.

The phone rang. "Russ, Russ, how ya doin'? When ya comin' in?" said Seaver. "Terrific. Terrific. No, don't lug any tennis racquet. We've got plenty. And we've got plenty of tennis balls too. Don't worry about it. You're excited? Hey, I'm excited! Terrific. Terrific."

When Seaver hung up, he turned to a guest in his office. "When I found out I made the Hall of Fame," said Seaver, "Russ was one of the first people I called. He still lives in Fresno. I said, 'You gotta be here. You gotta come as my guest.' He said, 'But I've never been farther east than Las Vegas.' I said, 'This'll be a first for you.'"

And then Seaver told the story about the caller, Russ Scheidt. For the road to Cooperstown for Seaver started with Russ Scheidt on Arthur Avenue in Fresno, California. "Russ lived across the street from me, and he was the first kid I can remember playing catch with," said Seaver. "I was five years old, he was six years old, and neither of us was allowed to cross the street. So we threw the ball back and forth from my side of the street to his." Seaver laughed, a high-pitched, boyish laugh that he has never lost.

A few years after that, said Seaver, Scheidt took his younger pal under his wing in the Little League. "We were both on the North Fresno Rotary team, and he showed me how to wear the baseball cap and the socks—the socks were way down on the tops of my shoes—and how to walk in the rubber spikes. He kind of polished me up a little bit."

Other Players Were Better

Seaver spoke about how he was late maturing, and that while he was a good player in the Little League, he was no "phenom."

"I was a shrimp in those days, and I needed all the power I could muster to throw the ball," Seaver said. That led to his low-slung, knee-dragging, piston-like pitching style. "It was a blessing in disguise," he said.

He was still small in high school. About a year ahead of him in Fresno were high school stars—and future major leaguers—Wade

Blasingame and Dick Selma. "They were the guys striking out 18, 19 guys a game," he said. "I didn't make the varsity in high school until I was a senior. I was on the junior varsity until then. And in my senior year I was 6-foot-5, or 5-foot-4, and I made all-city, but they probably didn't have anyone else to choose."

Seaver was at loose ends when he graduated from high school. "I had no offers to play baseball, and I had been only an average student and I was not sure what I wanted to do with my life," he said. The rain beat heavily on the window behind. "All of my brothers and sisters had gone to college—Katie to Stanford, Charles to Berkeley, Carol to UCLA—and I was the baby, and I had no plans for college. So my father booted my butt into the Marines. I was seventeen years old."

Junior College Detour

When Seaver got to Camp Pendleton—with Russ Scheidt, in fact—he soon made a discovery. After the drilling, after the commands, after the K.P., he said to himself, "So this is what dad was talking about." "This" meaning that life without direction was not going to be a day at the beach.

In a year he had grown from 5-foot-7 and 160 pounds, to 6-foot-1 and 200 pounds. He served six months in the Marines. "When I got out I knew exactly what I wanted to do: go to USC and become a dentist."

First, though, he went to Fresno City College, a junior college, and fulfilled what he said was "one of the first real goals I had in life. That was to pay for my education. And I did. Tuition was $10."

But it was at Fresno, he said, "that my world really exploded." He pitched for the school team and had a 10–2 record, and was offered a scholarship by USC. It was also at junior college that he met Nancy. He went to USC the next year, 1965. "And a year and a half later," he said,

"I was pitching in the major league All-Star Game in Anaheim in '67. Took me 15 innings to get into the game, but I made it."

He had starred at USC for one year with an 11–2 record, and then was signed by the Mets. He spent one year at Jacksonville in Class AAA—as did Nancy, since they had gotten married that year—and then came up to the Mets in the spring of 1967.

Seaver now went into the hallway to get the two shopping bags full of baseballs. They lay on the floor in front of his small trophies alcove. On the walls were photographs of important moments and people in his life.

Influenced by Hodges

There was a picture of Sandy Koufax and him. "I admired him so much, just the way he went about his work, with such professionalism, such consistency," Seaver said. "I remember when my season in Jacksonville ended and I went home and the Dodgers were playing. Sandy Koufax was pitching. I took Nancy to the game at Dodgers Stadium. Remember, we had just finished an entire season. And she was thinking, 'Another ball game? What have I gotten myself into?'"

Seaver pointed to a picture of Gil Hodges and him and said: "He was my most important influence in professional ball. He was a pro's pro. He became the Mets' manager in my second season. I was beating Marichal and the Giants something like 7–1 at Shea and thought I got a little gay on the mound. I wound up winning, 7–6. Gil called me into his office. He said, 'I was disappointed in you. That's not the way a professional goes about his business. It doesn't matter if you're ahead 10–1 or 2–1, whether it's April or September, whether it's 30 degrees or 90 degrees, whether it's a Monday afternoon in Chicago or a Friday night in Los Angeles, you still give the same level of effort.' I've never forgotten that."

Professor Aaron

Seaver moved in front of a picture of Hank Aaron and him. "He was my idol, like Koufax, a picture of consistency," he said. "The first time I faced him, I was a rookie, and I got him to hit into a double play on a sinker down and in. I could have lit up a victory cigar, I was so proud of myself. I figured I had his number. And he figured I was figuring that, too, because I threw him the same pitch in the same spot the next time he came to bat in the game and he whacked it into the left-field stands for a three-run homer. Another piece of education."

Seaver talked about his closeness to some teammates, like Bud Harrelson and Jerry Grote and coach Rube Walker of the Mets, and Carlton Fisk of the White Sox and Tommy Hume of the Reds. And opponents, too. There was a picture of Steve Carlton on the wall and Seaver recalled:

"One day with the Reds I was in the dugout and I caught Lefty's attention in the Phillies' dugout. Neither of us was pitching that day. I motioned for him to meet me in the runway behind the stands. I said, 'Lefty, I'm having a lot of trouble with my slider. Can you help me?' He asked about the release points, whether my fingers were on top of the ball, and was I squeezing properly? I don't remember now, but it probably helped."

Departure From the Mets

Seaver talked about leaving the Mets the first time, in 1977, and the bitter disappointment with management. "But I'm glad I left, in retrospect," he said. "It was good for me in that I got out of a bad situation for me, and it was good for the Mets. They were in disarray and soon they got new management. I guess we all needed a fresh outlook."

He pointed to a picture of him putting on his White Sox jacket at the edge of the dugout at Yankee Stadium in 1986, and one of his two daughters, Annie, then 11 years old, leaning toward him in her front-row seat. "This was after the eighth inning when I had just struck out Winfield with two men on and two outs, and I was leading 4–1 and going for my 300th win," he said. "At this moment, I was saying to Annie, 'Just three more outs.' And she said, 'Good, then we can go home and go swimming!'"

Seaver now dipped into the shopping bags to place baseball after baseball on the two long wooden shelves. Each one was marked. This one was from his 1978 no-hitter for the Reds—"the only one I ever pitched." And another was from the 1970 game in which he tied a major league record with 19 strikeouts, against San Diego. "This is from my 285th, and this one from my 20th win in 1975," he said, laying them in the racks. There were a number of All-Star Game balls. And one from the 1960 Babe Ruth League city champions of Fresno. And the ball he hit for his first major league home run, in 1970. "Must've gone into the Shea Stadium bullpen."

He picked up another ball. It read, "To Kenny. Best wishes, Tom Seaver." He looked at it oddly. "I don't know who Kenny is. Whoever he is, he must have sent it back."

He laughed and tossed Kenny's ball back into the shopping bag and began to pull out other balls, balls that had lined the road for George Thomas Seaver, the road that, in forty-seven years, has taken him from Arthur Avenue and Russ Scheidt in Fresno to Main Street and Babe Ruth in Cooperstown.

Moe Berg: "The Catcher Was Highly Mysterious"

December 14, 1989

In the baseball press boxes at Shea Stadium and Yankee Stadium in the 1960s and early 1970s, a man wearing a black suit, a black tie, black shoes—the ensemble never varied—with black hair and a touch of gray at the temples, black eyebrows rather closely knit, and a warm smile, an elegant demeanor, a high intelligence and an air of mystery was often seen.

His name was Moe Berg. He was a baseball player whose seventeen years in the major leagues with the Dodgers, Indians, Senators, White Sox, and Red Sox produced a lifetime batting average of .243, with 11 stolen bases and 6 home runs.

Before 1989 leaves us, it should be recalled that this is the 50th anniversary of the end of Moe Berg's playing career, a career, aptly depicted by a recent letter writer, Terry Hauser, as "unmatched for marginality."

Berg remains of interest, even 16 1/2 years after his death at age seventy. Several years ago a biography was written on him. For years various producers have discussed making a film of his life. And people still love to tell Moe Berg stories.

The late Bus Saidt, of the *Trenton Times*, a friend of Berg's, recalled how Moe would simply materialize in places. "Almost like from behind a pillar," Saidt said. And disappear just as quickly.

Lawrence Golden describes waiting on Moe numerous times "in a deli across from the Waldorf."

"A solitary figure," penned Golden in a note, "and he always ordered pastrami and eggs well and rye thin."

To some, it was a mystery how Berg remained on teams as, first, a shortstop, and later a catcher. But managers liked him around for his wisdom. He knew the pitchers, and could help the hitters. On occasion, he could also knock a pitch off the left-field fence.

Berg was a true scholar, unlike any other who has ever strapped on shin guards, or anything else, in the big leagues. He was a magna cum laude graduate of Princeton, a graduate of the Sorbonne, and, while still a ballplayer, a graduate in 1929 of the Columbia Law School.

He was also a linguist. Of Berg it was said, "He knew twelve languages but couldn't hit in any of them." And he was a spy. While on tour with an All-Star team to Japan in 1934 (Moe was brought along with Babe Ruth and others as an interpreter) he disguised himself in a kimono (black, of course) and snapped photos that were supposed to be helpful to American bombing missions during World War II.

Ruth's daughter, Julia, also on the trip, remembered Berg as "a marvelous dancer. He was awfully good at the fox-trot and Lindy."

In a photo of that All-Star team that hangs in the Baseball Hall of Fame, each of the players signed his name beside his picture. Moe, who was born in New York City of immigrant Jewish parents from the Ukraine, signed his name in flowing Japanese.

He was also described as working for the OSS (forerunner of the CIA) and going behind German lines during wartime and posing as a German-speaking nuclear scientist.

I sat with Berg often during games in the ball parks. He never discussed his spy days. When the topic was raised, he'd put his finger to his closed lips, as if to say, "Shh. Can't talk about it." But he'd quiz me on such things as the Greek name for Mercury; he was working the *Times* (of London) *Literary Supplement*'s crossword puzzle. And then he'd test me, in his gentle, agreeable and whimsical manner on why did I think the second baseman just moved one step to his right for the next batter? (I hadn't noticed.) I remember him relating a story that I read in his posthumous biography, *Athlete, Scholar, Spy*. But the authors only got part of it.

Berg once visited Einstein at Princeton. They had tea in a glass and the professor played the violin for Berg. At one point, notes the biography, Einstein said to his guest, "You teach me baseball and I'll teach you mathematics."

Moe, though, had added a kicker. He said, "Dr. Einstein told me, 'But let's forget it. I'm sure you'd learn mathematics faster than I'd learn baseball.'"

I asked Berg if he'd ever written for publication. "Only once," he said. "A treatise on Sanskrit." One day in a second-hand book store I ran across an old collection of *Atlantic Monthly* articles, "The Pocket Atlantic," and one, written in 1940, was entitled "Pitchers and Catchers." The author was Moe Berg.

The piece was all Moe, erudite, insightful and fun. Such as: "At first, the super speed of Grove obviated the necessity of pitching brains. But when his speed began to fade Lefty turned to his head. With his almost perfect control and the addition of his fork ball, Lefty fools the hitter with his cunning. With Montaigne, we conceive of Socrates in place of Alexander, of brain for brawn, wit for whip."

When I saw him at the ball park, I said, "Moe, you told me you never wrote for publication." And I produced the book. He looked at it, looked at me, and smiled. "You caught me, Ira" he said.

Hank Greenberg: A Kind of Beacon

September 7, 1986

One afternoon about ten years ago, Hank Greenberg, in tennis togs, stopped beside the pool of a Las Vegas hotel to chat with friends. Greenberg, then sixty-five years old and still vigorous at 6-foot-4 and 220 pounds, was there to participate in a celebrity tennis tournament.

The talk got around to 1947, when he played first base for the Pittsburgh Pirates. It was a terrible team, a team, he would recall, that in the clubhouse regularly had a record player blaring, and the favorite song was "Cigareetes, Whuskey, and Wild, Wild Women."

That was in Greenberg's last season as a baseball player, the end of a 13-year career in which he established himself as one of baseball's greatest sluggers and catapulted himself into Baseball's Hall of Fame.

"I wasn't used to this kind of team—this losing, and a lot of these guys drinking and carousing," said Greenberg. "I had been with the Tigers for 12 seasons, and we won four pennants and two World Series and everything was serious and bent on winning.

"Not the Pirates. Billy Herman was in his first year as a manager. He was a nice guy, maybe too nice, and he just locked the door of his office and didn't want to know what the players were doing.

"Well, one afternoon, one of the players got married and a bunch of the guys attended and got looped. We had a game that night. I think Kirby Higbe was pitching for us, and guys were making errors all over the place."

Now Greenberg stood, laughing, to demonstrate. "And Kirby—" Suddenly, Greenberg grabbed one leg, and began to hop around. "A cramp!" he moaned. "A cramp!"

He grimaced, yet still laughed—and was determined to finish the story. "Herman comes out to the mound to get Higbe out of there," said Greenberg. "Oh! Oh! My leg!—And Higbe—Higbe—Oh!" Greenberg's grabbing his leg and laughing as he nears the punch line. "Higbe says, 'I can't pitch when they're drunk out there.'" Greenberg is hopping here and there. "And Herman says, 'Who's drunk?' And Higbe—Higbe—Higbe says, 'Everyone!'"

And Greenberg collapsed into a chair, laughing and moaning, as he ended the story.

Last Thursday morning, Henry Benjamin Greenberg, born on Perry Street in Greenwich Village on January 1, 1911, and raised in the Bronx, came to another end. He died of cancer at age seventy-five, at his home in Beverly Hills, California. Like that story he told many years ago, his life was lived fully all the way to the end, and was filled with elements both funny and painful.

He had been a clumsy player in his youth, but with determination became a star. His high school coach at James Monroe once said, "Greenberg doesn't play baseball, he works at baseball." As a major leaguer, he hired ushers and peanut vendors to shag flies when he regularly took extra batting practice. He became a general manager with the Cleveland Indians and later part-owner of the Chicago White Sox, until his retirement from baseball in 1965. He learned the stock market so ably that he became a rich man from his investments.

I never saw Hank Greenberg play, but he was a legendary ballplayer to many, especially in Jewish households, like mine. He was the first truly great Jewish ballplayer and, ironically, a power hitter in the 1930s when the position of Jews in the world—especially, of course, in Hitler's Germany—grew weaker.

I remember my uncles talking about Greenberg's baseball exploits as if he were a kind of beacon for them—of the year he drove in a remarkable 183 runs, and of his homers. In 1938 he had 58 home runs with five games left in the season, and had a great shot to break Babe Ruth's record of 60. The rumor, said my uncles, was that because of anti-Semitism, pitchers wouldn't pitch to him down the stretch.

I once asked Hank about that. Not true, he said. "I got some hits and hit some balls hard, but I couldn't get one over the fence," he said. "In fact, there were people in baseball rooting for me to break the record." He recalled trying for an inside-the-park homer late in the season in which the umpire called him safe at home, "when I was really out."

But, he would recall, there were "remarks about my being a *sheenie* and a Jew all the time." During the 1935 World Series, it became so vicious that umpire George Moriarty went to the Cubs bench and made them stop.

Greenberg said he tried to carry himself with dignity because he understood that he was a symbol for many Jews in America. There were a few times, though, when he fought with his fists to stop remarks, on one occasion even battling a teammate.

Greenberg wasn't religious, but he believed he should observe Yom Kippur. He sat out a game that day in 1934, in the heat of a September pennant drive. That day, a Detroit newspaper bore a headline in Hebrew. Above it was the English translation: "Happy New Year, Hank."

When Greenberg returned from serving in the Army Air Corps during World War II, he rejoined the Tigers midway through the 1945 season. On the last day of the season, he hit a grand slam in the ninth inning to win the pennant for the Tigers.

In 1947, when Jackie Robinson broke the color barrier in the major leagues, Greenberg was at first base when the Dodgers played the Pirates for the first time that season.

Greenberg recalled, "Guys on our team were calling Jackie, 'Coal Mine. Hey, we'll get you, Coal Mine.' He got a hit and stood beside me on first base with his chin up, like a prince. I had a feeling for him because of the way I had been treated. I remember saying to him, 'Don't let them get you down. You're doing fine. Keep it up.'" Robinson later said that Greenberg was the first opposing player in the big leagues to give him encouragement. "Hank Greenberg," said Robinson, "has class. It stands out all over him."

Hank Greenberg was a special man in special times. He would have been a special man in any time.

Playing Pickup with Oscar

April 27, 1997

Indoors in a half-court basketball game a few years ago, I took one step to begin my dribble and heard a popping sound, like the shell of a Brazil nut being cracked.

The guy guarding me stopped. "What was that?" he asked.

"I don't know," I said, holding the ball. "But I think it was me." It was. I had severed the anterior cruciate ligament, the rubber band, so to speak, that connects the thigh to the calf. My doctor recommended against reconstructive surgery and gently suggested that, at fifty-two, my playing days were over.

I had played basketball since I was a small boy. And while I never became a pro—never close—I did become a starting player on my high-school and college teams, and would later play for my regiment in the Army, and in various amateur leagues and tournaments. Even now, in my so-called middle age, I was still playing in pickup games in parks and schoolyards and gymnasiums, long after many of my friends had stopped playing altogether.

But I couldn't accept that this was the end of the road of my basketball life. I mean, I knew I still had a lot of missed shots left in me. So I had arthroscopic surgery to repair cartilage that had been torn when I severed the ligament and, equipped with a $750 brace, worked for two years to bring my game back.

I did make one concession. I had been playing primarily with younger guys, some even in high school, and this concerned my parents, who are both past eighty. If you are going to continue playing, they said one day last spring, why don't you play with those of your own age? I said I would try.

There was a story I wanted to cover in Cincinnati, and so I decided to get in touch with an older fellow I knew there who might be up for a pickup game while I was in town. I had met him in the course of my work—he's fifty-eight, a year older than I am—and I learned a few years ago that he played recreational basketball at noontime at the YMCA. Well, I thought, I'll give it a shot.

"Hello, Oscar?" I said.

"Yes," came the long-distance reply.

Oscar Robertson owns three businesses in Cincinnati, and I had reached him at the office of Orchem, the Oscar Robertson chemical supplies company. "The Big O," as Robertson was called, was once regarded as the undisputed greatest all-around basketball player in history—until Michael Jordan came along.

Oscar and I chatted amiably for a bit before I managed to slip in the question, as nonchalantly as I could. "By the way, Oscar," I said, "are you still playing basketball?"

"Not to amount to much," he said.

"But you play?"

"Yeah. I play with guys of a certain age." He laughed softly. "Most of the guys are forty, forty-five and over."

"Guys like you who still enjoy the game?"

"Right. The way I play is, I always try to get a fast guard, one younger guy. And I fast-break guys to death. But I don't play as much as I used to. Some guys don't care to play with me."

"You mean, you're too good?"

"No, too rough."

"Too rough?"

"It's terrible. They're always calling all these fouls. I tell 'em: 'Whoever told you basketball was a noncontact sport? It isn't.'"

I laughed out loud. "Oscar, you sound just like someone in any of my games, complaining about the fouling. It's funny coming from one of the all-time greats." There was a kind of silence at the other end. I think he was getting steamed just thinking about the hackers.

I remember watching Robertson in college and in the pros, and marveling. At 6-foot-5 and 220 pounds, playing both guard and forward, he was strong, confident, effortless and competitive. He always seemed to get the shot he wanted, even when a battalion of players was storming him. He was never a flashy player, and was always fundamentally sound. He was a pleasure to watch.

Robertson had a patented spin move that I tried to imitate—still try, in fact. You're on the base line dribbling the ball and your back is to your defender. And then you spin around him, hooking your hand on his hip. Oscar did it so quickly and smoothly that he was rarely called for it. When I do it, I usually end up with a foul called on me, or an argument. That is the difference between pluck and genius.

After having been a three-time All-America, college player of the year and three-time major college scoring champion—with a 34-point average—at the University of Cincinnati, Robertson went on to play ten years for the Cincinnati Royals in the NBA. He scored 30 points a game for the Royals, at the time an output second only to the titanic Wilt Chamberlain, and along with that he averaged about 10 rebounds and 11 assists a game. That is, he averaged a triple-double for five years— and something close to that for his entire 14-year pro career. Robertson broke Bob Cousy's record for most all-time assists, and he held the record until Magic Johnson topped it. Oscar was traded to Milwaukee in 1970 and, teaming with Kareem Abdul-Jabbar, helped the Bucks win the NBA championship.

Robertson retired from the NBA in 1974 but didn't give the game up, as so many star players do. Oscar just switched from arenas like Madison Square Garden and the Los Angeles Forum and Chicago Stadium to the Cincy Y, of all places.

I asked Oscar what his game is like today.

"I can still shoot," he said. "I hit the three-point shot right behind the circle. Most pickup players don't understand how to guard a guy and they sag off you and I kill 'em with the outside shot."

Do you drive? I asked. He said: "I drive if I'm 15 feet in or closer. But at the top of the key it takes too long"—how true! I thought—"and guys hack you to death."

I asked him if he'd take me up to play in his game at the Y when I came to town.

170

Interviewing former World Light Heavyweight boxing champion Archie Moore, 1987.

Former World Heavyweight boxing champion Joe Frazier, with me and my wife, Dolly, 2002.

Playing pickup basketball with tennis star Martina Navratilova in the gym of SMU, 1982.

Playing with Navratilova and basketball legend Nancy Lieberman, who thought the game would help develop good movements which Martina could employ in tennis (which she agreed). Lieberman would shout instructions to Martina, including "Get up on him, Tini!"

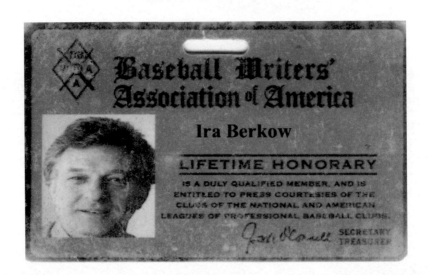

With Hall of Famer Rod Carew (center) in 1978, and the Minnesota Twins scout Herb Stein, who initially signed Carew to a professional contract.

With the lovely Rachel Robinson, widow of Jackie Robinson, 1983.

With legendary running back Red Grange, 1983.

At dinner with double gold-medal Olympic skater Katarina Witt, 1995.

Speaking with tennis champion John McEnroe.

With Walt "Clyde" Frazier, in a Sports and Society class that I conducted at NYU, 1977.

Interviewing former Boston Celtic Hall of Famer Sam Jones, 1987.

In conversation with former New York Knicks head coach Red Holzman in 1991. We became close friends after his coaching days.

In a Cincinnati Royals locker room with the great Oscar Robertson, 1970.

With Oscar Robertson after playing a full-court pickup basketball game
in a Cincinnati YMCA, 1995.

At a Chicago Bulls practice session with Michael Jordan, 1996.

A sketch of me drawn by noted artist LeRoy Neiman, July 30, 1999.

With LeRoy Neiman, with a race horse and exercise rider in the background, one early morning at Belmont Park, 1999.

With Kentucky Derby and Preakness Stakes winner
Smarty Jones, alongside trainer John Servis, 2004.

Interviewing golf champion Greg Norman in 1987.

PRESS

BUTCH LEWIS
BLP
PRODUCTIONS

TYSON vs. SPINKS

TRUMP PLAZA

ONCE AND FOR ALL • JUNE 27, 1988

```
TRUMP  PLAZA  WELCOMES:
Ira Berkow
Journalist
New York Times
SECTION: N ROW:     2 SEAT:     9
№    0605
```

Speaking with Pete Rose in 1985. *(Photo courtesy by Dick Schaap)*

With former Yankee catcher Yogi Berra, wearing Roosevelt University (Chicago) shirts (request by then president of Roosevelt U., Charles Middleton, a long-time Yankee fan), 2010.

In 1970, New York Mets star pitcher Tom Seaver wrote a weekly column for the national syndicate Newspaper Enterprise Assn., of which I was the sports columnist and sports editor. Many years later, Seaver autographed this photo: "To Ira—A long-standing friend! Between us—311 Wins in the 'Bigs.' Best, Tom Seaver"

May 8, 1985

Dear Champ:

I assume that you saw the New York Times piece I did on you
from our interview in your home. If not, please let me know
and I'll send you copies. Thank you for your time and patience.
You remain one of the world's most interesting ~~people~~ figures —
yes, I said £ "figures."

Also, please find enclosed the three letters that I borrowed
from you.

With warm regards,

Ira Berkow
Ira Berkow

*send 2 or 3
copies*

Muhammad Ali
Thank you

May 30-85

Ira and Dolly Berkow shortly after our wedding, 1978.

"Like I said, the games are kinda rough," he cautioned.

"I think I can manage," I replied, not knowing if in fact I could.

"OK, any time," Oscar said. "Just call ahead. I'll round up some guys to play with."

I arrived early for the noontime game with Oscar in order to limber up. After all, if I were going to sing with Luciano Pavarotti, I'd want to get in a few extra notes before going on stage.

I went to my locker and began to dress. I was adjusting my knee brace when I looked up and saw Oscar come through the door. As we greeted each other, I noticed that he seemed broader than I remembered him in his playing days, and of course older, with flecks of gray in his hair. His hand was large and his shake firm. He wore a plaid summer sport jacket, tan slipover shirt, tan pants, brown loafers and a smile that was, well, cryptic. As if to say: are you sure you really want to do this? Why did it remind me of a cat's grin, and why did I feel like the mouse?

Like a lot of older gyms, this one had a regulation-size basketball court but with only a little room to shoot on the four baskets—two on each side—that hung parallel to the court. I noticed signs on the yellow-painted walls: FIGHTING WILL RESULT IN IMMEDIATE SUSPENSION, and NO CUSSING. Yes, I thought to myself, a typical Pickup Game Heaven.

The squeak of sneakers and the faintly gamy smell of sweat were clear indications that a game was in progress. It was a full-court game, and I took in the caliber of play. It was pretty good, though not of the highest level, even by Y standards. There were some older players who looked as if they might be in their fifties, and some younger ones, including, Robertson later pointed out to me, one very good thirty-one-year-old. This was Tim McGee, a wiry, 5-foot-10 veteran wide receiver for the Cincinnati Bengals and a onetime high-school basketball standout in Cleveland.

Shortly after I got in the gym, Oscar appeared. He dressed plainly, in gray T-shirt, gray shorts and white sneakers. And when we warmed up, he took that jump shot that was so familiar and seemed nearly impossible to block. He cradled the ball in his right hand like a waiter carrying a tray of Champagne glasses. He seemed to hang in the air, not as high as Michael Jordan—not nearly as high now, to be sure, or even then—but just as inaccessible. It was the shot I had seen him take and score against stars like Jerry West and Bob Cousy and Wilt Chamberlain. The ball snapped through the net with an uncommon but customary authority. The one difference, however, was the discernible paunch under his shirt. He told me he tipped the scales now at about 250, some 30 pounds over his playing weight.

"Oscar," I said, "the floor feels a little slippery, or is it my sneakers?"

"This is the Y," he said. "They never mop it."

Then he spit on the wooden floor—my eyes widened at this—and rubbed the sole of each foot into it. "For traction," he said. Naturally, I did the same. It worked, too.

Oscar had written both our names on a sheet of paper that hung on the wall. Good, I thought, we would be playing together. Since the winning team stays, you get a better workout if you win, and the chances of winning with Oscar Robertson on my side in a pickup game, I figured, would be substantially better than if he weren't.

We played and lost, 10–6.

Oscar never seemed to get fully in the game. I felt a little nervous, as I always do in a game in a new place, with new people. There is always that thing about proving myself, or at least demonstrating that I belong. Like starting a new job.

The first time I got the ball on offense, I passed to Oscar in the corner. He missed the shot. He took another and missed that one too. He was playing their tallest man—someone about 6-foot-8—and muscling him out for rebounds. ("I don't jump much anymore," he said. "I just lean into people. And these guys up here don't really know how to box out.") As for me, I took a jump shot that hit the rim and bounced away. I took another and missed. My shots were just off, and I wasn't feeling confident. I have no doubt that Oscar sensed it. "They'll fall," he said to me, as we backpedaled on defense.

The third time down, I passed to Oscar, who motioned that I come around him. I did, and he set a wide screen with his ample body. He cleared out my man, and his man and, it seemed, everyone else in the gym. He was setting me up for the shot. I don't remember ever getting a screen like that. I felt all alone, as if I were in an empty meadow. I was buoyed. Oscar was, as the saying goes, trying to "get me off." I'd like to think he saw that I had a shot, and that he'd make use of it.

I shot from about 17 feet away. All net.

But Oscar didn't quite seem to be taking charge. Tim McGee, meanwhile, made three straight shots, on twisting, athletic moves. "Get him!" Oscar called out to the man guarding McGee. "He's scoring all the points." I was not, I am happy to report, guarding Tim McGee. McGee told me later that Oscar has mellowed in the last few years. "When I first came up to the Y ten years ago, he still had an NBA mentality," he recalled. "He'd holler at you if you missed a layup. He was in charge. Oh yeah. He's a little cooler now."

The Big O, one of the highest scorers in history, was shut out in our game. Didn't make a single hoop in three tries. But Oscar still had some Oscar left in him. And it became clearer when we were waiting for next.

He was critical of some of the play. "That guy hasn't passed the ball yet," he said of one player. "Look at that," he said, indicating another player, "he doesn't even try to get back on defense. Unbelievable."

But Oscar was also enjoying the camaraderie. "Kill 'em, Freddie," he called out to one guy. Freddie, a lawyer, tried to ignore him. Oscar needled a few others. "Oh, oh," he said, like an announcer, as one team scored several straight baskets, "the tide is turning."

In the second game we played, Oscar got more into it. A teammate was fast-breaking, and Oscar threw a perfect lob pass from half-court that sailed just over the outstretched fingers of the defender. I had the ball and he set a pick for a teammate to cut to the basket, and looked at me and pointed to the cutting teammate. I hit him with the pass for a basket. But on another occasion I threw a no-look pass that was wide of the mark. Oscar said nothing. He did shout to me, "Cut through," on one play, but I didn't do it quick enough and didn't get the ball.

At one point, I had the ball near half-court and looked to pass. Somehow, Tim McGee seemed to go from one end of the court to the other at the speed of light and stole the ball out of my hands. Outstanding athletes—especially those in top shape—are shocking to the layman in their quickness and strength; especially to the slowing layman.

I was feeling foolish and worthless after that steal, when, on the very next play, McGee stole the ball from Oscar! Off the dribble! Oscar looked not so much sheepish as disgusted with himself as he watched McGee put in a layup. The next time down, Oscar was pounding his dribble in that no-nonsense manner I remembered from his playing days. He got into the lane and scored on a jumper. He hit two more shots, including one on a rebound—after he missed three straight shots under the basket, getting the rebound each time. He was determined to make the shot.

Oscar's court vision was remarkable. He seemed to know where everyone was, when to get them the ball and how—lob pass, bounce pass, chest pass. And always with economy of movement. There wasn't an ounce of flab to his game. Never was. Oscar dribbling the ball between his legs would be as unimaginable as Pavarotti doing rap.

When Robertson was double-teamed, he always found the open man to pass to. When he was an active player, he once told me, "I always know who is guarding my teammates, and so when I'm double-teamed I naturally know who's open." He said it as though to say, "Well, doesn't everybody?"

Oscar threw me a sweet, crisp pass at the chest, just in my stride, and I hit another jumper. I missed my next two shots, however. With the score tied at 9—and the game on the line—I passed the ball to Oscar at the top of the key. He went up for the jumper without hesitation and, with the same perfect mechanics he had employed a million times, swished it for the game winner. We won the next game, too, 10–7, and I had my best results, scoring three baskets, including the game-ender, a fadeaway one-hander on the baseline in which I started to drive to the basket and then pulled up.

According to the rules in that gym, the winning team has to relinquish the court after two wins, but we'd been there for more than an hour and it was enough for both of us. Oscar's shirt was splotched with sweat; I could see he was tired. I think I was sapped as much from the tension and anticipation as from the games themselves.

"How about some lunch," Oscar said.

Oscar had said nothing about anything I did on the court, except for his "They'll fall." Which was enough. It elevated my spirits, and, along with his screens and passes, it also elevated my game. I imagine he gave me points for hustling, for I made certain I always got back quickly on defense, though, near the end, the brawny, 250-pound Oscar was having some problems doing so himself.

"It's really a simple game," he said to me as we went into the locker room. "It's rebounding and defense and maintaining control of the ball."

It's a simple game for Oscar, and, perhaps, in their fields, the same could be said for Picasso and Mozart. It's somewhat more difficult for the rest of us.

But I saw that Oscar still enjoyed the game, still delighted in the competition; it wasn't the NBA but it was still a decent run, even for him. He still enjoyed mixing with the other players in a familiar setting, just as he had when he first began playing as a boy in the "Dust Bowl" playground of Indianapolis, his hometown. And he maintained a competitive sense, even toward the pros of today. When I asked Oscar about Michael Jordan, who has averaged 32 points a game in his career, he said he was a great player.

I asked him how many points Jordan would have scored in Oscar's era.

"We had fewer teams and the talent wasn't as diluted as it is today," he replied. "So I think Jordan would have scored about 20 a game."

"Twenty a game?" I said. "But you scored 30 a game in that era."

"Well," said Oscar, with a shrug, "I handled the ball more than he does."

After we parted, I remembered something Oscar had told me near the end of his career. I had mentioned that his career scoring average was dropping. In his last season, he averaged 16 points a game, down from 30 after his first nine seasons in the league.

"I don't feel too bad that it's dropping," he said. "It's to be expected. I'm getting older." He paused. "But you know, it happens to everybody."

"What happens to everybody?" I asked.

"Autumn," he said.

When Ruby Missed the Final Four

April 1, 1989

This is the 30th anniversary of the year that neither my friend Ron Rubenstein nor I played in the Final Four. I recalled this recently when I saw the booklet "Final Four Records," a history of the Division I men's basketball tournament, published by the NCAA and put out to coincide with today's semifinal games.

In the section, "All-Time Final Four Player Roster," I checked the listing under "Louisville," and there, listed alphabetically several notches below "Pervis Ellison '86," and Darrell Griffith '80," I found the entry "Ron Rubenstein '59."

Rubenstein was a dark-haired, 6-foot-1 sophomore guard for the University of Louisville. He had been a starter, then suffered a leg injury that put him on the sideline. When Louisville played West Virginia and Jerry West in the 1959 NCAA semifinals, Rubenstein was a spectator.

I followed this rather closely. In such circumstances, many of us keep an eye on someone we know. I had played with Rubenstein in parks and schoolyards, and just two years earlier we competed in a Public League high school game in Chicago. I was a member of the Sullivan Tigers and he was a star for our nearby rival, the Senn Bulldogs.

He was one of the best players in the state, a swift, strong driver and deft outside shooter. I guarded him for part of the game, and, with my teeth clenched and my eyes blazing with competitive fire, I helped keep him to about 30 points as Senn beat us rather handily. The fact that Rubenstein—Ruby, as we called him—didn't play most of the last quarter may have contributed to my holding down his scoring.

He went to Louisville. I went somewhere else, never, it turned out, getting even close to being on a roster in the Final Four. Nor, for that matter, did anyone else I ever played with or against in school, other than Howie Carl, a standout at DePaul, who was in two NCAA tournaments, but with teams that were eliminated early.

So Rubenstein was unique among my contemporaries in the neighborhood, the only one on a team roster in the Final Four. These are the connections, the sometimes slim threads that often bind us to special events.

Rubenstein, for me, was a kind of distant basketball cousin. In the 1959 semifinal games, West Virginia beat Louisville, and California defeated Cincinnati. The Cincinnati star, of course, was Oscar Robertson. And Rubenstein earlier in the year played against Oscar Robertson, a step in the levels of the game that I found extraordinary, even uplifting.

I once met a former teammate of Rubenstein at Louisville, Bud Olsen, who told me this story: Just before a game against Cincinnati, the Louisville coach, Peck Hickman, gave the team a pep talk that ended with, "And remember, Robertson puts his jockey strap on the same way you guys do." Robertson scored virtually at will as Cincinnati won. In the locker room later Rubenstein turned to Olsen and said, "I don't care what Coach says, Robertson has to put his jockey strap on differently."

Smooth, but Not Slick

Six of the most beautiful, in the sense of artistic, athletes I've ever covered, who seemed to sweep across their athletic fields with grace as well as power, were Arthur Ashe, Roger Federer, Rod Carew, Sandy Koufax, Larry Bird, and Walt "Clyde" Frazier.

* * *

In October of 1992, I accompanied Arthur Ashe on a plane ride to Buffalo, New York, where he was headed to speak at a community college in Niagara. Several months prior he had been diagnosed with the HIV virus, after a faulty and life-threatening blood transfusion for a heart transplant. Arthur Ashe had a well-deserved history of being a thoughtful, caring and wise man. I had known Ashe casually and enjoyed his company.

On the way to and from the talk, I had the opportunity to speak with him about a range of topics, and would put that into a story I was writing for *The Times*. At the Buffalo airport before boarding back to New York, Ashe spotted a popcorn vendor. "Love popcorn," he said. And we stopped so he could purchase popcorn. On the airplane, sitting side by side, we talked and Ashe also popped the popcorn into his mouth. When finished, he discarded the empty box into the waste bag that the flight attendant provided.

I thought about the popcorn incident. At the time, there were rumors, unjustified by science, that the HIV was contagious if one would eat from the same plate as one infected, or drink from that person's glass. In general, most people eating from a box of popcorn would ask a companion if he or she would like a bite. Ashe didn't. I wondered if he was being sensitive to my possible aversion to contracting HIV from a handful of popcorn.

After writing the story, I called Ashe to check some facts. I then mentioned the popcorn and that I was aware that he had not asked me to share.

"I didn't offer you any?" he said.

"Yes, you didn't offer me any."

"Oh," he said, "Sorry. That was rude of me."

Well, Ashe was known as a crafty tennis player. And he may have been crafty—and sensitive—about not putting me in an embarrassing position of having to refuse popcorn—after all, who doesn't like popcorn? For me, the preponderance of evidence is on the latter supposition.

The Changing Faces of Arthur Ashe

October 25, 1992

They were seated around the kitchen table—Arthur Ashe; his wife, Jeanne, and their daughter, Camera, now six years old. This was a short time ago and the conversation was unremarkable, about what Jeanne and Arthur had done that day, and what Camera was doing in school. Jeanne looked at Camera and then casually turned back to Arthur, and saw that he had begun to cry.

"Camera didn't question it, because she knew that her father had been troubled, though I don't think she was quite sure of the depth of it," Jeanne Ashe recalled. "Then Arthur reached over and held her hand.

And I rubbed his back. It was one of the few times I have ever seen Arthur cry.

"Nothing was said."

As the gauzy cloudscape outside the airplane window slipped by, Arthur Ashe thumbed through his appointment book. He was flying from New York City to a recent speaking engagement upstate at Niagara County Community College, where posters on the small, rural campus in Sanborn, New York, read: "Today at 12:30 in the Fine Arts Auditorium/Arthur Ashe/US Tennis Champion and AIDS Victim/Discussion on AIDS and the Right to Privacy."

These are new and very trying times for Ashe—in a lifetime that has been full of new and often trying times. But it is also a life that has been, by any account, extraordinary.

At forty-nine years old, Ashe, as the world knows, found himself last April feeling virtually compelled to reveal that he had contracted AIDS. The disease was apparently transmitted through a blood transfusion that Ashe received after he underwent heart-bypass surgery in 1983.

After overcoming his anger over the belief that his privacy had been invaded, that he had been pushed to go public because a newspaper, *USA Today*, was pursuing the story that he had the disease, Ashe, as he has done with virtually everything else in his life, has made adjustments.

He has become a leading spokesman for education about AIDS, a man as consumed by helping those who will come after him as he once was determined to live his life on his own terms.

He talks frequently on college campuses and elsewhere, and he does so openly, and patiently, about what he knows and what he has learned, both about himself and the disease.

"I'm amazed at Arthur," Seth Abraham, the president of Time Warner Sports, and a close friend, had said earlier. "Barriers just don't exist for him. They don't impede him, don't block him, don't hem him in. He feels that there's just too much in life that he must do. And time is an element."

So Ashe has quit asking certain questions.

"When I first learned that I had contracted this supposedly terminal illness, in 1988," Ashe said, "I used to ask my doctor every few months if I had time enough to plan to take my daughter to Disneyland, or to play in a celebrity golf tournament, or to take part in a seminar on race, or some other matter. But I don't anymore. I've fallen into a kind of routine. I know I'll be sick with diarrhea and fatigue about once every five or six days. And this has been going on for several years. So I've learned not to panic when I feel bad. When the symptoms change, when I'm sick two or three times a week, then I might again have to bring up the subject of longevity with my doctor."

Arthur Ashe has always been lean, and he is thinner now, down to 147 pounds from 153 when he was playing tennis and confounding observers who wondered how he summoned so much power into a serve that could whistle at 115 miles an hour. That serve helped propel him to become the first black man to win the United States Open, in 1968, and Wimbledon, in 1975, and to be ranked No. 1 in the world.

"I weigh a little less than I used to, but I know I look even thinner because the muscle mass has diminished," Ashe said. "It happens with most retired athletes. I play golf now, and have given up tennis completely. I love golf. I'll play golf in a minute. I'd miss a meal to play golf." His eyes, behind aviator glasses, twinkled. "Sometimes I have."

He remains surprisingly active for someone who has suffered three heart attacks—the last, a relatively mild one, only six weeks ago—undergone two heart-bypass operations, one a quadruple and the second a double, and is coping with AIDS.

Ashe takes two drugs regularly, AZT and DDI, to try to slow the breakdown of his immune system. He takes a larger quantity of natural vitamins. In all, for his heart and because of AIDS, he consumes about 30 pills a day. His prescription drug bill is $18,000 a year.

Then and Now Triumphs Range Beyond Tennis

As the lone black male tennis star in the 1960s and 1970s, Ashe carried a burden that sometimes made him uncomfortable, but he carried it with dignity. He was a role model and a source of inspiration to blacks as well as whites. The story is by now well known: how a youth from segregated Richmond rose swiftly through the ranks, sometimes being refused entry in junior tournaments held in the South, to triumph in the nearly all-white tennis world.

Since the de facto end of his tennis career in 1979—after he suffered a heart attack, while ranked seventh in the world, at age thirty-six—Ashe had been involved in numerous social causes. Now that his condition is known, his life, his schedule, have become even fuller.

In his window seat in the airplane, Ashe mentioned that he had a dentist's appointment the following day. Arthur Ashe's going to the dentist is different from most people going to the dentist.

"The dentist comes out like he's going to war," Ashe said with a little smile. "He wears a long green surgical gown, a mask, goggles, latex gloves—well, he's always worn gloves—and his assistant is dressed the same way. No, it doesn't bother me. That's the way they should dress. I mean, he's going to poke around in there, and he might draw blood and he'd be foolish not to use all the health precautions he can. But he's been great. And he's shown courage.

"I don't mean just physically because he still treats me, and some doctors would not. I mean that because he still treats me, he's lost business. A number of his patients have left him because of me."

Ashe looked down at his appointment book, which is brimming: there is a function for the Arthur Ashe Foundation for the Defeat of

AIDS; one for the Safe Passage Foundation, which he founded to deal with problems in inner cities, and one for a black athletic organization that he has recently helped organize with the former Knick guard Dick Barnett.

Ashe handed his companion an article on AIDS in which it said that people with the disease feel an odd sense of liberation, that they can pursue activities and say things with candor that might have inhibited them before.

"Absolutely true," he said.

As an athlete, Ashe had transcended the sport, taking a stand for the end of apartheid and becoming the first black athlete to play in an integrated sporting event in South Africa, in 1973. When a delegation of Americans assembled to visit Nelson Mandela in October 1991, the black leader requested that Ashe be among them.

And just a day before the most recent heart attack, Ashe was arrested, handcuffed and placed in jail for a few hours in Washington while taking part in a demonstration in front of the White House. He was protesting the Administration's policy on restrictions of Haitian immigrants.

Now, en route to his speech upstate, he was pursuing another cause, the one of helping educate people about AIDS.

Ashe has known that he has AIDS since 1988. It was then that he underwent brain surgery after his right arm became paralyzed. The surgery revealed a parasitic infection that quickly led to a diagnosis of AIDS. But Ashe had not planned to reveal his illness until, he said, the time came when he would be noticeably changed by the disease physically, and then would have to confront obvious questions.

He said that he thought it was a private matter because he was no longer an active athlete whose performance would be affected by his having AIDS. But when USA Today asked him to confirm or deny a rumor that he had AIDS, he decided it was only a matter of time before the word was out, and he scheduled a news conference the next day to make his own announcement. He wanted, as much as he could, to control the dissemination of the information.

"Rumors and half-truths have been floating about concerning my medical condition," he said at the news conference April 8. He then made his announcement.

After the plane landed in Buffalo, Ashe was met by a Niagara County Community College student who took him into his confidence.

"Mr. Ashe," said the student, "my brother has AIDS, and he's dying. But my parents don't know it. He's told me, but he doesn't want to tell them."

"How did he contract it?" Ashe asked. "I mean, what was the opportunistic infection that revealed it?"

"He's gay," said the student. "I think it was a liver problem he had been in the hospital for."

"Do your parents know he's gay."

"Yes. Yes, they do."

"I think they can handle that he's dying," said Ashe. "He's probably afraid to tell them because he feels he'd be rejected by them. But I don't believe he would be. And he'd feel unbelievably good, knowing that he was being supported. People in this situation need as much support as they can get to bear up under it. It would be a big relief for him."

"He's afraid that my mother's health couldn't take it."

"Mothers hold up surprisingly well," Ashe said, evenly. "Their love is almost unqualified. I'm not one to give advice, but I think you should tell your parents about it. Does your brother work?"

"No. He gets a welfare check."

"I think he should try to get a job," Ashe said. "Otherwise, he just sits around collecting a check and watching the clock tick away. If he felt useful, he'd feel much better. It's important to be productive."

Some 300 students and faculty members—close to capacity—appeared for Ashe's talk in the college's auditorium. Much of the talk was about the most basic aspects of living with AIDS.

"I've had a religious faith, growing up in the South and black and having the church as a focal point of your life," Ashe said. "And I was reminded of something Jesus said on the cross: 'My God, my God, why hast thou forsaken me?' Remember, Jesus was poor, humble and of a despised minority. I wasn't poor in that my father was a policeman, but we certainly weren't rich. And Jesus asked the question, in effect, of why must the innocent suffer. And I'm not so innocent—I mean, I'm hardly a perfect human being—but you ask about yourself, 'Why me?' And I think, 'Why not me?'"

"Why should I be spared what some others have been inflicted with," he continued. "And I have to think of all the good of my life, of having a great wife and daughter, and family and friends, and winning Wimbledon and the US Open and playing for and coaching the Davis Cup team, and getting a free scholarship to UCLA—all kinds of good things. You could also ask about this, 'Why me?' Sometimes there are no explanations for things, especially for the bad."

Sometimes, he said, paraphrasing a bumper sticker, stuff happens.

Ashe believes he contracted HIV, the virus that causes AIDS, when he underwent heart-bypass surgery in 1983 and was given a blood transfusion. At the time, hospitals were not checking blood samples for HIV. That test began nationwide two years later.

"Just yesterday," Ashe went on, "literally, just yesterday, my daughter, Camera, who is six years old, asked me, 'Daddy, how did you get AIDS?'

"To use a sports analogy, this came out of not deep left field, but deep center field. But I was glad to hear she was asking. The more open the better. I know that she had asked her mother questions about me, and we've talked to her about my illness in a way that we hoped would penetrate a six-year-old's mind. And so now I told her what had happened, how the blood they gave me in the hospital was someone else's blood and it was 'bad.' She immediately perked up. 'And the person had AIDS?' I said yes. She sat a little longer. 'Are you sure?' I said, 'Oh yes, that's how I got it.' And then she mercifully went to sleep."

It was recalled that earlier, Ashe spoke about his wife and his daughter, and how doctors have said that he posed no danger to them. Each has tested negative for HIV.

"But one day," he said, "my daughter may be a danger to me. I couldn't go near her if she got a communicable disease."

In that earlier conversation, recalling the April news conference and her husband's starting to cry as he made his announcement, Jeanne Ashe had pointed out that "it was only when he came to the part about Camera."

"I think a lot of things flashed through his mind," she said. "They're really close, and he wanted to be able to see her graduate—from elementary school, from high school, from college. And he wanted to be around to be a grandfather, too. I think his mortality really hit him at that moment."

Back at Niagara Community College, Ashe said he remembered with anger that the Reagan administration had said that the "nation's blood supply was safe." "And it wasn't," said Ashe. "The medical community was slow to react. If it had been a more mainstream sickness, they would have been quicker." In the question-and-answer period, he was asked about the rights of privacy in his case. "Just because it's newsworthy doesn't mean it should be printed," he said. "Sometimes the media goes too far."

At that moment, the April news conference was recalled. At one point as he made his announcement, the often stoical-appearing Ashe had been forced to stop while reading his message—pausing at the part about his daughter—and put his fingers to his temple to prevent himself from sobbing. His wife had risen from her chair and had begun to read his statement for him. After a few moments, Ashe had continued his reading.

In the community college auditorium six months later, Ashe was asked, "What about your daughter, and the cruelty of other children?"

"That was also a grave concern of ours," Ashe said. "But there has been no problem at all, not at her school or anywhere else. Camera is never without supervision from adults. And people have been wonderful."

Does he ever need counseling?

"I remember sitting on my hospital bed when I was told I had AIDS," he said. "It was the day after I'd had brain surgery, and I'd experienced a paralysis in my hand, and as it turned out it was all related to AIDS. It was hard to believe, of course. But I never needed counseling. I'm able to function normally. I told myself, 'Just adjust and deal with it.'

"I wasn't trying to be macho. When you've gone through all I've gone through, like the heart operations, you learn that if someone can help you, damn it, get help. But emotionally I've been able to deal with a lot of things in my life. I viewed this as just one more challenge.

"There have been tons of these things in my life. And here's another one. I've learned to be self-reliant. It was kind of forced on me. The first moment that comes to mind in this regard was when I was twelve years old. And I went with my first tennis instructor, Ron Charity, to enter a USTA-sanctioned tournament for twelve-and-under at Byrd Park in Richmond. Byrd Park was a white park. It was a nice, warm, sunny spring day. And I remember the head of the tournament—a white man named Sam Wood—he's long gone now, but he was a nice, kindly gentleman. And he was apologetic, but he said, 'No.' There was no integration in Virginia then and he said, 'I'm sorry, but a law is a law.'"

Ashe continued: "I began to learn that I couldn't rely on others, that I had to take charge of my life. If I wanted to be a tennis player—and I did, passionately—that I'd have to leave there. In my senior year of high school, it was arranged for me to go to St. Louis. I knew that if

I couldn't play indoors in the winter, that the white kids would pass me by. I'm not bitter about any of that now. It's all in the past. But I learned that I couldn't let circumstances dictate my life for me. I have a minister—he's more of a friend—whom I'll talk over some personal things with. But in effect, I've become my own counselor."

Did he see himself as a victim?

"No," he said, "I see myself as a patient."

His lecture had consumed an hour and a half. After he answered the last question, the audience in the darkened theater rose and began to applaud—standing and clapping for long minutes, moved by the candor, warmth and strength of the man under the lights, in front. Arthur Ashe stood listening to the applause echo through the auditorium, then gathered up his notes and left the stage.

A 'Good Man' Who Transcended Sport

February 11, 1993 / Richmond, Virginia

There were more than 6,500 people in the Arthur Ashe Athletic Center, sitting, standing, fanning themselves with programs on a warm winter day and stopping to wipe their eyes with handkerchiefs. They came for a funeral service this afternoon, fittingly called "A Celebration of the Life of Arthur Robert Ashe Jr.," and clearly more suited for a statesman than for a man once simply ranked as the best tennis player in the world.

Decidedly, Ashe, who died Saturday at forty-nine of the complications of AIDS, was being celebrated last for being a tennis champion. Mostly, he was recalled as a dignified, courageous and "good man," the term used by Andrew Young, the former United States delegate to the United Nations, who delivered the eulogy. "Everything Arthur Ashe did, he did for a group or cause bigger than himself," said Young.

While tennis figures like Rod Laver, Stan Smith, Pancho Segura, Yannick Noah, Charlie Pasarell, Bob Lutz, Donald Dell, and Dennis

Ralston, among others, were in attendance, so were Ron Brown, the Secretary of Commerce; Senators Bill Bradley and Charles Robb; Gov. L. Douglas Wilder of Virginia, the Rev. Jesse Jackson, Ethel Kennedy, Mayor David N. Dinkins of New York, and LeRoy Walker, president of the United States Olympic Committee.

A letter from President Clinton was read, saying that Ashe "represented the very best of America."

Ashe's battles against racism and discrimination in sports and out of sports, his stand against apartheid in South Africa, his having been jailed just last summer in a protest in front of the White House regarding United States policy on Haitian refugees, his commitment to education and youths in tennis, were also cited and applauded. As was the work that defined and dominated the last year of his life: his efforts to end the ignorance concerning AIDS, the disease he said he contracted after a tainted blood transfusion following heart surgery.

"I remember his favorite T-shirt," said Smith, a close friend and Davis Cup partner. "It read, 'I Am a Citizen of the World.'"

The service was held in a sports arena the city built in 1981 and named after its native son. It is in the heart of Richmond, the city where Ashe was born and raised and which, despite his becoming a world figure and world traveler, he always called home.

The speakers in the three-hour service included friends and family. The audience, with Ashe's widow, Jeanne, and six-year-old daughter, Camera, close by the stage, heard sermon-like reminiscences and scripture and theological readings from religious leaders, and sometimes swayed to gospel songs sung by the Richmond public schools' mass choir and several solos by adults.

"This is a real African-American religious and cultural experience," Young said. "And it is quite appropriate for the world-class hero who came back, who had gloriously triumphed over adversity."

But Young also asked how many people like Ashe might have been produced in places like Richmond had not the obstacles of segregation existed, as they did for much of Ashe's youth in this city.

Other speakers mentioned Ashe's strength and quiet dignity in the face of discrimination. One friend and fellow tennis player, Linwood Simpson, recalled a time in Kalamazoo, Michigan, when Ashe was eighteen and had a chance to make the junior Davis Cup team, the first black to attain such an honor.

"I won a match in three hours and then was called back to play again, when most of the others hadn't even played one match," said Simpson. "I was thirteen years old, in a younger division, but I was angry at the injustice. Arthur, even then, even at the young age of eighteen, took me aside. 'Linwood,' he said, 'We're out here for a reason. We have to stand tall.'"

At this point there was applause from the crowd.

"Arthur said: 'We can't be bitter about this. We can't waste our energies on this nonsense.'"

And Ashe never did. He became the lone black male champion playing in what Ron Brown called "an utterly white game, a virtually all-white sport, and winning." Those remarks brought more applause.

Praise From Dinkins

Dinkins said Ashe was "one of the most decent human beings I have ever known."

Jackson celebrated Ashe by saying that "he did not allow a broken society to break his spirit." Said Jackson: "He had a power the tennis racquet cannot compare with. He had a faith."

Wilder said: "His fate touched him with greatness. His enduring message is 'If I can do it, you can do it.'"

Smith called Ashe, a champion of Wimbledon and the United States and Australian Opens, "the most intelligent player I think who's ever lived." Smith recalled how Ashe used that intelligence to found and lead, as president, the professional tennis players' union.

"The Respect of Silence"

Brown said simply, "His is one of the few names in the world that commands the respect of silence."

"He took the burden of race," said Young, "and wore it as a cloak of dignity." Young concluded the service: "Hallelujah, Arthur Ashe. Hallelujah."

Then the crowd emptied into the warm, bright Richmond afternoon. The funeral procession drove to the Woodlawn Cemetery where Arthur Robert Ashe Jr. was laid to rest.

* * *

What may be lost in the memory of Arthur Ashe, a crusader for human rights and a distinguished citizen of the world, is the beauty and grace of his tennis game. It was never more in evidence when, as a decided underdog to Jimmy Connors in the finals of the 1975 Wimbledon, he not only out-thought the doughty defending champion Conners, but had him chasing drop shots, lobs and corner shots as sixth-seeded Ashe earned a 6–1, 6–1, 5–7, 6–4 championship. It's my view, and I know I am not alone in this, that one of the few who performed on the artistic level of Ashe is Roger Federer, winner of 20 Grand Slams, who sometimes seems to float on the court as he whips blistering winners to the corners. Perhaps one of the greatest shots, if not the greatest, in the entire history of tennis was witnessed by millions in a US Open semifinals. I discussed it with Federer, who is as gracious in conversation as he is graceful in chasing a tennis ball while brandishing a racquet.

Roger Federer and "The Shot"

Original publication

It had been six years, in 2015, since top-seeded Roger Federer, then going for his sixth straight US Open championship, had hit, with two points needed to win in the semifinals against fourth-seed Novak Djokovic, what he had called "the greatest shot I ever hit in my life." Tennis followers often still refer to it as "The Shot," and need no further explanation.

In the intervening years for Federer, often nonpareil years at the highest level of tennis competition, he has never said that he ever hit a shot to equal it. Ergo, as we alleged savants of the press box might have it, one might conclude that if the arguably greatest tennis player of all time hits his greatest shot, it may arguably be the greatest tennis shot ever stroked by man or woman.

I remember that, watching the match on a sunny, windy Sunday afternoon on September 13, 2009, in the Billie Jean King Stadium in Flushing Meadows in Queens, New York, I found myself leaping from my seat in amazement, along with essentially every one of the capacity crowd of some 23,000. Another who leaped straight up as though on a pogo stick was Federer himself, in half (at minimum) disbelief. Djokovic, in yellow shirt, grinned with (also at minimum) disbelief and, since he had to serve, held the tennis ball to his mouth to keep, conceivably, from shouting in both unfettered appreciation and utter despair.

I had always wondered if our most cherished athletes had indeed eyes in the back of their heads, some sort of gifted anticipation or instinct. I recall Giants center fielder Willie Mays racing back in the 1954 World Series and raising his glove at just the right time to snare a long fly ball and without actually seeing where the ball was when he caught it. I remember Lakers star Jerry West stealing a pass that he didn't see coming in a playoff game against the Knicks, but knew where it was, and raised his hand at just the right moment to intercept it. Or Tiger Woods hitting a fairway shot around a forest of trees and without seeing the hole and having the ball land a foot from the flag—I guess that was seeing through the trees with Superman vision, perhaps another version of eyes in the back of a great athlete's head.

Before the beginning of the Open in 2015, I wanted to ask Federer purely out of curiosity a question that I had often pondered—did he indeed have eyes in the back of his head, or how else did he hit that game-winning shot? The score of the match was then 7–6, 7–5, 6–5 with the twenty-eight-year-old Federer ahead 0–30. In red shirt, black shorts and black head band, and with his customary balletic grace, he returned a drop shot at the net and then Djokovic stroked a lob volley that sent Federer racing to the base line.

About two feet beyond the baseline, back to the court, and with the ball hardly an inch from the ground, Federer not only hit the ball between his legs over the net but hit it to the unassailable right of Djokovic and into the far corner for a winner. On the next point, Federer hit a rocket forehand return of a Djokovic second serve into the same neighborhood as his wondrous, previous shot. Djokovic stood, stunned. Game, set, match.

In a televised interview immediately afterward, Federer said it was his greatest shot, given the difficulty of the shot and in a crucial moment in this Grand Slam event. "It was unbelievable," he said, in complete modesty.

Now, six years later, there was a news conference that I attended and when it was over I asked one of Federer's agents to have a word with him. "I have one question to ask him," I said. They said No, as he was being whisked out. Federer heard me, and, in the adjoining hallway, said kindly, "Yes, what is it?" I believe he saw that I had raised my hand to ask a question in the interview room and wasn't called on. He was now, in his ever-gentlemanly manner, calling on me.

I now recalled to him that shot in 2009—"Was it 2009?" he asked. I said, Yes, that I had looked it up to be sure. What did he see on that shot? Federer, leaning against the wall to recall that moment of a return with obvious pleasure, said: "As I ran back, I knew Novak would be closing in on the net. I thought about returning with a lob, but then I thought `I gotta go big,' that I'd try a passing shot.'"

He said it in such a way that he seemed to assume that he knew exactly where the net was in his mind's eye, that, in other words, to just clear the net wasn't the problem. "I figured Novak would be in the middle at the net and so when I went to hit the ball between my legs I angled my racket to hit it to the right of him, hopefully out of his reach. I wanted to hit it hard, but not necessarily in that corner. But that's where I hit it. In the corner. I was as surprised as anyone." Chris Clarey covering the match for *The Times* wrote, sagely, that Federer's leap and shout after the shot was "with the delight of a performance artist who had produced something transcendent."

Whatever the reasons—anticlimactic perhaps?—Federer in the following day's final lost to Argentina's Juan Martin del Potro in five sets. Federer was denied his sixth straight US Open title, but not his place in tennis shot-making history.

* * *

Ted Williams once said of the difference in style between him and Rod Carew: "When I first saw Carew in the late '60s . . . he was a little too lackadaisical to suit me. He still *looks* lackadaisical. It's his style. He's so smooth he seems to be doing it without trying. Some guys—Pete Rose is one, and I put myself in this category—have to snort and fume to get everything going. Carew doesn't."

The Fluid Style of Rod Carew: In Total Control at Bat

May 16, 1983

Rod Carew at bat tickles the fancy, unless, naturally, one is sitting in the foe's dugout, or facing him from the pitcher's mound. The California Angels' first baseman, one of the most remarkable and successful hitters of the last three decades, is off to perhaps the best start of any batter in baseball history. Carew was hitting nearly .500—.500!—after his first 100 times up this season.

Carew is kaleidoscopic at the plate. A left-handed hitter, Carew seems to have an infinite variety of batting stances, each depending on the pitcher and the situation.

One stance has him midway in the batter's box, crouching low, fingers flexing on the bat, as if he's plopped on a milk stool and handling an udder.

A second stance is straight up, like a park statue. A third finds Carew leaning—tilting—far back in the box, bat held flat and nearly parallel to the waist. Sometimes his teammate, Reggie Jackson, can't contain his amusement. "Lay down, Rod," calls Jackson, "lay down."

To Birdie Tebbetts, the former catcher and manager and Yankee scout who now keeps his eyes peeled for the Cleveland Indians, Carew hits with a tennis racquet.

"He serves the ball to right field, he lobs it to left, he does about anything he wants with the ball," said Tebbetts. "I have never seen him when he hasn't been in control of the pitcher. Or should I say in control of his own mind at the plate. He studies the pitchers, concentrates on the ball, and has the confidence—the great hitter's arrogance—that every time up he's going to get a base hit."

Following yesterday's game, Rodney Cline Carew, at the senescent age of thirty-seven, was batting .442, with 50 hits in 113 times up. Only

Jimmie Foxx in 1932 and Stan Musial in 1958 started a season better—both getting 50 hits in their first 107 times up.

Yet the terrific start this year comes after what must be one of the most disappointing seasons of his career—and one that has added to the criticism by some that this spray, or "singles" hitter, doesn't drive in runs like a home-run slugger.

Carew has an ambition to play in the World Series. He has been on four teams that lost in the league playoffs, one step from the World Series. The fourth team was the Angels of last season, who, after going ahead two games to nothing against the Brewers, lost the next three games and the playoffs.

The fifth and final game came down to the ninth inning, with the Brewers ahead, 4–3. The Angels put a runner on second base, with two outs, and Rod Carew coming to bat.

The capacity crowd of 54,968 fans at County Stadium in Milwaukee quieted, millions more watched on television. And Carew faced a hefty hard-throwing rookie relief pitcher named Peter Ladd. Before the game, Carew had called his wife, Marilyn, from her seat in the stands. "No matter what happens," Carew said, "no tears. OK? Someone's got to win, and someone's got to lose." "For the last couple of weeks of the division race and the playoffs," Marilyn would recall, "I was a wreck. All the wives were. It was such a tight race and the games were close and we wanted our guys to win so much."

Carew, meanwhile, would try to remain cool. When he came to bat against Ladd and with the season in the balance, he didn't feel undue pressure, he said. "I know I'm going to hit the ball," he said. "I just wanted to hit it hard. After that, you can't dictate to the ball to go into this hole, or to take a crazy bounce over a guy's shoulder."

He expected Ladd to be throwing as hard as he could. There would be nothing cute—no sinkers, sliders, or floaters—not in this situation.

He lined one foul down the left-field line. He took a ball, and then another strike. All on fastballs. On the following pitch, Ladd threw a fastball waist high and on the outer part of the plate.

He swung and made good contact. He hit it sharply. Just what he wanted to do. The ball took one bounce and landed right in the glove of the shortstop, Robin Yount.

"As soon as I hit it," Carew recalled, "I said to myself, 'It's over.'" The wives were waiting for the players in the hotel lobby in Milwaukee after the game. "The players were very quiet," said Marilyn Carew, "and the wives, well, we were all crying. It was like at a funeral." Carew, though, said that he tried not to dwell on it. "You just can't spend any time second-guessing yourself," he said. "We did the best we could—I tried the hardest I could—and there was nothing more we could do."

And when he arrived home in Anaheim, said Carew, his three children—he has three daughters, Charryse, nine, Stephanie, seven, and Michelle, five—were delighted to see him, and to know he didn't have to play baseball any more that year. "Now you can take us to the mall," said Michelle.

"It helps give you perspective," said Carew, with a laugh.

Carew was sitting on the dugout bench before a recent game, his long musician's fingers casually holding a bat between his legs, and recalled this.

His family, for the most part, gives Carew his diversion from the ball park and sometimes even from his own, deeply sensitive nature. In the game against Oakland recently when he went 4 for 5 and hit a grand-slam homer, he called home afterward and told his daughter Charryse.

"Daddy," she said. "I had the same stats." He thought she was kidding. She wasn't. In her Bobby Soxers' softball league, Charryse Carew also went 4-for-5 and belted a grand slam. Some of the girls who pitch against Charryse Carew must surely appreciate how someone like Bob

Stanley, the Red Sox' ace relief pitcher, feels about her father. When asked what kind of success he has had with Carew over the years, Stanley, who has been facing Carew for seven years, replied, "Success? Rod owns me."

A goodly number of pitchers admit to being in Stanley's category in relation to Carew. Now in his 17th season in the major leagues, still graceful, still fluid, Carew has a .331 lifetime average. Second to him among active players is Brett, at .316. Carew has won seven batting titles—his first was in 1969, and then he won six in seven years in the '70s. Only four men have equaled or surpassed his number of batting titles: Rogers Hornsby and Stan Musial, seven each, Honus Wagner with eight, and Ty Cobb, 12.

Despite this, Carew has suffered the criticism of some sportswriters, and been jeered by some fans. One of the jabs at Carew is, as mentioned, that he does not hit in the clutch—that is, that he doesn't drive in a lot of runs. "That's damn stupid," said Tebbetts. "He's a lead-off hitter mostly. A guy in that position is supposed to get on base, or keep a rally going—or start one. That's exactly what Carew does."

Carew's high for runs batted in was in 1977 with the Twins when, batting third and fourth in the lineup, he knocked in 100 runs. Last year, batting first, he had 44 runs batted in.

A team statistic last season showed that Carew batted .239 with men in scoring position. "That's a phony statistic," said Tebbetts. "The only thing that means anything along those lines is what a batter does with a man on third with less than two outs. Then, it's his responsibility to somehow get the runner in, by hitting it past a drawn-in infield, or uppercutting to hit a fly ball so the man on third can tag up and score. And in seventeen years of watching Carew, I have rarely seen him not get the runner in in a situation like that."

In a clutch situation, Dennis Eckersley, the Red Sox ace starting pitcher, says he would rather face a power hitter than someone like Carew.

"The big hitters air it out," said Eckersley. "You have a chance of striking them out. With Carew, you know he's going to hit the ball—and probably hit it hard. You just hope it goes at somebody."

This season, Carew has had a better start even than in 1977 when he finished the year at .388—with 239 hits in 616 times at bat. He was just seven hits short of becoming the first batter since Ted Williams in 1941 to bat .400 or better.

Carew is healthier than he has been in seasons past. He played almost all of last year, for example, with two cracked bones in his right hand, the guiding hand of the bat for a left-handed batter. He was virtually hitting one-handed, and still managed a .319 batting average, third in the league, and at one point hit in 25 straight games, the longest streak in the majors in 1982. And it was the 14th straight season Carew has hit over .300, an achievement bettered by only five other players.

Despite this, at Anaheim Stadium he has been the target at times of the condemnation of some fans. Just before the players' strike in 1981, the Angels were obviously disappointing the fans and were booed. Carew told a reporter that he felt the fans were fickle. Not all the fans, but some. It is not an earthshaking insight, to say the least. Yet the story received throbbing headlines locally, and Carew became a prime target of abuse. It became so foul, in fact, that he had to be escorted by security officers to his car after a game.

Now, with the Angels at the top of the American League West and Carew leading the league's batters, he is cheered. Proving, ironically, his original contention.

The Carews have lived in Anaheim for five years now, ever since the parsimonious Twins traded Carew to California—before he could become a free agent. The owner of the Angels, Gene Autry, who used to warble "Tumbling Tumbleweed" for a living, opened his saddle bags, it is said, to pay Carew nearly $1 million a year. It is doubtful that even a one-time cowboy troubadour would keep money in saddle bags, but it is true that he paid Carew that sweet salary.

(An aside: Carew hit only 3 homers last season and has just 87 for his career. Tebbetts, among other baseball people, feels that Carew could have hit 25 or 30 homers a year if he had wanted to—he's that strong. Did Tebbetts think Carew perhaps made a mistake and should have gone for more homers?

("If you audited his bank account," said Tebbetts, "I'm sure you'd find that he followed the right path.")

This is the last year of Carew's five-year contract with the Angels. Carew has said that he might retire, or that he might move on.

It is unlikely that with, surely, some five good seasons left in his bat, he would call it quits. Especially for the recompense he commands.

Carew is not foolish about money. He is careful with it now that he has it. He has not forgotten his boyhood in Gatun, Panama. He was so poor that at school he would walk beside the wall of the corridor because he was embarrassed at the sound made by the flapping soles of his only pair of shoes.

And with a father who, he said, beat him and abused him and finally left the home, Carew remembers that it was on the ball field that his talents flourished. "I felt there," he said, "like I was king."

He has never squandered his abilities. Carew, lean at 6 foot tall, still trains hard. His weight—about 178—is nearly the same as when he broke in to the majors seventeen years ago. "Sickening, isn't it?" said Marilyn Carew, with undisguised envy.

Carew says he still takes extra batting practice and still practices bunting diligently. He remains one of the best bunters in the game. He bunts the ball with a backspin, so that almost no matter how close the third baseman plays, he can usually beat out a hit. In the year he batted

.388 he bunted safely nine times with two strikes on him. He has also stolen home 17 times, the last time in 1981.

"Now," he said, "the pitchers always stretch when I'm on third. I don't think I'll steal home again—unless I have to." He doesn't, of course, run quite as well as he once did, but he says he runs smarter. "I'm more conscious of where the outfielders are playing when I'm on base, and I don't take such wide turns anymore running around the bases. I'm still learning."

But it is his hitting that continues to set him apart. A telling example of Carew's virtuosity at bat came in a game last Tuesday night against the Red Sox at Fenway Park. Carew had been on the bench resting a sore knee, the result of a collision at first base a few days before. It was the top of the ninth now, the game was tied, 5–5, and the Angels' manager, John McNamara, sent Carew up to pinch hit.

The pitcher was Luis Aponte, a twenty-eight-year-old right-handed reliever with a little more than a year's major league experience. Carew, in the red-billed plastic batting helmet glistening under the stadium lights, gray uniform, and red baseball shoes, crouched near the back of the batter's box. It was probably taken from somewhere in the middle of his batting-stance book.

Carew had faced Aponte before and had observed him. He is aware of how some pitchers will throw a fastball close to overhand, but drop a little for their slider and drop even more for their sinker.

Carew's eyesight is sharp enough to follow the rotation of the ball—at up to 90 miles an hour—from the moment it leaves the pitcher's hand just 60-feet-6-inches away. "He picks up the ball better than most," Eckersley had said. "And his wrists are so quick that even if you fool him, he has time to recover."

Now, Aponte threw a slider down and in. Carew saw it clearly and fouled it down the first-base line. "It was a nasty pitch," said Carew. "A good pitcher's pitch. I knew it wasn't the kind of pitch I could do much with. Some hitters will try to do what they can with even a pitch that's tough. I don't. I can foul it off, or just take it."

Fred Lynn, the Angels' slugging outfielder, said that every hitter generally gets one pitch each time up that he can hit. The good hitters consistently take advantage of it. He had said that this season, Carew was getting hits on that one pitch. And that first against Aponte was not for him.

Nor was the second, a ball. The third pitch was another good one by Aponte. "It was a sinker down at the outside corner," said Carew. And he fouled it down the third-base line.

The next pitch was a forkball that broke wickedly inside at the wrists. Carew, who had choked up on the bat with two strikes, strode, then halted his swing.

Ball two. "Last year," he said, "I couldn't have stopped because my hand hurt so much. I'd have punched out and walked back to the dugout."

"It was a perfect pitch," Aponte said after the game. "I think any other hitter in the big leagues would have gone for that 1-2 fork."

Now it was 2-2. Aponte threw four more strong pitches. None was to Carew's liking and, with uncanny bat control, he fouled off each one. "I could sense his frustration now," said Carew. "He had thrown me some great pitches, and I was still standing up there." It was true, and Aponte would acknowledge that he had "thrown Carew everything but the kitchen sink." Then Aponte wound up and whistled in a fastball. Carew saw it as clearly as if it were a cantaloupe tossed to him. The ball came in waist high and a little on the outside of the plate. Delicious. Carew smacked it in the alley in left-center. It hit the wall at 390 feet on one bounce.

Carew pulled up with a double, and scored when Juan Beniquez, the next batter, singled. It decided the game. The Angels won by that

6–5 score. "I didn't give in to him," Carew said afterward of Aponte. "I made him give in to me." It was a very fine job—for many baseball followers, the stamp of Rodney Cline Carew.

* * *

Carew finished the 1983 season with a .339 batting average. He retired as an active player in 1985, with a lifetime .328 batting average, and 3,053 career hits. He was inducted in the Baseball Hall of Fame in 1991.

Koufax Is No Garbo

July 3, 1985

There was something special about Sandy Koufax. On Monday night, in the Cracker Jack Old-Timers Baseball Classic at RFK Stadium here, he was chosen as the honorary captain of the National League team, a singular plum among such teammates as Henry Aaron and Ernie Banks and Warren Spahn. Koufax retains that special quality, apparently, even among his peers.

Perhaps it has something to do with an almost Biblical cycle to his baseball career. Koufax didn't quite have seven years thin and ill favored, and seven years of great plenty, but he did have six of each.

Miraculously, it seemed, he went from a pitcher of enormous but uncontrolled potential—catchers wore shin-guards when warming him up because so many of his pitches bounced in the dirt in front of them— to a star of the greatest mastery.

"What was it like facing Koufax? It was frightenin'," Banks, the former star Cub, recalled at the Cracker Jack, which the National League won, 7–3. "He had that tremendous fastball that would rise, and a great curveball that started at the eyes and broke to the ankles. In the end, you knew you were going to be embarrassed. You were either going to strike out or foul out."

Koufax's record was 36–40 in his first six seasons, 129–47 in his last six.

Maybe that special quality of Koufax also had to do with his poise and grit on the mound: the memory remains vivid of his breaking a World Series record in 1963 by striking out 15 Yankees in a game. Maybe the special quality also was enhanced by the air of distinction with which he comported himself, even to the way he adjusted his cap front and back, with two fingers of each hand, like knotting a bow tie.

And maybe the quality also had something to do with the way he retired, at the young age of 30, after having been named the Cy Young Award winner in 1966 for the third time in four years, after having led the major leagues in victories with 27, and earned run average, 1.73, and games started and games completed and innings pitched and strike-outs, with 317, and after having helped pitch the Los Angeles Dodgers to a pennant, their second straight.

He suffered from an arthritic elbow, and doctors feared that if he continued pitching he could cause permanent damage to his arm.

And so, virtually at the height of his career, Koufax retired. And moved to a small town in Maine. Here was the toast of New York and Los Angeles departing the bright lights for what seemed to some the life of Greta Garbo.

To some, he became a kind of mystery man.

"What was so mysterious?" he asked, dressing for the game in the Cracker Jack clubhouse. "I wasn't running away, or hiding from the police. Maine is not another world. A lot of people lived there, and still do."

He said yes, he sought some privacy. "I never liked being shoved and pushed in crowds," he said. "But I was around for six years doing Saturday afternoon baseball telecasts with NBC.

"And now I work for the Dodgers. I'm a pitching coach with the team in spring training and a minor-league pitching instructor during the summer months. I'm around. What's the mystery?"

Red Schoendienst came by. "Sandy," he said, "looks like you can go out there and still pump the heat."

Koufax smiled. At 6 foot, 185 pounds, he does look fit. He was tan and slim and perhaps only the hair on his head, more salt than pepper now, gives an indication that on his next birthday, December 30, he will be fifty years old.

He spoke about traveling as a pitching instructor and working with young players. Bill Schweppe, the Dodgers' vice president in charge of minor league operations, said that Koufax was effective with kids once they got past their awe of him. He mentioned Koufax's low-key approach that puts players at ease.

"In the minor leagues, the players are on the way up and they've all got their dreams," said Koufax. "It's a very positive thing. They want to learn. But I don't know how much I've helped anyone. I can show them some mechanics, but no one can make a big league ballplayer. In the end it's up to the individual. They help themselves. But it's satisfying to see improvement."

He had said that he became a better pitcher when he learned to control his temper and his frustration. "Maybe it was just a matter of getting older," he said. "I see young players getting angry with themselves the way I did, and I wish I could tell them how to curb it. But there's no secret formula."

Koufax grew up in Brooklyn, joined the Dodgers there in 1955, at age nineteen, and never played a day in the minor leagues. "If I walked five guys in a major league game, it was terrible," he said, "but if I had done that in the minors, where I should have been, it would have been fine—a learning experience."

He contends that there was no single turning point. "I had a good spring in 1961," he said, "and it seemed that management was finally going to let me pitch every fourth day. Before, if I didn't do well in an outing, I might not pitch for three weeks. That didn't help me. I kept telling the Dodgers that I needed a routine. Your control is dependent on consistency."

In his younger, more inept days, a story goes that Koufax, who is Jewish, said he wasn't sure whether he was a *shlemiel* or a *shlamazel*. In Yiddish, a *shlemiel* is someone who spills soup on people, a *shlamazel* is someone who has soup spilled on him.

"Or is it vice versa?" Koufax said smiling. "I really don't remember if I ever said that, but there were times when I felt that way."

As he spoke, a television crew came by and began shooting him from the side. The bright light made him blink. He turned to the three men. "Don't television people ever ask?" he said, with a half smile.

"I'm sorry," said the man who apparently was head of the crew. He introduced himself. Koufax shook his hand, and said, "At least let me put on my shirt before you continue."

Later, he was asked if he still goes back to Maine. "Every year," he said. "I still love it."

* * *

With Koufax and his wife, Jane, I once mentioned to him that the writer James Thurber allegedly said that "The majority of American males put themselves to sleep by striking out the batting order of the New York Yankees." Koufax said he'd never heard that. "I asked, "Had you ever dreamed of that?" "No," he said, "I hadn't." "But you did it," I said. He shrugged in acknowledgment. I said, "Sandy, what do you dream about?" He pointed to Jane. "Her," he said. Sandy Koufax was clever not only on the pitching mound.

That Quiet Moment for Larry Bird

August 19, 1992

If, as has been said, it is the quiet moments, the moments out of the spotlight, that most define character, then this was one of them:

It was a few years ago, when Larry Bird was still healthy, still untroubled by the back problems that forced him yesterday, at age thirty-five, to untie his basketball sneakers for the last time. Bird, as usual, had come onto the court in Boston Garden two hours before the game, under the dim lights, to shoot alone for 45 minutes, working on his moves and priming his mind for the game ahead. His only audience was the working men who put up the baskets and lay down the parquet floor.

It was considered unusual then to spend so much time working out before a game, although many have since followed suit. And Bird didn't fool around. You could see the intensity in his face, his eyes narrowed at the hoop, the familiar and smooth Swiss-clock release and follow-through.

A team trainer fed him the ball. Bird now began his routine shooting from the right side of the court and swung around to the left. He made one shot, another and another.

The working men, about eight or ten of them, had stopped putting up tables at courtside, and watched, as they often did. They now counted among themselves: Ten in a row, 15, 18, 20, 22, 24 . . . On the next shot, from the top of the key, Bird missed.

"Boo!" chimed the working men. "Boo!" Bird turned, looked at them, and began to laugh. So did they.

It saddened many when Larry Bird announced his retirement yesterday. Many will miss him very much, but it's my impression that few will miss him more than those laborers.

Larry Bird was first, like them, a working man, one who gave the paying customer and the paying boss and his coach their money's worth. And those working men at courtside understood and appreciated that, just as Bird understood what it meant to be a working man. He was a garbage collector who became a kind of Rembrandt as an artist and a craftsman and an athlete.

When Bird dropped out of Indiana University, he was employed for a while as a garbage collector in his hometown, French Lick, Indiana, part of the working class, if not the underclass.

But some special quality within made him strive to be different, to go beyond just being an athlete: Was it to prove something after the suicide of his father when Bird was in his teens? Or watching his mother work to support the family? Or some Midwestern ethic, or inborn pride?

And while he sometimes appeared plodding as he ran down the court and was less than the best jumper, his instincts, his zeal, his technique and his killer will made up for whatever he lacked.

Bird became more than a great athlete, he became a champion. He became perhaps the best college basketball player in the country at Indiana State, and, for his 13 seasons with the Boston Celtics, one of the best pros ever.

It was said about Bird, just as it was about Bill Russell before him, and Magic Johnson his contemporary, that he made the other players around him better.

He did it by all the prescribed verities of team play: hitting the open man (remember how he stole the ball from the Pistons and hit the streaking Dennis Johnson for the winning basket in the playoff game?), hustling so hard that he seemed to be in two places at one time (remember the shot he missed from the top of the key and he got the rebound at the base line, and scored?), being absolutely reliable in the clutch (remember—oh, there were too many times to remember just one!).

Statistics, while impressive, never told the story of Larry Bird. He never had to score 50 points in a game to be sensational, although he did that, too. One no-look, chest-high, touch pass to a man cutting behind him was enough.

If there is one most telling statistic, however, it is that he completely flipflopped the Celtics in his rookie year.

The season before he joined the team, the Celtics in 1978–79 had a 29–53 record, and finished last in the Atlantic Division. The next season, with virtually the same cast, but with Bird, they were 61–21 and finished first, the greatest team turnaround in National Basketball Association history to that point.

There have been other great players, and there are other great players, and there will be other great players, but it is doubtful whether there will ever be another quite like Larry Bird. It's sad that he's going, but it was a deep pleasure to have had him. Just ask the guys who put up the baskets and lay down the parquet floor at Boston Garden.

* * *

Larry Bird is the only person in NBA history to be named Rookie of the Year, regular-season MVP, NBA Finals MVP, All-Star Game MVP, Coach of the Year (Indiana Pacers, 1998), and Executive of the Year (President of Basketball Operations, Pacers, 2012). I once was in his Pacers office in his executive period and mentioned to him that, like him, I worked as a garbage collector in summers in my school days in Chicago. "I know you did as well, in French Lick," I said. "My wife thinks I idealize the job, but I was a young guy, working with men, having to carry my weight in those alleys, built up some muscle, and eventually got used to the smell. I loved it." The often-stoic Bird rose from his desk, all 6-foot-9 of him, and said, "I loved it, too!"

Clyde's "Ultimate Cool"

February 6, 1987

The memories of Walt (Clyde) Frazier playing his quietly exciting basketball for the Knicks come back in a flood for any fan, especially now, the day after he has been elected to the Basketball Hall of Fame.

There was the time he hit this clutch shot with one second left to win the game, the time he threw that pass or got that rebound or made that steal to turn the game around.

And of course, there was the seventh game of the National Basketball Association championship series in 1970, when, with Willis Reed ailing, Frazier scored 36 points, grabbed seven rebounds, and added a sensational 19 assists as the Knicks won their first title.

He ran the offense. "It's Clyde's ball," Reed once said, "he lets the rest of us play with it sometimes."

Frazier did it in his seemingly cool fashion. But for all that, the game that sticks out in this reporter's memory is one in which he played against the Knicks.

After ten years with two championship teams in New York, he was sent to the Cleveland Cavaliers as compensation for a free agent, Jim Cleamons, on October 3, 1977.

Frazier, at thirty-two, was past his salad days, the team chemistry had changed, and he was distraught—he had built his life here, and now learned of the deal second-hand—and was incommunicado for several days before reporting to the Cavaliers, the lowly Cavs. Shortly after, he returned to Madison Square Garden, this time in a strange uniform.

When he was announced before the game, the cheers nearly brought the roof down.

Clyde, cool Clyde, showed, customarily, little emotion. But he was pumped. He scored 28 points, made five steals, as the Cavaliers won in overtime, 117–112. As the buzzer sounded ending the game, Clyde, cool, cool Clyde, thrust a fist in the air and leaped and yelped and raced off the court, with the crowd again cheering madly for this special opponent.

But he wouldn't have many more great basketball days, and he never quite seemed to heal from a stress fracture to a foot, or from his sudden departure from New York, and although he hung on for a few more seasons, he would never be the Frazier we knew.

His easy style made it seem to some that he wasn't always trying as hard as he could. Some said that he could make so many steals because he gambled and, if he missed, well, there was Willis Reed to back him up.

But Frazier was clever as a defensive player. He would, for example, lull a player into a sense of security. He would capture the rhythm of an opponent's dribble. And although he could make the steal now, he might decide to wait, to use the steal off the dribble for a crucial moment later in the game. Thus those clutch, late-game snatchings. One player he had trouble with, however, was Lenny Wilkens, who, ironically, was one of those who was nominated for the Hall, but didn't get the required number of votes.

Once, before heading off to do a piece on Wilkens—then the coach of Seattle—I asked Frazier if he had a question for him.

"You know, Wilkens was a lefty and he always went left," said Frazier. "But I could never stop him. Ask him why."

I did. "He always knew I was going left," said Wilkens, "but he never knew when." Frazier delighted in the response. Frazier was able to laugh at himself, and in that way, although he greatly enjoyed the world of the star in Manhattan, could retain some perspective.

Despite his pink Eldorado ("the Clydemobile"), and his black mink coat and his wide wardrobe of lids and kicks and suits (including the black cowskin suit with poncho and silver studs), there were moments when Frazier could still be seen as the kid who grew up in Atlanta, the oldest of nine children—he and his brother, Keith, the youngest, were the only boys in the family.

Walt helped his mother diaper and cook for the babies, and then went into the schoolyard where he learned to dribble an erratic basketball that kept bouncing off the stones.

And he was the guy who didn't sulk and quit when he didn't make grades and lost eligibility for a time at Southern Illinois. Instead, he played with the varsity only on defense, and labored so hard at it that he would become a superb defensive player. And when he came to the Knicks, after having led Southern Illinois to the National Invitation Tournament championship in 1967, he seemed lost in the big city, and on a team in disarray. He was often afraid to shoot. But with the help of a new coach, Red Holzman, Frazier regained confidence, a career opened up, and he would be rated among the best guards ever, with Oscar Robertson, Jerry West, and Bob Cousy.

Frazier once recalled a time when he picked up two kids hitchhiking in the Catskills, where he had a basketball camp. The kids—they were about twelve or thirteen years old—sank into the white leather seats of his Cadillac. They were coming from playing basketball and were very quiet.

"I got a feeling they knew who I was," recalled Frazier, "but they didn't say anything. Cool cats. I didn't say anything, either. I stopped to let them out, and they thanked me for the ride. As I drove away, I saw them in the rear-view mirror. They were jumping up and down and slapping palms. Cool cats to the end."

With his election to the Hall of Fame, Clyde Frazier, the ultimate Cool Cat, can now forgivably slap palms, too.

Cheering for Soccer While the Toast Burns

June 19, 2002

I remember soccer. I played it on occasion many years ago in grade school gym class in our gravel-strewn schoolyard. I remember that when Mr. Kennedy, our gym teacher, told us what was on the agenda for the period—no baseball, no football—it was as if we were being sentenced to soccer.

I remember the bruises from my playmates who mistook my shins for the ball, and, surely, the compensatory bruises I inflicted. I remember the header that I struck with my eye, and the one with my ear. But I don't think those stinging memories are the reason soccer today is as compelling for me as watching a man with a jackhammer dig a hole in a street. You stop for a moment, and move on quickly.

No, after all, I was hit in the head with a baseball and I've been spiked. In football I've been pummeled. But those two sports, to name two, still hold a lure for me as an adult.

And there are other sports that I engaged in only somewhat, like boxing and golf, that I find intriguing. But here we are in the midst of much hoopla about the United States soccer team in the quarter-finals of the World Cup—the first time it has reached such heights since Hoover was president. Newspapers and television stations in America are paying extravagant amounts of money to cover it, and the aproned, spatula-holding cooks in Greek coffee shops that I frequent are out of the kitchen and rooted to the television set and cheering passionately in a medley of languages while I'm concerned that my toast is burning.

Most Americans I know feel the same way I do. Beyond the ethnic conclaves, soccer has little enduring interest for Americans as a spectator sport. For those who grew up with soccer—either playing it in their countries abroad, or having a foreign-born parent stimulate interest at an early age—it is nearly a matter of life or death. In fact, when a Colombian player accidentally kicked a goal into his own net in 1994, he was so hated at home that he was murdered soon after.

Some who love soccer hold to the belief that the legions of soccer-indifferent here are philistines or chauvinists, or decided dolts.

The arguments are plentiful. One is espoused by Danny Ahn, a South Korean friend, who owns a photo shop in my neighborhood. He believes that soccer is boring to Americans because we like violence in our sports, and soccer has virtually none (other than the fans who love a good riot in the stands and in the streets).

Yes, football is popular among the team sports, but hockey, except for pockets of fans, hardly competes as our national pastime (check the perennially dismal television ratings), and it's dripping with gore. Basketball is tough but not really bloody, and baseball is more noted for its grace and hitting and pitching power than its occasional dusters and dust-ups.

When I first got into the newspaper business, in 1965, I was assigned to write an article about soccer as the next big sport in America. It was supposed to be the next big sport in the 1970s, and '80s, and '90s—and some are calling it that today.

But after a brief romance with fans, and after the Pelés and Beckenbauers have come and gone, we are left with players with names that do not resonate. And it's not because they are invariably foreign-sounding, either. We have embraced the Suzukis and Nowitzkis in other team sports in places from Seattle to Dallas.

It is because there is a disconnect with the sport. "Look, Ma, no hands" somehow doesn't do it for the American sports enthusiast. And it's one thing for the scoring in soccer to be minimal, but when they do produce a goal, it's as if they've overthrown a despot. They go berserk, ripping off their clothes, shrieking around the stadium and then, for good measure, piling on top of one another. And this is only halfway through the first half.

The fact is, while soccer has become popular with some moms and a ton of tots, it seems to lose spectator interest when the children reach adulthood. We got a little excited when the United States women won the World Cup in 1999, but that has faded. The longtime cultural ties to team sports like baseball (as tedious as soccer sometimes) and football and basketball take up a great chunk of our emotional and mental time.

They are in our blood the way soccer is for most of the rest of the world, which didn't grow up with the other sports.

We would need a sports transfusion to change, but regardless of how far the American team advances in this World Cup, the paramedics still appear a long, long way off.

* * *

The US Men's and Women's soccer teams have indeed stirred worldwide interest as they competed valiantly for and/or won World Cup championships in the last two decades since the above column was written. And statistics show that the American professional soccer league, MLS, gets the third highest average attendance of any sport in America after Major League Baseball and the National Football League, yet I maintain that, from my admittedly anecdotal research, interest in those special exploits arguably remains relatively limited, especially compared to the fandom for such longtime sports that Americans, from my experience, hold most dear, such as baseball, football and basketball, or even golf, tennis and hockey and, to an increasingly lesser extent, boxing, once at the top rung of interest to American sports fans. The Ultimate Fighting Championships—of which I am no fan (punching *and* kicking, too)—seems on the rise as well.

Am I right about soccer? Well, a number of years ago, following a biography I wrote of Red Smith, sportswriter supreme, a man named Serge Kulmetycki of Mt. Clemens, Michigan, sent me a note that Red Smith had written him in a response to a boxing question.

Dear Mr. Kulmetycki:

One day I remarked to the late Frank Graham, a great sportswriter, that I thought that Sugar Ray Robinson was the best fighter that I had ever seen.

"Perhaps," Frank said, "but Benny Leonard would have beaten him as a lightweight. Jimmy McLarnin would have beaten him as a welterweight, and Mickey Walker and Billy Conn would have beaten him as a middleweight."

"I don't know whether you're right," I said.

"Neither do I," Frank Graham said.

Yours, Red Smith.

On soccer, at this point, I'm with those two guys.

Part II: Heroes Behind Bars

Some of our most heralded athletic stars have wound up in various kinds of adversity, including prison sentences like, famously, O. J. Simpson, Mike Tyson, and Pete Rose.

O. J. Simpson: The Former "Lifesaver of the Month"

I first met Simpson when he was a college football player, well before his various legal charges and convictions that captivated the nation.

"O. J. SIMPSON, ALL-AMERICAN, STARS AS USC BEATS ARCH-RIVAL UCLA"

"The only thing I'm thinking is that I don't want to be killed," said Simpson. This was the lead of my nationally syndicated sports column dated November 27, 1968, following his reaction to the adulation of him following a football game in which he typically starred. It was a remark that some twenty-five years later would embody tragic irony, when he would be put on trial for the murder, slashing the necks of and stabbing, an ex-wife, Nicole Brown Simpson, and a friend of hers, Ron Goldman.

The twenty-one-year-old Simpson, still in sweat-stained T-shirt, with shoulder pads and cleats on the floor, was talking to me in front of his locker in the Los Angeles Memorial Coliseum, after the senior University of Southern California All-American running back had run circles around archrival UCLA. Wearing the yellow number 32 on his red jersey, and sometimes cradling the ball wide in his arm as though on a wing, he had twisted and dodged and fled tacklers, in a 28–16 triumph—and, the following month, after leading the nation in rushing for the second consecutive year, he was in route to winning the Heisman Trophy, emblematic of the best college football player in the nation.

With a welcoming smile, and handsome, genial looks that would one day put him into Hollywood movies and television commercials and broadcasting, he was describing a scene at game's end in between being carried off the field on the shoulders of fans and then struggling to run through the adoring, grasping crowd to get to the locker room. It seemed that a good portion of the 75,000 game spectators had descended excitedly onto the field. Someone was wrenching off the strap of his helmet for a souvenir. Simpson gave it to him in self-defense. A second tugged at his wrist band. He gave it to him. A third was untying his shoe lace. But no dice there.

"I enjoy it, sure," he was saying, about the adulation. "Sometimes I think it could get dangerous. Like that thing about untying my shoe. I could trip and fall. But I'm patient with the kids because I was just such a kid growing up in San Francisco."

Growing up in a project in the rugged Potrero Hills neighborhood, Orenthal James Simpson was and was not such a kid. As a teenager he was a member of the "Persian Warriors" gang and was arrested several times for a variety of infractions, and was also incarcerated for several days in the San Francisco Youth Guidance Center.

"I snuck into all the 49er games. When I got older I'd scalp tickets. But I changed. And it was mostly Marquerite who changed me."

Marquerite Whitley, who grew up in the same area as Simpson, had an expanded take on the young O. J. Marquerite was, by the time of that USC-UCLA game, Mrs. O. J. Simpson, and eight months pregnant. She waited for him after the game in the runway outside the locker room. "She waits two and three hours after every game because Simpson is patient with reporters and well-wishers who, like the kids on the field, engulf him," I wrote. "Throughout it all, he answers questions with animation and thought."

"I remember that at first I hated O. J." Marquerite told me, as she sat in a folding chair in the fog and smog-filled night. "He was a tough, always wanting to fight. Once I was at a party and he and his friends were not allowed in. So they broke windows and came in. It broke up a nice party."

(In a *Playboy* magazine interview, in 1976, Simpson said, "I never infringed on people. I only beat up dudes who deserved it . . . At least once a week, usually on Friday or Saturday night. If there weren't no fight, it wasn't no weekend.")

"Well, we started dating anyway," Marquerite told me outside the Coliseum, "but my mother was not thrilled about it. He'd come over on Sundays dressed—uh, very casually. Let me put it this way, in jeans and sandals. My mother is very religious and she thought you have to wear a suit and tie on Sunday. O. J. started doing that.

"My mother felt that any boy I was dating ought to go to church. O. J. started doing that, too."

Simpson and Marquerite married on June 27, 1967, she was eighteen and he twenty. But at least one thinghad changed from their courtship. "He doesn't go to church every Sunday anymore," she said, with a wry smile.

"In those days, O. J. would ask odd questions. Once he asked if I had any girlfriends. I said I had a lot of associates. But I was very close with my mother, still am. O. J. had a previous girlfriend who said she had lots of girlfriends. But he felt that none were true friends, because girls are envious. Later he told me he was impressed with my honesty.

"He would ask my advice on things, for instance. When he graduated high school"—Simpson was an all-city running back for Galileo High School—"his grades weren't good enough for USC, where he had his heart set on going. So he went to junior college. But he got many offers from schools like Arizona and Utah. One college even offered to send us to Hawaii for our honeymoon.

"It was tempting, let me tell you. But I thought that he should stay in junior college so that he could eventually get into USC." Which is what happened.

"Things are different from those days," she continued. "What I miss is all the time we used to spend together. We'd go boating, take walks, study at my house. Now, he comes home and is so tired he can hardly talk.And on Sundays we nurse his wounds."

Simpson finally emerged from the locker room. He sought out Marquerite, threw an arm around her and kissed her. A boy who—like Marquerite—had waited for hours for Simpson shyly asked for an autograph, and said, "I am a fan of the other team, but I thought you were great."

"That's a real man," said Simpson, signing the boy's program. "Not many people would say that." And Marquerite and Simpson went off to nurse his wounds.

(It was remarkable to think that this stupendous running back had contracted rickets when he was two years old, his legs skinny and bowlegged and pigeon-toed. His mother, Eunice, a hospital orderly (his father didn't live with the family), couldn't afford braces, so she made her boy wear a pair of shoes connected by an iron bar for a few hours almost every day until he was five.)

The next time I spoke with Simpson was on another late November afternoon five years later, 1973, for an article for that same syndicate. A lot had changed. He and Marquerite had two children. He had been a No. 1 selection in the National Football League draft of 1969, and had become an All-Pro with the Buffalo Bills. Now Simpson, who had rushed for stunning yardage all season but especially in games this November in pursuit of an NFL record, was to receive an award, the Lifesaver of the Month, sponsored by the candy maker. (One wondered, however, who Simpson was saving that month, since the Bills had lost three of their four November games.)

Life had lately been relatively filled with profound football incident for Simpson, in this his fifth pro season. I wrote that "every time he makes a move, a swivel of his hips, he hears the echoes of Jim Brown. It is Brown's single-season NFL rushing record of 1,863 yards that Simpson has been flirting with to fracture." He needed 417 yards in the last three games of the season to break the record.

Simpson soon arrived in the restaurant. At 6-foot-1, 210 pounds, he was broad-shouldered and natty in dark pants, dark shirt open wide at the color and light-patterned sport jacket, and, I wrote, "a nice electricity in demeanor and smile."

At one point, talking about his running style, he said, "I used to be criticized for jitter-bugging when I got to the line of scrimmage. Some people said I should hit the hole. But there were no holes, so I danced along the line looking for a place to scoot. But I don't look for trouble.

"I'm not a runner like Larry Brown. Sometimes me and Carl Garrett and Mercury Morris we'll sit around and kid Larry. His style is to run over eleven guys. He runs into people. I run away from them.

"Early in the season I was having trouble getting my head together. I started thinking about the record while on the field. I remember I was having a miserable first half against Baltimore. I went and sat at the end of the bench and began to talk to myself. I told myself to concentrate on the present game and not on Jim Brown's past."

About two weeks later, Sunday, December 16, Simpson was in New York again. This time in Queens, in Shea Stadium, where the Bills would be playing the last game of the regular season, against the New York Jets. Having gained 1,803 yards in the previous 13 league games, Simpson was 61 yards shy of breaking the record which, it was assumed, he would reach easily, since he was averaging almost 140 yards rushing per game. The question was would he become the first player in NFL history to gain 2,000 yards in a season? He needed 197. The week before, in blizzard in Buffalo, he skidded through it for 219 yards.

I remember it being a cold day for that Shea Stadium game, temperature below freezing, and snow blowing at a blizzard level. Not necessarily ideal for running. But with 4:26 left in the first quarter, Simpson broke Brown's record on a six-yard run. He kept piling up yardage. Speculation was rife in the press box. Would time run out before he could reach 2,000? Would his line hold? Would the Jets defense stiffen? This was answered when with 5:56 left in the fourth quarter Simpson cracked through the Jets' defense for seven yards, for 2003 yards for the season and a record that would never be broken. The NFL went to a 16-game schedule in 1978 and a few runners have amassed 2,000-plus yards in a season, but they needed two more games than Simpson had to do it.

After the game, Simpson was besieged for an interview, in a tight boiler room in the bowels of Shea Stadium. Simpson insisted that his linemen, who had blocked for him, fit into the room, and be a part of the newsmaking. He seemed thoughtful and appreciative. The following July, when the Bills showed up for training camp, "The Juice" gave each of his "Electric Company" (the linemen so-named) a gold bracelet. It had their name, number and an inscription, "O. J. We Did It. 2,000 Yards."

For many of us reporters, there had rarely been an athlete as gracious and generous—with his time and his money—as O. J. Simpson. It seemed that the bad boy of his teen days in San Francisco was well behind him. He played four more seasons with the Bills, and two more lackluster years due to injuries with his hometown 49ers—a Hall of Fame 11-year-career—retiring in 1979, at age, thirty-two, with a lifetime now to nurse his wounds, as Marguerite had described it in his college days. But he was also going to nurse those wounds without Marguerite, since they were divorced in 1979.

Simpson's post-football career seemed as illustrious, in another way. He was featured in commercials and Hollywood films. He became the first African-American athlete to be merchandised on so broad a scale. He once said, "I'm not black, I'm O. J."

In 1985, the 38-year-old Simpson married a statuesque blonde, twenty-six-year-old Nicole Brown. They had children, and for all we knew, his life was as mythical as Ozzie and Harriet. In 1989, however, he was charged with domestic violence. According to police reports Simpson beat his wife so badly she needed to be hospitalized. When the police arrived after the beating, the records show, Mrs. Simpson ran out of the bushes, yelling, "He's going to kill me. He's going to kill me." She had called the police eight other times because of beatings, and fearing for her life.

The 1989 conflict ended with Simpson pleading no contest to spousal abuse, was sentenced to 120 hours of community service and two years' probation. It was the only time I and many of my colleagues heard of such abuse, and it was generally assumed that this was an aberration, just a blip in the otherwise serene life of the Simpsons. The couple issued a joint statement following the sentence: "Our marriage is as strong as the day we were married, if not stronger."

It was perhaps a year or so later that I saw O. J. and Nicole and two of their small children, a girl and a boy, in Los Angeles airport terminal waiting for a flight. O. J. chased after the playful kids. I asked him if it was harder running into the line in a football game or running after the kids? "At my age, it's running after the kids!" He was then about forty-five, and with legs that withstood years of bruising tackles. Simpson and Brown were divorced in 1992.

The next time I was aware of Simpson was a few years later, in June 1994, when he was the target of the infamous white Bronco chase by Los Angeles police, following the savage murders of Nicole and Ron Goldman.

In one of the most notorious trials in American legal history, Simpson was acquitted of the murders, on October 3, 1995. As the trial had proceeded to a rapt country, I happened to be with the Hall of Fame pitcher Bob Feller. We talked baseball, and then, almost with no other context, I said, "Did O. J. do it?" He was taken aback for a moment, and then replied, "If he didn't, who did?" That response echoed my sense as well.

A few years after the trial, I spoke with Simpson's lead defense counsel, Johnnie Cochran, who, by most accounts, performed brilliantly—and successfully.

"I think that very often these days the lives of outstanding athletes have been far different from others, and I think African-Americans are no exception," he said. "They are catered to much of their lives, from a young age. And someone like O. J. Simpson, even though he had transcended the African American culture and had assimilated into some other kind of world, ascended a pedestal. And there is often a sense of invincibility among outstanding athletes, a sense of immortality. I saw it in even the best. I think even Magic Johnson, who has been in many ways a model citizen, had the attitude that he could do things, and there is no way he'll be caught. In his case, it was HIV.

"But I think power does that," he continued, "gives this idea of being immortal and invincible. It's a real tough thing. I see that in athletes and it's troubling because they have to realize—part of it is that they are young, too—that one wrong turn, one incident, could change your life."

I asked Cochran if Simpson was in fact guilty. He smiled. "The jury spoke," he said. In fact, there were no other suspects to the murders then, and there are none now.

But Simpson faced another trial regarding the murders, this one a civil suit brought for the "wrongful deaths" of Nicole and Ron Goldman, brought by their families. In February 1997, the jury ordered Simpson to pay $33.5 million in compensatory and punitive damages.

Simpson was pretty much out of the news until September 2007, when he was arrested for having been embroiled in a plot to regain what he believed was memorabilia belonging to him. He and an accomplice broke into a Las Vegas hotel room at gun point and confronted the memorabilia collectors. Simpson was arrested shortly after for kidnapping and armed robbery. He was sentenced to thirty-three years in prison, with parole possible after nine years. The renowned football star wearing number 32 on his jersey had become Prisoner No. 026489727 in the Nevada Department of Corrections system. He was paroled in 2017.

There had been numerous instances of sports stars demonstrating at some point in their life and times a vulnerability that is all too common among human beings generally. While Simpson's case that deals with murder is to be sure not common, the shock or surprise that comes with the knowledge of such a fact often is.

On June 25, 1994, shortly after Simpson's arrest for the murders, I wrote the following in my "Sports of the Times" column.

The Worship of False Gods
June 25, 1994

I was struck with a statement in another newspaper the other day about O. J. Simpson, which said that "it had taken courage for him to run against men who were twice his size."

The writer went on to say that "it took no courage at all to murder the mother of two children and a companion, if in fact he was the one who did it. And it took no courage to repeatedly beat and terrorize the same woman, which we know for certain that he did."

It took no courage, however, for him to play football games, other than those required in summoning up his particular skills in that game, which is nothing more than a game, regardless of how society has often painted such games.

O. J. Simpson was blessed with immense athletic skills. He was strong, he was fast, he was shifty. He was one of the most talented running backs ever, combining the swivel hips of Gale Sayers with the torpedo-like thrusts of Jim Brown. Simpson, in full football armor, also had blockers blocking for him. When he was with the Buffalo Bills, Simpson called his offensive linemen "the Electric Company," because "they turn the Juice loose."

But it is not uncommon to equate athletic talent with courage. It is done all the time by those in the game to perpetuate their economic base or aggrandize themselves, by the fans as a form of hero worship, and by the press, wittingly or not. Even one of the best sportswriters ever, Red Smith, once looked back and said he, too, at times, had been guilty of "godding up the players."

Sometimes we are so entranced with skill that we ascribe larger elements to those fortunate enough to have been born with them. We seek to make icons of them. "Like a young god, Hercules—something like that," said Willy Loman, about his son, Biff, a high-school football player, in "Death of a Salesman." "And the sun, the sun all around him. Remember how he waved to me . . . and the cheers when they came out—Loman! Loman! Loman! God Almighty . . . A star like that, magnificent, can never really fade away." But Biff did, disastrously.

When Charles Barkley appeared in a television commercial and said that he didn't want to be looked upon as a role model, for people really didn't know him, he received criticism from some quarters. How dare he! And yet all we know of Barkley, and all we knew of Simpson, is that they were sports stars.

But what and who are sports heroes? Was Mickey Mantle, who hit home runs but didn't look after himself or his family, a hero? Was menacing Giants linebacker Lawrence Taylor, who said he lusted to slam rivals so hard that their snot flew?

David Cone, All-Star pitcher, once told me that what he did wasn't courageous but a father or mother who gets up every morning to go to work to put food on the table for his family is courageous.

People who risk their lives in battle are courageous. During World War II, star baseball players like Hank Greenberg and Bob Feller enlisted in the military, and some, like the little-known Red Sox pitcher Earl (Lefty) Johnson, were awarded a Bronze Star for bravery in European action.

People who risk their lives on a ball field are courageous, as was Jackie Robinson, who braved death threats from those who were against his breaking the color barrier in the majors. Or Pee Wee Reese, who befriended Robinson.

People who overcome great handicaps, who refused to allow the world to tell them something is impossible, are courageous, like Jim Abbott, the one-handed pitcher of the Yankees.

Courage can come in the little moments, such as the time Jesse Barfield saw a female reporter maligned in the clubhouse and, risking a kind of ostracism, befriended her in a casual but powerful way.

Mainly, we must look to qualities beyond the playing field. And athletes can be as worthy of respect here as anyone else. Like Roberto Clemente flying off on a mercy mission to bring food and clothing to people in Central America who had suffered in an earthquake. Or Dave Bing, who has developed a business and has hired numerous minority group workers, far exceeding any accomplishment he has produced in his Hall of Fame basketball career.

If O. J. Simpson were to be admired for a special characteristic, it might have been his rise from ghetto gang leader to a heretofore contributing member of society.

"I remember that at first I hated O. J.," his first wife, Marquerite told me in 1968, when they were first married and he was at USC, "He was a tough, always wanting to fight."

But he changed. Or so we imagined.

After Three Years in Prison, Mike Tyson Gains His Freedom

March 26, 1995

Whether the blue dawn that broke like a thin ribbon across the Indiana horizon this morning was fitting symbolism for Mike Tyson upon his release from the Indiana Youth Center prison, only time and Tyson will be able to determine.

More than 200 reporters and camera crews, along with hundreds of curiosity seekers, some wearing T-shirts that read, "Tyson is Back," waited for hours in the cold and dark outside the low, red-brick administration building here about 18 miles east of Indianapolis to witness the 28-year-old Tyson step into a waiting black limousine after serving three years and six weeks of a six-year sentence for a rape conviction.

Tyson's departure at 6:15 a.m., with his retinue encircling him, was reminiscent of his scenes from the ring, except for the expression on the former champion's face. There was none of the arrogance and swagger so often associated with him, after having mercilessly dispatched an opponent, or on the witness stand at his trial in 1992, haughtily snatching a garment in evidence worn by his accuser, Desiree Washington, then an eighteen-year-old beauty pageant contestant at the Black Expo in Indianapolis and now a fifth-grade student teacher in Pawtucket, Rhode Island.

Followed by Don King, the boxing promoter and Tyson's Svengali, and surrounded by John Horne and Rory Holloway, Tyson's co-managers, and Fruit of Islam bodyguards, Tyson emerged from the doorway of the building. Wearing a dark suit and an crocheted, eggshell Islamic prayer cap, he was shielded from the cameras by a bodyguard who spread open his black leather coat.

Tyson's eyes darted momentarily to take in the spectacle.

On either side of the building were the 10-foot-high barbed wire fences that shown silvery in the wide expanse and many light stanchions of the prison area. Armed guards watched from nearby towers, and faces appeared from behind bars in the lighted windows of tiered cellblocks to observe the scene outside.

From around the country and from such places as Japan and Italy and England and Brazil, several hundred reporters and camera crews, restrained behind the kind of yellow tape familiar in crime or accident scenes, stood in the near-freezing morning amid vans and satellite dishes and glaring television lights to catch a glimpse of Tyson.

Several radio-station helicopters whirred overhead in the still-black sky that was illuminated with a sprinkling of stars and a quarter moon.

Before leaving prison, Tyson filled out the count form, which states that he will not be among the 1,130 prisoners who must be accounted for, and signed a probation form, and is on probation for the next four years. On Monday, he must report to his probation officer in Ohio.

"When I saw him before he left, he said, 'Goodbye, and thanks,' nothing more," said Phil Slavens, assistant superintendent for the prison, who noticed Tyson was reading Ring magazine in his cell.

Tyson did not acknowledge the crowd, but a statement was released that said: "I'm very happy to be out and on my way home. I want to thank everyone for their support. I will have more to say in the future. I'll see you all soon."

The limousine with King, Horne, Holloway, and Monica Turner, a Georgetown medical student whom Slavens said had visited Tyson before, arrived at 5:52 a.m. with members of the Fruit of Islam in a red Lincoln in front of it and a blue Buick in back. When Tyson climbed into the limo and the cars pulled away, there was a chase, some in cars and some on foot. There had been rumors that Tyson would join Muslims in prayer on the lawn of a dance studio across Moon Road from the prison. But that never materialized as the cars kept driving past the location.

Tyson's multicar entourage then sped to the headquarters of the Islamic Society of North America, a mosque about five miles from the prison. Tyson, who is said to have converted to Islam two years ago, was joined in prayers by Muhammad Ali, the former heavyweight champion and covert to Islam, and the rapper Hammer, who is not a Muslim. Tyson has not publicly declared his religious affiliation, though in 1988 he was formally baptized, with the Rev. Jesse Jackson presiding.

He then was flown by private jet from the Indianapolis International Airport to Youngstown-Warren Municipal Airport in Ohio and was driven to his 66-acre farm in Southington, near Youngstown.

Nine months ago, Tyson had attempted to have his prison sentence reduced. In an Indianapolis courthouse in which he was brought in blue prison clothes and handcuffs, Tyson told the judge he had witnessed things that "could totally drive" someone "insane."

Tyson, who once described himself as "the baddest man on the planet," told the court he had changed. "I was young, I was arrogant, I didn't treat people correctly," he said. "I've changed."

But Tyson, or offender No. 92335 in the Indiana Youth Center, wasn't convincing to the judge, Patricia J. Gifford, particularly because he had neglected to attend classes regularly for completion of a high school equivalency program that was part of the rehabilitation program and because, while he said he was "sorry" about the "situation," he never formally apologized to Washington, with whom he maintains he had consensual sex. Gifford ordered the fighter to complete his sentence.

But had he changed? "It seems he's matured," said Slavens. "He seemed at peace with himself."

Tyson would be trading in his 8-foot-by-10 1/2-foot prison cell for his 14-room estate in Southington. And he would be trading in his jobs of cleaning dormitories and handing out equipment in the prison gym, and his $75 every-other-week spending money, for a return to the arena, where fighters are lined up in hopes of exchanging punches with him in his first return fight for what some estimate could be as much as a combined $100 million payday. According to King's boxing director, Al Braverman, his first fight will be in late June or early July, against a ranking but probably not well-known fighter.

It had been a long and circuitous route for Tyson, often spectacular, sometimes tumultuous, invariably finding his way into the headlines for events he got involved in outside of the ring as frequently as in it.

He came from a broken home out of tough Amboy Street in the Brownsville section of Brooklyn, where, he had said, he grew up sometimes mugging old ladies. He was discovered by Cus D'Amato, the old and sometimes eccentric fight trainer, whom Tyson idolized, and who realized the enormous fighting potential of the teen-ager. On November 22, 1986, one year after D'Amato died, Tyson, at age twenty, became the youngest man to win the heavyweight championship, knocking out Trevor Berbick in two rounds.

Tyson entered the ring for his fights in black shorts and black shoes but with no robe or socks, as though so lustful to destroy his opponent he had no time to don the customary apparel.

He knocked out Michael Spinks in 91 seconds of the first round. He battered the former champion Larry Holmes in four rounds.

He was the elemental man, but with a kind of brilliance. He could be ironic, sometimes self-mocking and he was a keen student of pugilism, diligently viewing on film the styles and techniques not only of his opponents but of the great fighters of the past, including his predecessors of the heavyweight crown, from John L. Sullivan to Joe Louis to Ali.

He made an estimated $40 million and lived like a sultan, believing that anything he wanted, whenever he wanted it, was his by the birthright of his swift, menacing fists. His former manager, Bill Cayton, believes he has been "stripped clean" of almost all of his money.

His marriage and divorce to the actress Robin Givens made headlines around the world, and his wild forays, from conviction of fondling a woman in a bar—he was fined $100—to the rape conviction contributed to his notoriety.

And when he lost his title in one of the great upsets in sports history, to a journeyman, a 42–1 underdog named Buster Douglas, in February 1990, it was blamed on his disdain for conditioning. Before he could enter a scheduled fight to try to regain his crown from Evander Holyfield, he was convicted of raping Washington, whom he met as a guest celebrity to the Miss Black America pageant in Indianapolis. He invited her to his hotel room late one night and, because of the charge and conviction, didn't leave Indiana again until this morning.

"Mike Tyson may be the most recognizable person in the world," said Jeff Powell, a reporter for the *London Daily Mail*, and who was among the members of the media at the Indiana prison. "And part of it may be what Teddy Atlas, his former trainer, said: 'There is simply a fascination with Godzilla.'"

"Maybe," Camille Ewart, who had formally adopted Tyson when he lived in Catskill, New York, and trained under D'Amato, said at his sentence-modification hearing last June, "maybe prison will prove to be a good thing for Mike."

All the success, so early, Tyson admitted, was harmful. "It was like it all just dropped from the sky," he had said. "But I've learned."

As the cars pulled away from prison in the growing light of day, people shouted well-wishes after Tyson. Someone, perhaps lost, shouted, "Free the Juice!"

On the grass near the entrance to the prison, Slavens, the assistant prison superintendent, was saying that Tyson had been "a very, very unremarkable prisoner," other than that he would get up to 150 pieces of mail a day. "He had one small problem early on, but that's normal. Otherwise, he followed the rules."

Slavens was asked if he knew where Tyson was now headed.

"No," he said. "All I know is that he is off state property."

* * *

Tyson returned to the ring with mixed results. I caught up with him at the end of April 2002. I traveled to Maui, Hawaii, where Tyson was training to meet Lennox Lewis for the heavyweight championship. Tyson was staying at a beachfront hotel, with his suite at ground level. An interview with Tyson for several reporters, including me, had been arranged. He sat on a couch in a T-shirt, his muscles prominent. We reporters stood around him and asked questions. Sometimes he'd answer questions politely, sometimes with a bullying aspect. At one point he talked about his tough upbringing in a tough neighborhood in Brooklyn, which accounted for his troubles with the law and society in general. "I was a dog guy from the den of iniquity," he said.

I then said, "Your brother Rodney came from the same background but he became a pharmacist and never got into trouble. Shouldn't you take responsibility for your own actions?" Tyson stared hard at me, and eased forward. "You know, I could do anything I want with you," he said in a most threatening manner. "If we were in the slammer I could"— and he characterized a sexual assault—"and you couldn't do anything about it." "Ah, Mike," I said, "I just can't see us crazy in love—so why don't we drop the whole thing?" He smiled a gold-toothed grin, and relaxed back on the couch.

Lewis proved a tougher opponent than I would have been, knocking out Tyson in the eighth round.

Tyson's boxing career ended three years later, in which he compiled a record of 58 bouts, 50 wins, 44 by knockouts. He never regained the title.

The Flowering and Wilting of Pete Rose

On September 11, 1985, at Riverfront Stadium in Cincinnati, before a standing-room only crowd and under a twilight blue sky beribboned with pink clouds in the dusk, Pete Rose, the Reds' player-manager, came to the plate and lined a single into the left field off pitcher Eric Show of the San Diego Padres. It was the 4,192nd hit of Rose's career, and he passed Ty Cobb to break the all-time record of career hits. That was surely a highlight, if not *the* highlight, of Rose's astounding major-league career. But four years later he suffered a stunning fall from grace. Baseball commissioner Bart Giamatti banned him from baseball for gambling on the game. Rose could no longer be a part of an MLB team in any capacity, and, it turned out, he would lose his chance to enter the Baseball Hall of Fame.

In 1991 Rose was convicted of tax evasion for $345,000 in unreported income from personal appearances and selling baseball memorabilia and served a five-month sentence in the Marion, Illinois, federal prison camp, beginning in September of 1990 and ending on a cold, gray early morning on January 7, 1991. I covered it. He came out of the prison gate in jacket and jeans and sneakers and unsmiling. The famous No. 14 on the ball field who had been No. 01832061 in the penitentiary was about to get into an awaiting prison vehicle that would take him to a halfway house in Cincinnati when one of the reporters there shouted out, "How does it feel to be out of jail?" Rose, without changing expression, replied, "Great," and disappeared into the car.

The Meaning of Rose

September 1, 1985

Peter Edward Rose has averaged a little better than three hits every 10 times at bat over his 23-year career. He has maintained nearly that pace for much of this season. At the age of forty-four, an antique in baseball terms, he remains as consistent as a grandfather clock.

If the past is indeed prologue—and if he goes sock the way the clock goes tock—then very soon Rose will be stroking the 4,192nd hit of his career.

It is a career that in regular season play—that is, not counting Grapefruit League games and All-Star Games and playoff and World Series games—has included 13,765 times at bat and something like 25,000 innings played in 3,467 games. And, as he is proud to relate, he has played in more winning games, 1,925 than anyone in history— more winning games even than Joe DiMaggio.

Neither injuries nor slumps nor personal problems nor managing nor Father Time has stayed this dedicated courier from his appointed rounds.

In a swift-paced and not altogether shallow age inspired by television and capped with such as MTV and *Battle of the Network Stars*, when, according to Andy Warhol, everyone will be a celebrity for 15 minutes, Rose's durability and excellence stands out markedly.

When quite young the Reds' player-manager found something he loved—baseball, the hitting of a baseball, the thinking of baseball, the feel, the smell, the sights and the sounds of baseball—and he has stuck with it.

He also had the good fortune to be born bearing some gifts in this area—not an overabundance of physical skills, but just enough, it seems, so that with dedicated labor at his craft he developed it into, what, an art form? Perhaps. If he does not perform an art, then it's a skill that unquestionably provides huge pleasure to millions of people.

As for his motor skills, his hand-eye coordination, never minimize them. After all, he was in the major leagues at age twenty-two in 1963, and rookie of the year. This despite not being able to run fast—he has relatively few stolen bases for his career—but he learned to run well, and still goes from first to third on a hit as well as almost anyone. He couldn't hit far, so he learned to hit to holes, with terrific bat control and studious observation of pitchers. When he played the outfield, it was obvious he didn't have a powerful arm, but he charged all balls so that runners wouldn't presume to take an extra base on him.

Rose's hustle, his tenacity, his concentration, his daring, his resourcefulness, his nearly lustful joy at his occupation, at the job at hand, gives the paying customer his dollar's worth. Not an altogether common happenstance today. There are tailors and shoemakers and plumbers and account executives and bank presidents who cannot say the same.

What drives Rose? One late night, riding in a car, a companion asked him his motivation. "Pride," he said, simply. He said nothing else.

Coming up to the major leagues, and appearing odd to teammates and opponents for the way he ran out everything and ran everywhere, he was derisively called Hot Dog, and was fairly unpopular. He remained undaunted, remained his own man comfortable within himself and his style. And over the years a new nickname took hold, one which would reflect the respect for the only man who started at five different positions in all-star games—he played where his team needed him, and did it without remonstration. That new nickname was Charlie Hustle.

Rose is narrowly focused, and makes no apologies. "I don't talk when I'm sitting with people about the stock market or physics or stuff like that, but I listen," he said. "When they want to talk about baseball, or sports, then I'll contribute. I'll never put my foot in my mouth talking about those things."

He embraces baseball. In the famous, exciting and beautiful sixth game of the 1975 World Series, Rose at one late point turned to the Red Sox catcher, Carlton Fisk, and said, "Isn't it a thrill just to be playing in a game like this?"

If one play characterizes Rose, beyond the sliding face first into second base, or snapping his glove decisively as he catches a throw, or running home with his cap in the dust and his longish, grayish hair flying in the wind, or even his widely controversial collisions in crucial moments at second base and home plate, it would be the play on the foul ball in the 1980 World Series.

He was with the Phillies then and Frank White of the Royals popped one up high near the dugout. The catcher, Bob Boone, clanking like a knight in his armor, hurried to catch it. The ball eventually dropped from the heavens, hit Boone's waiting glove and then bounced off. But just before the ball hit the ground, Pete Rose, the first baseman, suddenly materialized, snared it for the out.

It caught fans and players by surprise. The play was so starkly simple in its beauty, in its execution, and so unexpected. But it demonstrated the essence of the ardent Pete Rose—he leaves little to chance.

Years later, recalling that moment, Rose seemed less than impressed with himself. What was I supposed to do, he said in his direct manner and in so many words, stand at first base with my thumb curiously nestled?

Another moment: Recently, Rose was kneeling at the batting cage alongside Shawon Dunston, the twenty-two-year-old rookie shortstop for the Cubs. Dunston, highly publicized and under pressure, has been a disappointment. The rookie had now sought out the veteran. They chatted for some time.

What did Rose say? Dunston was asked. "Have fun," said Dunston. Meanwhile, Rose slugs on.

"Some people think I'm actually going to stop playing when I get the record," said Rose. "Hell, I wouldn't think of it. This is my business. I keep going. Who knows? The day after I get the record, I might get four hits."

Pete Rose Waits to Hear the Verdict

March 25, 1989 / Plant City, Florida

The ancient Greeks had a saying that until a man is dead, do not yet call him happy, call him lucky. I thought about this in relation to Pete Rose, and how happy he had seemed.

No man appeared more possessed of what he was about than Pete Rose. He had baseball, and that's all, essentially, he seemed to need.

He was Charlie Hustle. He ran to first base on a walk, as if he couldn't wait to get there. He didn't slide into a base, he dived for it. He didn't catch a ball in the outfield, he snatched it. And at the plate, in that low crouch, he waited to hit the ball with, as Red Smith described it, "an almost lascivious enthusiasm."

"Pete Rose has a twelve-year-old heart in a eighty-eight-year-old man's body," Tug McGraw observed about ten years ago.

"I'd go through hell in a gasoline suit to play baseball," Rose had said.

Then one day in August 1986, hitting only .219, and after twenty-four years in the big leagues with a .303 lifetime average, and having played more games than anyone in history, and batted more times than anyone, and hit more hits than anyone, he stopped playing.

He was the manager of the Reds, and he never again put Pete Rose's name on the lineup card, never again asked him to pinch-hit.

Yet Rose still has never announced his retirement. It's as if he couldn't bear it, as if that twelve-year-old heart still holds out the possibility that one day he'll crack the lineup again.

He still had baseball, however. As manager, he was still in uniform, still in knickered pants, still wearing that funny baseball cap with the button on top and the bill that shielded the eyes from the sun, even during night games.

Now, though, something has changed. His banter, his joking sound not, as in the past, to come from the heart. Pete Rose, while he sat the other day on a dugout bench in Plant City, Florida, the home of the Cincinnati Reds in spring training, was different from any time in memory. Despite a brave front, the look in his eyes is that of a man who has been deeply shaken, who is frightened.

The office of the baseball commissioner has been carrying on for a few months a "full investigation into serious allegations" concerning Pete Rose and gambling. In the current issue of *Sports Illustrated*, a source is quoted as saying that Rose, while in the dugout during a game, would give hand signals for betting purposes to a friend in the stands.

Other reports say that Rose, who admittedly bet fairly heavily on horse and dog racing, owes bookmakers $500,000 to $750,000.

His first wife, Karolyn, was recently quoted in a magazine as saying that Rose had once received a dead fish in the mail, apparently from a bookie threatening Rose if he didn't pay his debt. She later denied the quote.

Rose is supposed to have sold his red Corvette, a gift from the team owner, Marge Schott, that bore the license plate PR4192, emblematic of Rose's breaking Ty Cobb's career base hit record of 4,191.

And Rose, who has made millions from baseball, is supposed to have taken out a second mortgage for $150,000 on his home in Cincinnati.

Rose's den at home has been filled pridefully with his extensive baseball memorabilia. So it was stunning to hear his reply when someone asked whether it was true that he had sold the showcase items, the bat and ball with which he broke Cobb's record. The sale price was said to be $175,000. "No comment," said Rose.

And it was "No comment" on whether he bet on baseball games.

"It's not true," said John Franco, the Reds' ace relief pitcher. "It's just a bunch of hearsay coming from the media."

"It's coming from the commissioner's office," he was reminded.

Franco grunted. "It's not true," he said again. For a moment he sounded like the boy calling to Shoeless Joe Jackson after the news that the White Sox star was one of those named in the throwing of the 1919 World Series: "Say it ain't so, Joe."

Few know the facts. Did Rose have serious gambling debts? And did they cause him to gamble on baseball, or give gamblers information about baseball?

If such things can be proved, then Rose could be suspended from baseball for one year or life. "It would kill him, if they took baseball away from him," said Karolyn Rose.

Only Pete Rose knows the full depth of his gambling involvement and compulsion, though he may not know fully what the commissioner has in his files. An announcement is expected soon, and rightly should be, since justice delayed is justice denied.

Meanwhile, Pete Rose, with eyes no longer laughing, sits in the dugout and waits, like the rest of us, to hear.

* * *

On August 25, 1989, commissioner Giamatti held a news conference in which he read his decision to ban Rose. Giamatti's opening sentences told the story: "The banishment for life of Pete Rose from baseball is the sad end of a sorry episode. One of the game's greatest players has engaged in a variety of acts which have stained the game, and he must now live with the consequences of those acts." A corollary to the banishment was what I viewed as an unfair consequence regarding Rose's deserved eligibility into the Baseball Hall of Fame in Cooperstown.

The Thumb in Baseball's Hall of Fame

February 4, 1991

Thumbs will surely go down today in the meeting room of the board of directors of the Baseball Hall of Fame, and bury the hopes of Pete Rose. The board has gathered to act on the recommendation by a special committee that anyone (read that "Rose") who is on baseball's permanently ineligible list be ineligible for the Hall of Fame.

The Hall of Fame group seems dead set against the likes of Rose appearing on the ballot, on which, under normal circumstances, he would have been included for the first time in December.

The controversy, a purely subjective and at core a simplistic issue, concerns a group of people voting to supposedly deify baseball players. Nonetheless, the Rose case has touched the ethics, morals, emotions, and logic of a surprisingly large segment of the national populace, some of whom don't have the slightest interest in ball games.

Much of the focus involves the whole point of a Hall of Fame. Is it a place to honor only the performance on the field of great ballplayers? Or is it to honor great ballplayers who were good citizens as well?

Thumbs-downers say, Since Rose was banished from baseball for allegedly gambling on games and possibly on his own team, he should not be allowed to hang in the shrine.

Thumbs-uppers, like me, say, Let Rose be banished from further participation in baseball, but his activities off the field have nothing to do with his play on the field.

Thumbs-downers say, Well, when he was a manager, he might have influenced games by his use of pitchers.

Rose, however, had been considered for the Hall of Fame strictly as a player, not as a manager. Was it then his bad luck that after his playing days he got a job in which he remained in uniform? Had he become a plumber or a lawyer, say, after he hung up his spikes, and was found gambling, he would most likely not be in the pickle he now finds himself.

But, it is rightly contended, there was a brief overlap in his 24-year playing career when he was a player-manager.

Yes, but nowhere has Rose ever been accused of throwing a game or trying as a player to do anything but his best to win. He was incontestably (at this writing, anyway) Charlie Hustle to the end, and the man who got more base hits than anyone else in the history of the game.

Well, there's a clause on the ballot that says "character, integrity, sportsmanship and contributions to the game" must be considered.

It is not spelled out whether this means on-the-field only, or on-the-field and off-the-field both. If it means both, then of course a number of bad actors who were great pitchers and hitters should be thrown out. And if it means good players who were outstanding citizens, then some like Dr. Bobby Brown, or Saul Rogovin, the pitcher-turned-school teacher, should be in. If it means on-the-field only, then no one played with more character, integrity or sportsmanship than Rose (some of his severest criticism leveled at him, in fact, was that he played too hard—even in an exhibition like an All-Star Game). As for "contributions to the game," Pete Rose, according to one of the latest electees, Rod Carew, "is baseball."

OK, but Rose knew the rules, posted on the clubhouse doors, which say No Gambling.

But there are separate entities. Nowhere on those rules does it say, "And if you gamble, then you will not be eligible for the Hall of Fame." It just says you are subject to suspension or banishment.

But precedent of the Black Sox players established that those deeply involved in gambling would not only be thrown out of baseball, but made ineligible for the Hall of Fame.

The Black Sox players, it happened, weren't thrown out because they gambled. Their crime was fixing the 1919 World Series games for gamblers. They did it for the payoffs, and played dishonestly, or accepted the gamblers' money to play dishonestly. There was, again, no taint whatsoever of that with Rose.

Some half-thumbs-downers say, Then put on Rose's plaque in the Hall that he was banished.

If we included negatives, then, in spite of the romance of the hall, perhaps traits ranging from immoral behavior to striking out should be mentioned on other players' plaques.

Some half-thumbs-downers say, But it would be embarrassing to have Rose honored at the Hall of Fame ceremonies.

The Hall of Fame is an honor, but an honor achieved purely through sweat on the field. At the ceremony, one may ask instead of applaud.

Others say, If Rose is elected, it shouldn't be on the first ballot.

This is conceivably to make Rose suffer because he has been bad. But if one is good enough to be in the Hall of Fame, he should be good enough to be elected on the first ballot. For too many years, a majority of electors felt that no one should be chosen on the first ballot. Joe DiMaggio, for example, was not elected on the first ballot. It was unjust then and it's unjust now.

* * *

Pete Rose has spent the latter part of his life living in Las Vegas, and working in a store in a hotel there signing autographs for a price. For years on end he would travel to Cooperstown on induction weekend and sit in front of a sporting goods store and sign autographs, still on the outside looking in.

Part III: In Troubled Waters

Tonya Harding: Did She or Didn't She?

On the late morning of January 6, 1994, twenty-four-year-old Nancy Kerrigan, sometimes called "The Snow Queen" for her clean-cut demeanor, finished her work out on the ice of the Cobo Arena in Detroit. She was preparing to compete the next day in the US Figure Skating Championships, where, it was anticipated, her major rival would be Tonya Harding, then twenty-three, who even described herself as "rough-hewn," and with a hardscrabble background that gave her an aura of being "from the other side of the tracks," and whose skating style was more muscular than Kerrigan's regal. They would also be vying for spots on the Olympic team for the Olympic Games scheduled in about six weeks in Lillehammer, Norway.

The two had competed numerous times against each other, with Kerrigan often coming out on top, as she had in the 1992 Olympics with Kerrigan earning a bronze for third place, and Harding finishing fourth. Two skaters would be picked. A fourth-place showing would, of course, eliminate that skater, whomever it would be. Michelle Kwan was considered competitive for a spot, but Kerrigan seemed the surest bet.

Harding had completed her warmups that day and was elsewhere taking a nap. Kerrigan, in white skating dress, white ribbon in her hair and white skates, came off the ice and went through a blue curtain on the way to the dressing room when suddenly a beefy man with what was described as a police baton clubbed her in the right knee, as she screamed in pain and moaned "Why? Why?" It was dubbed "The Whack Heard Round the World."

It would soon be discovered that a plot by Harding's ex-husband, Jeff Gillooly and her bodyguard, Shawn Eckardt, had been hatched to try to dispense with Harding's arch rival. Some two weeks later, with the FBI working on anonymous tips, Gillooly and Eckardt confessed, with Eckardt determined as the assailant.

Harding, to be sure, was a suspect. She proclaimed her innocence in the plot but public reaction to her was swift and abundantly suspicious. In a national Harris Poll taken around that time the result was expressed in the headline "2-to-1 Majority Say US Olympic Committee Should Not Let Tonya Harding Skate in Lillehammer."

Two of the conclusions: "By 61–31 percent, most people believe that Tonya Harding should not be allowed by the US Olympic Committee to represent the country at the Winter Olympics." And: "Only 16 percent of all adults believe that Tonya Harding did not know in advance of the plan to attack Nancy Kerrigan. Almost three-quarters of the public (72 percent) believe she did know. The replies of men and women to this question were very similar."

I believe that sports commentators around the country were even more strongly convinced that Harding was a participant in the crime, and should not represent the US at the Olympics. I took a different view, one that landed me on numerous radio and television programs, often debating another sportswriter. One, *Face the Nation*, with moderator Bob Schieffer, had me head-to-head against *Sports Illustrated*'s esteemed Frank Deford, who had said on his NPR radio show that Harding had been "convicted of arranging the assault," which she had not been.

Is the Case For Harding Open-Shut?

January 28, 1994

This is a true story: In January 1957 there was a terrible murder in Chicago. Two teenage sisters, Barbara and Patricia Grimes, were found in a culvert in a park, their nude bodies frozen. A citywide search for the killer or killers was begun. Headlines screamed as suspects were rounded up. People were in panic. Who committed this dastardly deed, and why?

Finally, a twenty-one-year-old Skid Row illiterate bum and sometime dishwasher named Benny Bedwell, who wore long sideburns like Elvis Presley, was arrested. "We got our man!" the sheriff gloated. Bedwell denied the charge but after more questioning, he confessed: "Yes, I murdered the girls."

He said, among other things, that he had taken them out the night of the crime and fed them hot dogs. The coroner wondered about this, because there was no trace of hot dogs in their systems. Witnesses said Bedwell was at such and such a place when the murders were supposed to have occurred miles away.

Soon after, a chagrined police department released Benny Bedwell from custody. Bedwell later made another confession: that he had said he committed the murders because, a lonely and forgotten man, he relished the attention.

I've never forgotten this. I was seventeen at the time and, like almost everyone else in Chicago, I had been convinced without a doubt that Bedwell had done it. It was a powerful lesson: something that seems black and white just may not be so. One must wait until all the facts are established.

I remember an old movie, *12 Angry Men*, in which 12 jurors are sequestered to decide what appears to be an open-and-shut case. A

Hispanic youth is charged with murder. There are witnesses. Eleven jurors know that he did it, and want to hurry home and finish this business. One juror, Henry Fonda, has questions. One by one they all begin to have questions. Turns out the kid did not commit the crime.

That was fiction, though it apparently was based on fact. As for current facts: a prosecutor in California said he had an open-and-shut case regarding the Menendez brothers in the confessed killing of their parents. Turns out two separate juries did not convict on murder, but were, as the foremen said, "hopelessly deadlocked."

There were shocking decisions to many in the Yankel Rosenbaum murder trial in Brooklyn, the first Rodney King trial, the Lorena Bobbitt trial, the William Kennedy Smith case, to name a few. Now, on a different level, but one that has captured the imagination of the country, we have another case, one that, to many, appears open-and-shut: Tonya Harding knew about the plot to knock out Nancy Kerrigan, her chief rival, from the figure-skating national championships.

How do we know this? Well, for one thing, her former husband and live-in mate, Jeff Gillooly, said so. While accepting a plea bargain for a single charge of racketeering, Gillooly admitted to "intent to commit perjury." He also admitted lying to authorities. And he admitted all this for several reasons, one of which, to quote a Chicago trial lawyer named Barry Holt, was to "sing for his supper." The maximum punishment for racketeering in Oregon, as Judge Donald H. Londer told Gillooly in the Portland courtroom, is twenty years and $300,000; he agreed to two years and $100,000. So how credible is Gillooly?

Harding, meanwhile, in the face of a national barrage against her, including much of the press and public opinion, has also admitted "not telling the whole truth" when first interrogated by authorities. First she said she knew nothing of the attack, but later said she found out about it several days after the assault (but didn't come forward for fear of reprisal by Gillooly, whom she said was a wife-beater, and Gillooly's family).

In Oregon, failure to report a crime is not a crime in itself. And while, as some say, this may not be "good sportsmanship" it should hardly be enough to keep her from skating in the Olympics, where integrity is of such a high level that many believe Harding, regardless of how well she skated, could never at this point get a fair shake from the judges.

Nor, at this point, should all the hearsay and circumstantial evidence and statements by Gillooly and his gang (statements from a co-conspirator do not necessarily carry the same weight as from an independent, uninvolved witness). Harding has maintained her innocence in the assault plot. She has rebutted all the testimony. She has not been indicted or convicted.

The American legal principle of innocent until proved guilty, while obviously tiresome to many, remains fundamental. And if the United States Olympic Committee members truly represent American values, then they cannot turn their backs on it.

* * *

I had traveled to Lillehammer to cover the Olympics and, to be sure, was, like so many of my colleagues, drawn to the events involving women's figure skating. On February. 16, as the drama built, I wrote the following:

The Judge Can't Be The Czar

February 16, 1994

As Tonya Harding prepares to arrive in this favored land of frozen fjords, reindeer salami, and people bundled and masked like burglars against the cold, there will be included in her baggage, on paper or in her head, Circuit Court Judge Patrick D. Gilroy's Judgment of Dismissal issued last Saturday afternoon in Clackamas County, Oregon.

It is her ticket to skate in the Winter Olympics. But with it comes further evidence that a new world is dawning in sports, and that athletes in the United States—and perhaps those under international governing bodies, as well—may be assured they will be treated fairly, subject to the same democratic laws and judgments as anyone else. Sports, in other words, are not above the law. Not even the Olympics.

The days may be dwindling when athletes are treated arbitrarily, when, say, a swimmer may be dismissed from the Olympic team by an imperious sports czar for drinking champagne on a ship, or a sprinter banned for a positive drug test that he asserts was a laboratory error.

The United States Olympic Committee had leveled seven administrative charges against Harding regarding sportsmanship and ethical code violations and had scheduled a hearing on her participation in the Olympics. She responded with a lawsuit against the USOC. In helping to settle the dispute, Judge Gilroy acknowledged that the case was "difficult."

"The USOC has the right and obligation to oversee and discipline certain conduct of its Olympic athletes," he said. But, he added, "Tonya Harding has the right to a fair and impartial hearing regarding claimed ethical violations and the right to prepare adequately for same."

It seems apparent that the judge did not want to upset altogether the ability of sports groups to sanction athletes for, say, using an improper sled. But when the matter is larger, infringing on true due process, or the principle that one is innocent until proved guilty, then it must answer, as they say in the Hebrew National frankfurter commercials, to a higher authority. In this case, the courts. The sense of it was that the USOC, acting as judge and jury, with conceivably private agendas, could not necessarily be expected to administer "a fair and impartial hearing."

Some of the reasoning behind this is that sports such as the Olympics are now beyond games. The Olympics are big business, from the host cities and nations standing to profit by millions of dollars, to manufacturers' logos on athletes' uniforms, to the inclusion of uncontested professional athletes, to those who may dream of making a fortune from their gold medals.

"I don't know if there is such a thing as a true amateur anymore," said Albert Grimaldi, the bobsledder otherwise known as the Prince of Monaco, and a member of the board of the International Olympic Committee. "Most of us at this level train as hard and as long as any professionals." And many reap the financial rewards. "I didn't know there was real money in skating until a few years ago when I started getting endorsements," said Nancy Kerrigan. "I had just thought that the only money I'd ever make from skating was to teach it."

With this comes a yearning for fair treatment by athletes. When Vegard Ulvang, the Norwegian cross-country skier and a triple Olympic gold-medal winner, recently criticized the IOC as "undemocratic," it drew assent from many other athletes. One day, if dissatisfaction increases, Olympic athletes might go on strike, like coal miners, or even ballplayers.

The USOC officially stated that it compromised on the Harding issue because it was drawing too much attention from the Games.

It compromised, in fact, because it understood that Butch Reynolds, the aggrieved sprinter, won a judgment against the International Amateur Athletic Federation of $27 million in a Federal court in 1992.

It compromised because its "sportsmanship" code was seemingly too vague to stand up in an impartial hearing. Harding has not been charged with a crime and has denied having prior knowledge of the vicious attack on Kerrigan on January 6. While Harding admitted learning a few days after the attack that her former husband, Jeff Gillooly, and several of his associates had been involved in it, she also contends she didn't come forward immediately because he had threatened her life, which police records state he had done in 1991.

Could the USOC hearing board say to her summarily: Sorry but you're disqualified because the Olympic skating competition is more important than your alleged fear for your life?

Maybe. Which is why a court had to help settle the dispute. And which is why courts may play an ever-greater role in the world of sports.

* * *

And as the competition for women's figure skating drew ever closer, the drama continued to build.

An Angry Kerrigan Emerges

February 25, 1994 / Lillehamer, Norway

It began serenely. Nancy Kerrigan commenced her training session in the Olympic Amphitheater yesterday afternoon, skating in black leotard and with a dark, dancing ponytail to a Neil Diamond medley. It is the background music, and the skating routine, she will use tonight, a night in which she can win the Olympic gold medal. Just her being here seemed beyond imagination to many just seven weeks ago, when she was stalked and clubbed on the knee with a metal baton.

Now she spun, she soared, she floated, and received polite applause from the scattering of onlookers. She smiled, but it was hardly a genial smile. Kerrigan, in first place following the first of the two-day competition, appeared to be saying that she meant business.

On the ice with her were the other five top finishers from Wednesday's short program. They would stay on the periphery until their turn to skate their routines.

As Kerrigan's flashing blades swept her smoothly across the oval, someone suddenly screamed. Everyone stopped, except Kerrigan.

At the side of the rink, two skaters had collapsed. Oksana Baiul of Ukraine and Tanja Szewczenko of Germany moaned, the German doubled over and holding her stomach. It was quickly understood what had happened. The two, warming up and skating backward, had collided. Katarina Witt swiftly skated over to offer assistance. Surya Bonaly and Lu Chen stood nearby, frozen.

Kerrigan, glancing over her shoulder for a moment, took it in and sailed into the next part of her routine—a spiral, her trademark, in which she spins like a blender.

While Baiul left the ice on her own power, Szewczenko had to be helped by her doctor and coach. Strikingly, Kerrigan kept on.

"The routine was perfect," said Ben Wright. "Her concentration was unswerving." Wright is a retired figure-skating judge and referee who had worked nine straight Olympics until this one. "If she skates like this tomorrow, she'll win the gold."

Wright is from Boston, where he has observed Kerrigan since, he said, "she was a child."

"I see a resolve, a fortitude in her that I have never seen before," he said. "You can see the determination in her eyes. She has really matured, and I think it's been mainly since the incident."

When Kerrigan was clubbed, there were pictures of her slumping to the floor, crying, "Why? Why me?" This refrain echoed through the weeks and gave to some degree the sense that Kerrigan was a helpless victim. She has proved anything but that.

Under pressure that would have daunted a lesser athlete, perhaps a lesser person, Kerrigan executed a near-perfect routine Wednesday, closer to perfection than any of her rivals, including her lone American teammate, the lady in red, Tonya Harding, who is in 10th place. As the world knows, Harding's former husband, Jeff Gillooly, confessed to having planned the attack. He also accused Harding of complicity and giving the go-ahead to the plan to eliminate her main rival. Harding denied it and has not been charged.

Kerrigan, meanwhile, has never spoken negatively about Harding in public, though it is clear she possesses something less than love for her. Kerrigan has demonstrated, too, that she is no fragile, trembling Snow White on skates.

"The attack made Nancy mad," Evy Scotvold, her coach, said after practice. "She was angry that someone prevented her from defending her national title. And she's angry that someone tried to keep her from the Olympics. It was like someone was trying to rob her of these things."

After the clubbing, he said, Kerrigan wasn't sure how well she would heal, if she would be able to skate again, or well enough to satisfy the United States Olympic Committee. "She became impassioned," said Scotvold. "She started training harder than I have ever seen her. She knows what to do and how to do it. She's digging in."

Kerrigan has had a reputation for folding after the first day's competition, for losing focus, for lack of confidence—a fear of failure.

"What she did Wednesday gives her the knowledge that she can do the same in the long program," he said. "She's confident."

If Kerrigan had withdrawn into herself after the attack, saying she had lost heart, it would have been understandable. Monica Seles, who was stabbed in a maniacal attack, has been unable to return to competition. The mental trauma, more than the physical, is the barrier.

But regardless of how she skates tonight, Nancy Kerrigan has already performed remarkably, on and off the ice. The lady is a champ.

* * *

And the following day, the unexpected and inexplicable took place.

Harding, In Finale, Comes Up A Lace Shy

February 26, 1994

On the big, black scoreboard at one end of the Olympic Amphitheater tonight the following message appeared:

On the Ice: Tonya Harding USA

But on the ice, there was no Tonya Harding. There was no one at all. Harding was supposed to have been performing in the long program of the women's figure skating competition in the Winter Olympics. And the 6,000 or so spectators, a good number of them waving American flags, looked at each other, and some began the familiar rhythmic, impatient clap. The Harding saga continued, the mystery thickened.

But the reason was hardly the stuff of riveting plots.

"My lace broke," she explained later. "I cut it on the warmup, and then it broke as soon as I got off. I went to try and tighten it and it broke."

She and her coach, Diane Rawlinson, hurriedly sought another lace. "It was too small, but I tried to go out and skate with it anyway," Harding said. "I only had two minutes to get out there before I would be disqualified. So I just laced it as best as I could and went out there."

Plea to the Judges

So with only six seconds remaining before disqualification, Harding skated out, in burgundy costume with choker and rhinestones, to a chorus of mostly cheers. With that Pete Rose–like stocky, pugnacious aura, she went into her routine and at the first leap and whirl, a triple lutz, she didn't complete it. At this point, she broke the agenda and skated listlessly and in tears.

"I knew that if I was going to skate like that it was going to be very risky," she later explained, alluding to the short lace. "I could break my ankle easily. As soon as I did the triple lutz, I went to try it and there was nothing there. There was no support whatsoever. I just knew that I had to stop."

She skated over to the judges' tables and threw her leg up on the railing at the referee and pointed to her skate.

She began a tearful plea, explaining what appeared to be a tortured tale of her white skating boot with gold blade.

The skating judges huddled. Then came the announcement: Harding would be allowed to fix her skate and would perform again five skaters later.

Script Writer's Dream

If Harding were writing a script for a made-for-television movie based on her life, then her dramatic imagination was working overtime. After all, it seemed she needed a more compelling denouement than just coming in 10th, as she had, in Wednesday's technical program, virtually eliminating her from medal contention.

She returned later, with a longer lace. None of this was known by the crowd, which greeted her with some derisive whistles but mostly gentle applause.

But now she nailed the triple lutz that she had missed the first time around. And, despite a mistake or two, she completed her program in reasonably strong fashion. She smiled at the conclusion, and, with what appeared as much relief as exhilaration, held her hands together and threw the crowd a kiss.

Her scores were decent, and though it put her in second place at the time, the best six skaters, from Nancy Kerrigan and Oksana Baiul to Katarina Witt, were still to come. She would eventually drop to eighth overall in the competition .

"I got out there and left my problems behind," she said later. "I did the best under all the circumstances because I think I was ready to have a nervous breakdown before I went out the first time."

Her experience at the Olympics, she said, "was definitely worth it." She added, "I was really happy that at least one of my dreams came true, that I was able to be here. And if I didn't win a medal, that's OK."

She said that she had never given up, even though her connection to the clubbing attack on Kerrigan made her own participation here uncertain until the eve of the Games. Harding's former husband has pleaded guilty to one count of racketeering for his involvement in planning the attack. Harding has not been charged and maintains she had no advance knowledge of the assault.

"I'm not a quitter," she said. "I knew that if I went out and did my all, that there would be a possibility of getting a medal. My figure skating career is not over. I'm far from finished from figure skating and I want to be back for the next Olympics.

About Kerrigan, she said: "I'm really glad Nancy skated great. I hope she did it not only for herself but for her country and our team."

Did the pressure from the continuing criminal investigation affect her?

"I'm not going to answer that," she said.

As is the custom at these events for skaters, bouquets of flowers, about 30, a generous offering, were thrown onto the ice at the conclusion of Harding's performance. And then she skated off.

* * *

Gillooly pleaded guilty to racketeering in exchange for a 24-month sentence. Eckardt, and two other accomplices, Derrick Smith and Eugene Stant, friends of Eckhardt pleaded guilty to conspiracy to commit second-degree assault and began 18-month prison sentences. In March, Harding pleaded guilty to conspiracy to hinder prosecution. A judge placed her on probation for three years and ordered her to pay

$150,000 in fines. She also agreed to resign from the US Figure Skating Association.

In 2017, a major Hollywood film, *I, Tonya*, starring Margot Robbie as Tonya Harding, was released to generally critical acclaim, though some criticized it as being too sympathetic to Harding. Allison Janney, playing Harding's acerbic mother, LaVona Golden, won an Oscar for Best Supporting Actress. Harding went back home to Portland, Oregon, married for a third time, had a son, and tried a variety of pursuits to earn a living including singing, acting and a short stint in professional women's boxing. She also managed a wrestler, attempted a skating comeback as a professional, and drove into a ditch and served 10 days after failing a field sobriety test. Kerrigan married her manager, Jerry Solomon, and following the '94 Olympics went on tour, starring in "Champions on Ice" and "Broadway on Ice." In 2004 she was inducted into the US Figure Skating Hall of Fame, an honor denied Harding.

To this day, there has never been a scintilla of hard evidence that Tonya Harding was complicit in arranging the crime of clubbing Nancy Kerrigan.

At the '94 Olympics, one of the most heart-rending moments occurred when the former two-time gold-medal winning figure skater Katarina Witt, now twenty-eight years old—rather past her prime in skating terms—skated in the free skate (long) program to the recording, "Where Have All the Flowers Gone," the song an homage to now war-torn Sarajevo where, eight years earlier, she had won her first gold. That April, I had dinner with Witt for a *Times* feature story.

* * *

At the 1994 Olympics Katarina Witt, in her figure-skating routine to the song "Where Have All the Flowers Gone?" reminded us of the ongoing war in Eastern Europe.

Katarina Witt: Firepower Off the Ice

April 20, 1994

The moment arrived during dinner at our table for two when I looked across to Katarina Witt and said, "Katarina, tell me, what kind of man do you like?"

The figure skater, who has captivated judges and spectators alike with her both sizzling and poignant programs, met my eyes.

"Someone who I can steal horses with," she said.

Steal horses?

"It is a German expression," she explained. "Someone you can share everything with, that you can share all sides with. Someone that is honest, trustworthy, funny—a little bit of everything. He doesn't have to be handsome, doesn't have to be macho man. I hate macho man. I like a man who has weakness, who can cry. Men are taught not to cry. It is so stupid."

We had finished the main course at the Union Square Cafe—she had salmon, having decided against tuna since the nets that tuna fishermen use often snare dolphins. It is a problem that concerns her.

During dinner, other patrons walked by, looked, and then whispered to one another. Discreetly, a couple at another table stole glances. "Are you often recognized on the street?" she was asked.

"Not always," she said. "I mean, I don't walk around with my skates."

Her tartness is softened with a smile. At one point, a couple came over and the woman politely said: "We were happy to see you in the Olympics, Katarina—you did so well. Would you sign our napkin?" Obliging, Ms. Witt said, "Thank you."

Ms. Witt said that she especially enjoyed women showing appreciation for her skating. "Too many times women try to be competitive with each other," she said. "We should help support each other, rather than try to be better than each other."

She took a sip of her cappuccino. Her brown hair was pulled back into a ponytail. Her eyes are direct, her laugh quick and full, and there also lurks the substance of a highly competitive athlete—she has won four world figure-skating championships and two Olympic gold medals—and a woman confident in handling herself. She wore a black turtleneck sweater with a bright Versace vest of purple and green and yellow and red, and black designer jeans.

Ms. Witt was in New York between stops of the skating show Stars on Ice, in which she performs. But she is still buoyed from her achievement at the Winter Olympics in Lillehammer, Norway, in February.

Her performance in Lillehammer was unlike her presentations in previous Olympics. In Calgary in 1988, she skated to "Carmen" and, she admitted, "flirted my way through the program." On the ice in Lillehammer she exuded a different kind of passion when she skated to the anti-war song "Where Have All the Flowers Gone?" in the freestyle program.

Ms. Witt, at twenty-eight, is the virtual grande dame of the sport. Her stature seemed illuminated in a practice session in Lillehammer when two sixteen-year-old skaters, Oksana Baiul and Tanja Szewczenko, collided, and Ms. Witt hurried over to help. "I picked them up," she said, "and they were light as feathers."

In the technical program in the Lillehammer Olympics, she skated in what was for her an unusual guise. "I wore the Robin Hood—like a man's costume—because I didn't want to be accused of seducing the judges this time," she said. "And I like the Robin Hood character. So I wore an outfit up to my neck." She paused and, with a paradoxical smile, added: "But I think that leaves more to the imagination. Sexier than cleavage, no?"

But the freestyle program was different. Ms. Witt was the last skater to appear on the program. In her blood-red costume, before the 6,000 spectators in the arena and millions more watching on television,

Ms. Witt delivered what she called her "message of peace" for war-torn Sarajevo.

It was in 1984 in Sarajevo, then a pretty, gaily bannered town, that Ms. Witt, as an 18-year-old East German, won her first Olympic gold medal. "Now when you see the pictures on television of the people killed there, and houses bombed and children crying in pain, it breaks your heart," she said. "I wanted to say something about this. Send some message."

She had worked diligently for that opportunity in Lillehammer. "I did all those boring jumps in practice, week after week, over and over and over again," she said. "It was very hard on my body."

She knew she couldn't skate with the athleticism of some of the younger competitors. "It is a new generation of skaters," she said.

She believed, though, she could compete from an artistic standpoint. And while she felt she had little chance for a medal, she was skating, she said, for a "bigger purpose."

Though skating with customary grace, she missed the triple loop when her hand touched the ice, and turned her triple salchow into a double. When finished, she turned to the crowd with a wan smile. She spoke the words, "I am sorry." She felt she had failed. But the crowd thought otherwise; they were cheering.

"The whole building was clapping," she said. "I thought, 'Oh my God, they all understood what I wanted to say.'" She finished seventh in the competition, but was grateful for having achieved a goal.

She had come a long way from the grimness of Communist East Germany, and the sudden changes in her life precipitated by the collapse of the Berlin Wall and the end of Communism in East Germany in 1989. She had made the transition from the ice princess whom the Stasi, the East German secret police, monitored closely, to the "older, more mature" woman who now lives "spontaneously," and with, she says, "bewusst."

"*Bewusst* is a German word, I don't know how you translate, but it is living with a full mind, that you are aware of the moment and enjoying it," she said. "When I was younger, I thought of winning the competition and going on to another. I did not fully appreciate the experiences. But when I skated in Lillehammer, I wanted to be conscious of everything I was doing, and soak it in."

For all her accomplishments, some in Germany believe that she was once a spy, some a Communist apologist, some a seeker of faded glories.

"One day my father calls me in my apartment in Berlin," Ms. Witt said, "and he says, 'Katarina, did you see the newspaper this morning?' I said no. He said, 'It says you were a spy for the Stasi.' Never! I was followed constantly. They even bugged my hotel room, and in a report, said that I had sex with an American from 9 to 9:07. I was just talking with the man in English, but people who were monitoring this didn't speak English, didn't know what to report. So they said sex. I laughed when I heard this. It was so stupid. But they had contacted me to spy. I said, 'I am no spy, I am a skater.'"

Her privileged position in East Germany sometimes resulted in her being sniped at and booed in the West. "Some said I defended the old way because I had had special advantages," she said. "Sometimes I even now feel like a stranger in my country. But I knew there would be problems because I had seen the world as a skater. And now? A lot of people in eastern Germany have lost jobs, rents went up, food costs went up, unemployment went to 20 percent. Freedom is good, but it is not easy."

At the Olympics in Lillehammer, Ms. Witt had an opportunity to observe the other skaters. About Nancy Kerrigan, she said: "She needs to learn a lot. She's now a celebrity, not just a skater. She's stepping out of sports, and she meets the yellow press, who haven't followed the sport. It happened to me. They don't know me totally like the sports writers, and don't respect what you have done. They don't look at you so much as a skater, but as a person."

Ms. Witt said she couldn't believe it when Tonya Harding made the tearful appeal about her laces to the judges at rinkside. "I thought, 'Girl, get real,'" she said. "I was not sympathetic to her. She has now had three or four incidents in competition when something breaks—a blade, a dress, something. I know she has had a tough life, but a lot of people have had a tough life. I grew up, it wasn't a free country. I hope she gets with people who care about her, and help her make a new environment for her."

When Miss Baiul finished her freestyle program and came backstage, she was in tears. "I asked someone, 'What's wrong with Oksana?' They said, 'She just won the gold medal.' When I won the gold medal in '84 and '88, I was laughing for joy. Oksana, though, is a good skater for her age—no, an incredible skater. But maybe she will find she will need more personality. She is so young. She can be wonderful."

Ms. Witt's life now includes activities ranging from lending her name to save endangered animals to anti-war groups, to, well, the social whirl. For a while, she dated Richard Dean Anderson, star of the former television series *MacGyver*. "But he lived in Los Angeles, I lived in Berlin, and it was very difficult," she said. Of the other men she has been linked to, like Boris Becker, the German tennis star, she said: "It was just yellow press. Not true."

As for Alberto Tomba, who first sought her attentions at the Olympics in Calgary, she recalled: "He came backstage during the skating and I didn't know who he was, but he was wearing two gold medals around his neck. It was ridiculous. Nobody wears medals to another sport. I said, 'Wow, in which sport did you win those?' It was like shooting him with a gun. He was a big Italian hero, but I am not too interested in ski sport." She laughed. "We became friends. Not romantic friends, just friends."

Ms. Witt lives for most of her non skating year in Berlin, with two roommates—both men. "It is like something I would have done ten years ago, if I was in college and not skating and the Government would have allowed it," she said. "We are just friends, these guys, and when I'm not training, I'm going to the ballet, or a concert, or the movies. Like normal people."

She has also been looking for a part-time apartment in Manhattan and thinks she's found one overlooking Central Park. "You wouldn't believe the view—spectacular, right above the trees," she said.

A platter of cookies arrived at the table and Ms. Witt broke off a piece of the lone chocolate chip cookie—only a piece, ever mindful of her figure.

Over the last few years, she has skated in touring shows—her television version of "Carmen" with Brian Boitano won an Emmy—and has done figure-skating commentary on television. She plans to skate in shows for perhaps two more years. Then?

"I have some things on the table," she said cryptically. "I will let you know."

Ms. Witt says she will now leave the competitive stage to the younger skaters. "I don't want to compete," she said. "I want to skate for the joy. I get so nervous in competition. I get always sick. I had pressures enough in my life from skating."

She retains ambitions, to be sure, and dreams. "I want to see sunrises in the mountains," she said. "You never get to see such things enough in a lifetime. I want to see more.

"But right now, in the show I'm in, one of the programs I skate is my Sarajevo message, and the crowds go bananas. I know this is maybe naive, but one day I hope will be peace in the world. Maybe one day the flowers will come back."

Bob Knight: Degrees of Separation for Coach and Indiana

September 11, 2000

Zero tolerance, after nearly twenty-nine years of maximum tolerance at Indiana University, may not have much wiggle room. And after an incident last May—one of scores involving Bob Knight over the years—the president of the university, Myles Brand, said that Knight deserved a "last chance." If he does anything that is deemed embarrassing to the school, Brand said, he will be dismissed.

And Bob Knight seemingly, and perhaps finally, understood the possible ramifications of zero tolerance when he conducted a news conference on Friday to explain his grabbing an Indiana student by the arm and, possibly, spewing profanity at him. The student had said, "Hey, what's up, Knight?"

Knight apparently stopped the freshman, who was buying football tickets with friends, and admittedly held his arm and said: "Son, my name is not Knight to you. It's Coach Knight or it's Mr. Knight." The student, Kent Harvey, said that the grip was so tight that Knight's nails broke the skin on his arm.

Mike Davis, an assistant coach for Knight, witnessed this and said, "The grip was more like shaking hands." Some handshake, apparently.

Knight, who turns sixty soon, his gray hair cut short, a palpable paunch under his red sweater, on Friday drew a diagram on the chalkboard to demonstrate the closeness of having to pass the student in a corridor. He even desperately invoked a scene in church when he was a youngster—"some people may not believe that I was ever in church"—and talked about a high school coach of his who taught him the lesson of respecting elders. A lesson, it is apparent, that Knight has frequently forgotten.

But there he was, with a look in his eyes that reminded me of Richard Nixon trying to explain misdeeds—Pat's Republican cloth coat and that poor dog Checkers—a look, that is, of being trapped when guilty.

The fact is, Knight is a full professor at a highly regarded university. The fact that he is a coach of a basketball team that has won three National Collegiate Athletic Association titles, and that he has won more Division I games than any other active coach, is beside the point. If an English professor or a dean of students acted as Knight has over the years, he would surely have been out long ago. If Knight wants to make a point to a student about correct behavior, all he has to do is tell him, e-mail him or call his parents. But keep your hands off him. And if civility or professional behavior isn't incentive enough, then how about being under probation of zero tolerance?

But not Knight. Knight is out of control. If he doesn't have an emotional problem, then he surely has an ego problem. You don't have to be a psychologist to comprehend that. He said last spring that he didn't really have a problem with anger, but something else. "I've always been too confrontational," he said, "especially when I know I'm right."

So his problem, folks, is that he's always right. He has also believed that he could get away with anything—because he has, to the utter shame of Indiana University and other institutions where he has worked, and worked over people. But the buck has finally stopped. Brand, who announced Knight's dismissal yesterday, called Knight "defiant and hostile" and said the coach had shown a continued unwillingness to work within the guidelines of the athletic department.

In May, when Neil Reed, one of Knight's former players, charged that Knight had once choked him in a practice, Knight protested that it was a lie—that he had just held the young man's shoulder—and Knight's sycophantic assistant coaches and players also denied it had occurred. But a film of the incident exposed the lies of Knight and his supporters. Around the same time, it was learned that Knight had also intimidated a sixty-four-year-old secretary in the athletic department with foul language and had thrown a vase, and had gotten into abusive arguments and physical altercations with colleagues and subordinates.

Brand fined Knight $30,000, suspended him for three games and issued the zero tolerance warning.

Knight's numerous other incidents of physically and verbally abusing people have been a public scandal for years.

It goes back a long, long way. When Knight was starting out as a high school basketball coach in Ohio, a student in the school, Susan Wilkinson, recalled in a letter to me some time ago, that he used to "rant and rave" in the hallways.

"One particular time, I had the misfortune of being in the hall when he was throwing a student up against a locker," she wrote. "I couldn't equate this behavior with being in sports or being human. It scared me to death."

When Knight was a coach at West Point, his team played Boston College in Madison Square Garden. Bob Cousy, then coaching BC, recalled being shocked at halftime when he noticed that Knight had one of his players up against the wall and his hand at the boy's throat. Cousy continued to observe Knight through the years. "It's time to grow up," Cousy said of Knight a few years ago, "and he hasn't grown up."

In 1993, Knight pulled his son Patrick from a game and appeared to kick him in the shin.

Supporters of Knight say that at least he doesn't cheat and abides by NCAA rules. Cousy counters correctly: "That the only alternative to wholesale prostitution is to do it the way Bob Knight does? I certainly hope not."

Brand has, at length, answered in the affirmative.

Knight deserves a good rest, and a long-deserved retribution for acts that were neither scholarly nor cultured. At long last, someone in authority has had the courage to render to him what is fitting and proper.

No one, however, should take joy in Brand's decision. In the end, it is a sad and tragic—if not concluding—chapter in what should have been fully one of the most glorious careers in American sports.

* * *

In 2001 Knight was named head basketball coach at Texas Tech, where he avoided controversy for the most part, compiling a record of 138 wins in seven years, highlighted by a Sweet 16 appearance in the NCAA tournament (and losing to West Virginia). When Knight retired in 2008, he held the coaching record of 902 Division I wins, a record now held by Mike Krzyzewski of Duke. Knight is now third on that list behind Jim Boeheim of Syracuse.

The Darkest Blot

March 29, 1985

It is ironic that on the eve of college basketball's most glorious moment—the National Collegiate Athletic Association's Final Four games tomorrow and Monday—the specter of college basketball's greatest fear and disgrace is raised: the fixing of games.

In regard to the three Tulane basketball players arrested this week on charges of point-shaving in two games last month, there have been no indictments and no convictions. It is too early and too easy to judge and sentence them without benefit of the facts. Their day in court will come soon.

However, the arrests of the players—the New Orleans District Attorney said he believed it "quite possible" more would follow in Louisiana and other states—instantly and inevitably recalled the most famous of college basketball scandals, the 1951 fixes. At that time, an investigation showed that between 1947 and 1951, 32 players from seven colleges had fixed 86 games in 23 cities in 17 states: CCNY, LIU, NYU, Manhattan, Kentucky, Bradley, and Toledo.

Still, the lessons of 1951, too quickly forgotten or ignored—there were fixing scandals in 1961 and 1965 and 1979—remain as pertinent today as they were nearly thirty-three years ago when General Sessions Judge Saul S. Streit of New York handed down his sentences in a 63-page report.

Notwithstanding the element of individual greed or stupidity among some of the players, Judge Streit most forcefully condemned the hypocritical college athletic system.

He criticized the paltry education some of the players received: they were admitted to college on forged entrance papers. Some of them, as recalled in Zander Hollander's *The Modern Encyclopedia of Basketball*, remained eligible for basketball with IQs of 80. In his senior year, one of the players took an academic load consisting of public speaking, oil painting, rhythm and dance, and a music seminar.

Little has changed in some instances, as seen when schools are caught in the act of nefarious activity, such as the numbing cases with fictitious scholars at places like Southern California and New Mexico, where some athletes could barely write their names. Most recently, a 6-foot-10 basketball player named Chris Washburn is found to have been admitted to North Carolina State with an educational background that wouldn't qualify him for dog catcher, let alone Economics 101.

Judge Streit condemned the "athletic scholarship racket as the most fruitful device and scheme yet invented to destroy the amateur code." He called it "the darkest blot" on American college athletics and said that the coaches, their assistants and the alumni "go prospecting for athletic talent like miners searching for gold."

Little has changed. Hundreds and hundreds of college recruiters call, write, visit and camp on doorsteps to lure a prep kid blessed with the ability to jump high, run fast and throw accurately. When Moses Malone was a high school basketball player in Petersburg, Virginia, he recalled having to hide under his bed to escape college recruiters.

Judge Streit said that the coaches and the universities "must share responsibility" for the plight of college athletics. Coach Adolph Rupp and Kentucky boosters and alumni, it was then pointed out, would slip players $10 to $50 after a good game. And did they get it after a bad one? "No sir," Don Barnstable, one of the Kentucky players convicted of point-shaving, told Judge Streit. "You were lucky to get something to eat."

Little has changed. There are still financial inducements to players, whether they come in the form of cash payments, or cars, or fake jobs or coaches who can arbitrarily strip them of their scholarships.

Clair Bee, the coach of LIU then, wrote in the *Saturday Evening Post* in 1952 about those big games in Madison Square Garden with capacity crowds of 18,000: "'I'm bringing in all these people and playing my heart out for them,' the boys must have said to themselves. 'Clair Bee is getting all the credit and Ned Irish is getting all the gravy. Where do I come in?" Irish was then president of Madison Square Garden.

Of the three Tulane players arrested, one, the 6-foot-10 senior center John "Hot Rod" Williams is a potential first-round draft choice in the National Basketball Association. He said that he would never shave points because he had "too much to lose." That may be so, but in that first scandal, some of the best players in the country, from Alex Groza to Sherman White, shaved points.

In each of the scandals, memory was short and arrogance and greed were long. Regarding the latter, it has been said that slammers are filled with people who thought they wouldn't get caught. As for memory, there is an apt and much-quoted remark by the philosopher George Santayana: "Those who cannot remember the past are condemned to repeat it."

Apparently, no one sat with the 1951 fixers and went over the 1919 Black Sox scandal, which rocked baseball and the nation when the World Series was manipulated for profit.

Coaches at schools such as St. John's and Fordham bring in FBI officers before the season to talk to the players. Despite this, there is continuing dissatisfaction with the system. There are college athletes who, as in the days of Clair Bee, believe, and rightfully, that they are being underpaid. In many cases, the colleges exploit the athlete by using him without educating him. These athletes are not there to study at all, never were, and tuition, board, books and fees are insufficient pay when they might be helping the school make enormous sums of money: each Final Four school, for example, will get about three-quarters of a million dollars for its participation.

There will always be people who want more money than they have, no matter how much that is, but it is time that players get a bigger and an honest piece of the action. Pay them as the pros they are, and not as the amateurs the schools like to pretend they are.

In the end, nothing breeds dishonesty like dishonesty.

The Edwin Moses Case

January 24, 1985

Edwin Moses, one-time honor student and holder of a bachelor's degree in physics from Morehouse College, two-time Olympic gold medal winner, world-record holder and a man who has not been defeated in a 400-meter hurdles race since August 26, 1977 (109 races), has been shown to be vulnerable.

Edwin Moses, at age twenty-nine, is one of the most respected athletes in the world. The word "dignity" is mentioned as often in discussions about him as is the word "gifted." He is a man chosen to represent his country and his sport on the boards of the International Olympic Committee and the United States Olympic Committee, as well as being a spokesman for the United Way and the American Cancer Society and numerous commercial enterprises. But Edwin Moses has been shown to be vulnerable.

For one thing—at least once—Moses fell down at the job of tying his shoelace. This was in the 1983 track and field world championships held in Helsinki, Finland. He won his race despite a flopping shoelace that had come untied as he bounded over the hurdles.

But the world wasn't looking on at that, or at least the audience was nothing like the second time Moses's vulnerability became apparent. This occurred during the opening ceremonies of the 1984 Olympics. Moses had been given the distinct honor of reciting the competitors' oath before a crowd of more than 100,000 at the Los Angeles Coliseum and for an international television audience of nearly two billion.

Part way through the 43-word oath that he had memorized, he stumbled. Suddenly it was painfully obvious that he had forgotten the words. Moses, a lean 6-foot-2, stood ramrod straight. The look in his eyes was—calm? worried? It was hard to say. Then he gathered himself, clutched the rest of the oath as he had been clutching the white Olympic flag, and finished faultlessly.

To many, this was an indication of the inner man, a prideful man who had taken the trouble to memorize the oath—however short—and had the confidence to recite it before this unprecedented audience without benefit of notes. It seemed to speak also of his meticulous training habits, and of the enduring qualities that have made him an exemplary athlete.

Only he and Paavo Nurmi, the Flying Finn of more than half a century ago, have won individual Olympic gold medals in the same running event eight years apart. Moses's current winning streak is believed to be a record for any runner in any event.

Quietly, patiently, gently, Edwin Moses had continued to go about his business. Advertisers had flocked to him, wanting to associate their products with his name and impeccable reputation. He earned an estimated $1 million last year—legal under current amateur guidelines—and it was expected he would top that this year.

He also made time to visit schools and speak to youngsters about the necessity not to drop out, and to tell them that athletics should play a secondary role to academics. He talked of clean living and the harm that drugs can do to body and mind. He was also a spokesman for athletes, particularly those lesser known who were getting short-changed by some promoters.

He was a family man, married, and the son of educators from Dayton, Ohio.

Edwin Moses was a role model of the highest order.

Last year he won the prestigious Sullivan Award for amateur athlete of the year. This year, among other awards, he was named *Sports Illustrated*'s Sportsman of the Year and ABC's *Wide World of Sports* Athlete of the Year.

Then, suddenly, the incredible world of Edwin Moses collapsed-or seemed to. At 3:17 January 13, a Sunday morning, he was arrested in Los Angeles. According to a charge filed later, he had solicited an undercover policewoman who was posing as a prostitute. The charge is a misdemeanor, and those found guilty are often fined around $50. Moses was given a date for arraignment and released.

Moses had been returning from a meeting of the USOC that ended around 1:30 a.m. He and a few others went to a discotheque, and after awhile he left. On his way home, Moses, in his gray Mercedes, stopped at the corner of Sunset and Genessee. He said he stopped for a red light. He says that the woman came over and he turned down the window "eight inches" and "joked" with her. The police contend that he solicited her. He contends that there was no such intent.

273

The undisputed fact is that he never got out of the car. He never unlocked his door. He drove away. The woman was wired and the conversation was heard by two policemen in a car nearby. They followed Moses and two blocks later picked him up.

Now, Moses was hardly incognito. His license plate reads OLYMPYN. During the Olympics, he was on billboards throughout the Los Angeles area, hurdling at passersby in his red track suit. When he was picked up, one of the officers recognized him.

"The officer was dismayed that it was Moses," said Lieut. Dan Cook, a spokesman for the Los Angeles Police Department.

"When they saw it was Edwin," said Gordon Baskin, Moses's business manager, "I think they felt, 'This is a nice fish to fry.'"

Whatever, word of the arrest got out—Lieutenant Cook says he has no idea how—to a local television station. It was soon a big story, and growing. "It became," said Lieutenant Cook, "international."

Moses called his wife, Myrella, who came to his side. And almost immediately Moses began receiving numerous calls and telegrams of support, said Baskin.

One caller was Peter Ueberroth, former head of the Los Angeles Olympic Organizing Committee and now the baseball commissioner. "Edwin," said Ueberroth, in New York, "is a giving, decent human being. If he says he's innocent, I believe him. I told him that if there is anything I can do to help—if I have to go back to Los Angeles—I'll do it."

Moses goes to trial Febuary 8. He has pleaded not guilty.

"I have done nothing wrong, and that will be proven," Moses said Sunday, accepting his trophy on "*Wide World of Sports*." "This has hurt me deeply," he added in his straightforward manner, "but I'm going to be a champion no matter what."

* * *

A jury found Edwin Moses not guilty of the charged crime of solicitation. In 1999, Moses was ranked 47th on ESPN's *SportsCentury 50 Greatest Athletes*.

Jerry Smith: "The Courage of the Gentle"
August 31, 1986

The recent news that Jerry Smith has been suffering from AIDS for eight months was met with what, on the surface, might seem an unusual reaction from his former Redskins football teammates.

Smith, who has discussed his illness but not his life style, played tight end for the Redskins for 13 seasons, from 1965 to 1977. He caught so many passes, and in such clutch situations, that George Allen, who coached him for more than half his pro career, called him Home Run Smith.

Smith, who is forty-three years old, is seriously ill in Holy Cross Hospital in Silver Spring, Md. He has dropped from 210 pounds to 150.

"Certainly I'm not going to judge someone else's life style as it affected them," Calvin Hill, the former all-pro running back, told The Washington Post. "In terms of how Jerry affected me, both on and off the field, it was very positive. He was an effervescent, helpful guy who was concerned when other guys were down."

"I liked him then and I like him now, AIDS or no AIDS," said Dave Butz, a Redskins defensive tackle.

"If you love a guy," said Bobby Mitchell, a National Football League Hall of Fame receiver and now assistant general manager of the Redskins, "you love him. That's all there is to it. Jerry G. has been a very dear friend almost twenty years."

Those reactions might have come from some less brawny community. But football players? Hard-nosed tough guys? The image of American masculinity?

One of the players who was asked his reaction to Smith's illness, the former free safety Mark Murphy, said: "What Jerry has done, coming out and talking, takes a lot of courage. I think he's right. It will heighten the public's awareness about the disease."

But courage was demonstrated by those who were football friends and teammates of Jerry Smith's. It's a courage greater than plunging for a first down, or chasing down a breakaway runner. It's the courage of character, the courage not to accept stereotypes. It's the courage of true virility. Perhaps it is true, as Leo Rosten wrote in Captain Newman, Maryland, that "it is the weak who are cruel, and that gentleness is to be expected only from the strong."

A spokesman at Holy Cross Hospital said that every third phone call there has been for Jerry Smith. There were "lots of Redskins, ex-Redskins and friends" calling, he said. "It's been phenomenal."

Smith never said he was a homosexual, but it could have been easy for friends to reject what they readily believed to be a life style that may not have been consistent with their own, and not consistent with the image that they have fostered, or had thrust upon them.

And there will surely be some who in fact will now shy away from an association with Jerry Smith. The concern was expressed by his mother, Laverne, at his hospital bedside. Smith is scheduled to be inducted into the Washington Hall of Stars at RFK Stadium this fall. "Do you think when they find out," she asked, "they'll change their minds?" No, her son whispered. The hall committee has confirmed that there will be no change in plans.

The awareness grows that AIDS, which primarily afflicts homosexual men, can reach into the world of the arts, of law and law enforcement and industry and international business and politics and garbage collecting and sports, even football.

Will there be increased research from increased awareness of the disease, due in part to Smith's public acknowledgement?

Possibly, and it might begin in the most unexpected of places, the NFL Charities, which in the last ten years has committed $7 million to numerous causes, but none to AIDS research. Commissioner Pete Rozelle says it's now a possibility.

Beyond that, there is another important aspect to the Smith case. And Sam Huff, a former star linebacker, said it clearly: "I think it's time that people view football players as people. Because you can play football, what makes you a celebrity? Because you can block and tackle and run? We're people. Sometimes I think people forget that."

And there is a variety of people born with athletic talent. Nowhere is it written that only heterosexuals are allowed to be coordinated.

Dr. Bruce Oglivie, a retired professor of psychology at San Jose State, is a consultant to three National Basketball Association teams, the Portland Trail Blazers, the Milwaukee Bucks and the Golden State Warriors, and has been a consultant to half a dozen NFL teams over the last twenty years. "Incidents of homosexuality—or, at least bisexuality—have been known, of course, in athletics," he said. "But that shouldn't be surprising. About 6 percent of the male population in America is homosexual. I think it's safe to say that that same percentage of incidence would appear in any field you could name."

He said that some players have asked him about "coming out of the closet." He advised them that it was hazardous, given the potentially negative reaction by teams, the community and religious leaders. "You cannot anticipate how others would respond," he said. "The possibility is great that they would treat it as a threat to their idealized concept of masculinity, and what sports represents to them—the essence of manhood. It would fly in the face of the projected needs of the public, their fantasy of what a man should be."

Dr. Oglivie had recommended that they retain a private life style. Those few athletes—such as the former NFL running back Dave Kopay and the former Dodger outfielder Glenn Burke—who did acknowledge their homosexuality, did so after their playing career was over.

Dr. Oglivie said that he was heartened by the response of Smith's teammates.

"It indicated how much we've grown as people, and are willing to accept a diversion from ourselves," he said. "And that we don't measure the acceptability of a human being on the basis of a single dimension such as sexual orientation, one tiny, tiny segment of the totality of the human being.

"I think the response of these football players to Jerry Smith is a beautiful thing."

* * *

On a lighter side, it is possible to be not only in troubled waters, as the above section has indicated but, as the author finds himself, one may find oneself in troubled snows, as well.

Dilemma on the Slopes

January 10, 1991

It was reported in the news the other week that there are some 400,000 skiing injuries every year. This translates to the entire population of Pittsburgh walking around in neck braces, arm slings and casts on their legs. And those not walking would be hanging in traction.

There was an article in this space last Thursday about safety measures in skiing, including legislation concerning hit-and-run skiers, the wearing of helmets, lawsuits and other slope matters.

These accounts put me in mind of the time I went skiing.

It happened years ago when I was a young reporter at another organization. One day the sports editor asked if I had ever skied. I told him no, though I said I had skeetched.

It was called skeetching by the boys in my neighborhood, the word perhaps a combined form of skating and hitching. On icy city streets at night, we'd grab the back of a fender of a passing car, hunker down, and go for a ride, one's face turning lurid red when the taillight registered. This activity could be dangerous, though few of us considered it so.

I had also gone sledding, particularly near the train trestle, where a good slope was located. We belly-flopped onto our sleds, slid down the hill and swooped into the street. This could also be hazardous, since cars usually swerved to avoid hitting the low-flying sledders, but it was all part of that winter wonderland.

"Never skied? Great," said the sports editor. "Try it and write a story about doing it for the first time."

I had come to value life and limb, particularly mine, in a new way from my boyhood. I had also heard all about what happens to skiers. And so to my sports editor I replied, "No thanks."

"Here are your plane tickets," he explained. "You leave tomorrow."

It was a trip to a popular resort area in Colorado. In my young manhood I had also developed an aversion to spending much time out in the cold, and still prefer my wintertime activities indoors, like basketball, or tennis, or sleeping, and enjoying each of them in one piece.

Everyone at this resort in Colorado, though, when I arrived there, seemed so happy and red-cheeked, even those on crutches.

On D-Day, I climbed into my new ski pants, and swathed myself in several sweaters and a parka and stocking cap. I was fitted for skis and boots, and assigned an instructor named Lise, once a member of the Norwegian ski team. Lise had a charming accent and exuded a gentle confidence.

She described a site she would take me to for my first lesson which was some 12,000 feet above sea level. "Der iss a little trail vere you can luv de nature," she said.

We ascended into the blue in a double-chair lift that hung by a thread and did not have safety belts. Below, skiers sped down the pine-scattered mountain. Lise swung her legs like a naughty girl on a Ferris wheel. "Sving de feet to keep de circulation," said Lise. I swung and did not look down.

About half an hour later we reached the top of a mountain. I noticed signs that read "Caution" and "Danger." Another was marked "To Banzai Ridge." Close by was the little trail Lise had touted. The first lesson in skiing, I learned, is how to fall down. "If you don' fell de right vay," she said, "you can break de leg." She demonstrated the proper fall, hurtling herself into a snow bank.

I tried to imitate, but was rooted to the spot. I'd always been able to fall like a champ, especially when missing a curb, but not now. "Relax," Lise advised. I tried again, and eventually succeeded. "You felled very nice," she said.

Other things to learn: how to get up after falling (she lifted me under the arms); how to crouch, how to turn, how to stop. I did a little of everything, tasting some of the mountainside as I went along.

Finally, the lesson over, she said cheerfully that now I could ski back down. I looked and decided that the bottom of the mountain was about 14 miles almost straight down. It was like falling from the top of a tall building.

"I'm not skiing down this mountain," I said.

"But how else to go down?" Lise said.

"Those chairs," I said.

A long line of colorfully clad skiers rode up the lift, but a long line of empty red chairs rode down.

"The chairs going down is not for de people," she said.

Before she could say another word I leaped onto a lift chair, clutching my skis and poles, and started down, calling goodbye to Lise. As I descended, little girls and boys, matrons and college kids, in rising chair lifts, looked at me, hardly suppressing laughter. I pulled my stocking cap low to my eyes.

"What happened?" asked a man as we passed in the sky. "Broken binding?"

"Broken binding," I said, suddenly brightening. "Broken binding!"

All the rest of the way down, I met each gaze directly. "Broken binding," I repeated, shaking my head. "Some luck, huh?"

Haven't touched a pair of skis since.

Part IV: The Munich Olympics

Triumph and Tragedy

In late summer 1972 an extraordinary occurrence took place in Munich, Germany. That nation, and that city, was to host the 1972 Olympic Games, and the aspiration of the organizers were to erase all memory of the 1936 Olympic Games held in Berlin, which have commonly been called The Nazi Olympics. There would be no profusion of swastika flags hanging from buildings, no goose-stepping guards, and no Adolph Hitler.

In his insightful book, *The Nazi Olympics*, published in 1987, Richard D. Mandell writes in his introduction about the importance of these Games as an avatar for the rise of Nazism: "The Olympic Games of 1936 were an important spectacle in the establishment of an evil political regime. . . . Much of the success off the 1936 Olympics was due to the pursuit by the National Socialists of supremacy in mass pageantry. Hitler's success as a whole is inconceivable without the application of the contrived festivity that enveloped Nazism from beginning to end."

It was only thirty-six years after the Berlin Olympics, but the atmosphere had dramatically changed now in Munich (also the site, many remembered, of Hitler's attempt in 1923 in a local beer hall to overthrow, or institute a *putsch*, of the democratic Weimar Republic). The German word *gemutlichkeit*, meaning essentially friendliness and congeniality, was ascendant.

I had come to Munich to cover the Olympic Games, and was struck by how sincere the "happiness" environment was. I had arrived a week before the start of the Games. I was writing for a national feature service which had a lead time of about a week, so I had come early to get in my stories, which I wrote daily. The flags that flew were primarily the five-ringed Olympic banners. And while, to this Jew in Germany, anyone in a uniform—policeman, trolley car conductor, garbage collector—seemed, if not ominous, a bit discomforting, the Munich streets as well as the Olympic grounds, and the German people in general, were welcoming, patient, accommodating.

And so the popular Glockenspiel, the ornate clock in Marienplatz, the Munich central square, chimed hourly and the wooden dancers came out in old-world garb, and many of the townsmen still sported Tyrolean hats but some of the men and women were also dressed fashionably in Western modern. The young women were in short skirts and heels. No frumpy hausfraus. Overall, it seemed apparent that this was a vastly different Germany from three decades ago. There was no omen in the air that foretold tragedy, which indeed would transpire, and transfix and shock the world.

The press headquarters was housed in a large building and filled with computers and machines printing out information for reporters. The headquarters was crowded and raucous, yet seemed to be run with great efficiency, efficiency being a characteristic often applied to Germans. It was in press headquarters that I ran into the great sportswriter Red Smith and his wife Phyllis. I had been in Munich for several days. They had just arrived.

"I've got credentials, Phyllis doesn't, but do you think she could still get into the Olympic Village?" Red asked me.

"It's not too hard," I said. "I've seen people sneaking into the Village all the time. Security is not terrific. Even the guards try to be nice. No strong-arm stuff. When you and Phyllis get to the gate of the Village, just wave to the guards. They'll wave back, and you'll stroll in."

And so they did. The Village itself was a pleasure, with athletes from a multitude of nations, in their colorful sweats, seeking their own forms of gemutlichkeit, often trading trinkets and tokens from their countries, and trying to overcome any language barriers, and not infrequently reduced to hand gestures and laughter.

Security didn't seem a pressing concern; racial politics, however, was a concern. Black African nations threatened to boycott the 1972 if Rhodesia, with a white supremacist government, was allowed to participate. The International Olympic Committee, despite the vote by its hide-bound president Avery Brundage against the action, sent the Rhodesian contingent home.

So I went about talking with the athletes for my stories, charmed by men and women who would participate. Like the lone participant, a long-distance runner, from Upper Volta—where?—which is located in the hot, arid plains of West Africa. "We come to bring honor to our country," said Andre Bicaba, through a French translator. "Of course we cannot dream of a medal. Yet who can predict results? This is the wonder of sports."

And there was the Hungarian javelin thrower and gold medal winner in Mexico City, Angela Ranky, whose maiden name was Nemeth. I asked her if she was related to the famous American football player, Joe Namath, who was also of Hungarian background, and perhaps "a's" in Namath might easily have been transposed from "e's" by a customs official in Joe's family history. Nemeth Ranky knew of no family connection with Joe. "But," she said, "remember, all Hungarians are descended from Attila the Hun."

There was the twenty-one-year-old Northern Irish lightweight boxer Charlie Nash, from Derry, which is in the middle of the battleground between the Irish Republic Army and the British Army. He said that he at first had trouble sleeping in the Olympic Village because it was so tranquil. "The bombs and the shootin' goin' off at home were so frequent that they put me to sleep. If I don't hear a whale of a lot of shootin' I stay awake." His sleep in the Olympic Village was gradually restored.

The lone member of the Israel track team, Dr. Shaul Ladany, a balding, bespectacled thirty-six-year-old industrial management professor, competes as a 50-kilometer race walker. "Some friends call me *mishugey*, that's Hebrew for crazy, for this, uh, unusual sports activity," he told me. "But," he added with a wry smile, "crazy only in a specific area." While he was the lone track participant for Israel, he wasn't, as we would learn to our horror, the lone Israeli athlete to compete in Munich.

And there were the Americans, of course, including Jim Ryun, the miler, and Mark Spitz, the swimmer. Ryun's training was intense, and he told me he struggled every day to break what runners call "the pain barrier." Spitz, after winning a record seven gold medals in his events, and for fear of his life because he was Jewish, was whisked out of Munich under police protection.

Before the Olympic Games had begun, I had learned of a woman named Gisela Mauermayer, who worked as a librarian in the Munich Zoological Institute. As a discus thrower, she was once a powerful sports symbol for Germany during the 1936 Olympics. Six foot tall, blonde, and strong, she had seemed the embodiment of the Aryan model. I met with her, and she told me at the '36 Olympics she had felt great pressure "to live up to the responsibility to my country." She won the gold medal.

"I was very patriotic," she told me, in late August of `76. She was now fifty-eight years old, still fit and spoke softly, and with gentle blue eyes. "Germany had lost the first World War in 1918. And for a long time we had foreign occupation. Hitler was the man who had driven them out. Millions joined the Nazi party. My father and I joined not for profit but out of idealism. Years later it was not feasible to get out of the party, though we had wanted to. I saw that the Nazis were doing evil to people who could not defend themselves—beating them in the streets—like the Jews and others who did not have leanings toward the Nazis. She became a physical education teacher and grew deeply dismayed by the direction of the government. By 1938, she said, she had refused to join a Nazi teachers organization, but, given her stature as a Teutonic sports hero, she was not harassed.

"But it is still politics in the games," she said, with an unsuspecting prescience. "I am so sorry for it. I am sorry for the athletes who want only to compete. Every country will have the intention to show its political strengths and make political demonstrations. People did not learn from 1936. No so much has changed."

* * *

One day I took a day off from covering the Olympics to visit the Dachau concentration camp, located about ten miles northwest of Munich in the medieval suburb of Dachau. The town is quaint, the concentration buildings as they come into view as one approaches is fearsome, and sickening, knowing what terrors had been perpetrated inside those stolid walls behind three rows of barbed wire, with watch towers that scanned the compound with search lights as late as twenty-seven years before—it opened in March 1933, the first concentration camp of the Nazi regime, less than two months after Hitler came to power as Chancellor, and it began with the imprisoning of political dissidents and eventually Jews, gypsies, homosexuals, citizens of other countries considered enemies of the Nazis, and it wasn't until April 29, 1945, and the end of the war, that it was liberated by US forces. It is now a museum, a grim tourist attraction, as a kind of warning to future generations of the evils man may inflict on man.

Dachau was made to house 5,000 inmates, but usually some 12,000 were shoveled into meager barracks. The prisoners were flogged, starved, worked to exhaustion, skimpily clothed even in the most freezing weather. The lives of uncounted thousands ended in the camp crematoria.

On my visit I happened to run into a uniformed US Army PFC named Tony Rowland, from Spokane, Washington, who had recently come to Germany to join a military unit in a small Army base which borders the Dachau camp. Rowland, an affable eighteen-year-old with blond hair and broad shoulders, told me he had startled his company commander, a Lt. Wigley, with a strange offer of assistance. Rowland said he had a special knowledge of the area. He said that during World War II his father had been in this concentration camp. His father, he said, had been stationed here while a member of the SS, the feared elite Nazi police.

Lt. Wigley thanked Pfc. Rowland but did not see how he could use the information. "I just thought I could add to the general knowledge of the history, kind of first-person knowledge—coming from my dad, that is." His father, an enlisted man, had been a clerical worker for the SS and was assigned to Dachau in January 1945.

"When I wrote my dad that I was going to be stationed here," Rowland continued, "he wrote back that I should visit the concentration camp. He thinks people should always remember man's inhumanity to man, so that it won't happen again. He told me about one particular wall that I should see, where he watched 3,000 people lined up and shot to death.

"He said he saw terrible things. He said he saw Jews beaten to death, and chewed to death by the Nazi dogs. He saw people die from medical experiments on them. For instance, Nazi doctors were looking for a malaria cure, so they inoculated some prisoners with the disease. The experiments failed. The prisoners died.

"Dad was just a young guy—he's fifty-five now, so he must've been, what twenty-eight then—and he was scared stiff. He said he wanted to do something to stop that stuff. But he saw three of his buddies get caught plotting to overthrow the camp commandant. These guys got new striped uniforms. They became prisoners in the camp, not guests."

SS enlisted man Rowland and about thirty fellow troopers knew the future for the Germans was hopeless by mid-April 1945, said Pfc. Rowland. They escaped to nearby Augsburg and gave themselves up to the advancing US forces. After the war Rowland was brought to the United States and made to stand for war crimes. "He wasn't convicted and he was even allowed to stay in the states," said the younger Rowland.

He said his father is not ashamed of his past. "No," he said, ""I mean, I would've been scared to death, too, if I was in his boots. Once he got into the S. S. he couldn't get out. I respect him for telling me about it. It's like something I read in the paper the other day. It was a story about Dachau, and said that a lot of people, especially Germans, and Germans around here, wish the place would be torn down. People say it's twenty-seven years since the war ended, and, hell, let the grass grow over it. But the article also quoted this guy, don't remember his name, who said something like, 'If you don't remember the past, you're condemned to repeat it.' Dad used to tell me something like that, too."

Rowland said that some of his fellow soldiers looked forward to seeing the sights of Bavaria, seeing some of the Olympics, visiting the beer halls and trying their luck with the local frauleins. Others will go to the legalized brothels, like the one on Dachaustrasse, where they find the rates for patrons during the Olympics is up to 70 deutsche marks (about $23) from its usual 40 DMs (about $13). "A lot of the guys didn't even know Dachau existed, and a lot don't care," he said. "They say they don't want to get bogged down in history. Others say maybe things like this are still going on, like in 'Nam."

The transition back those 10 miles to Munich and the Olympics was indeed returning to another world, certainly a gayer and saner world than the criminality that embodied the Dachau concentration camp. Sure, there were problems among the nations represented in the Olympics—were the Russian and East German athletes really amateurs, of course not—but in the sweet atmosphere of games it seemed—wished?—that all problems could be worked out. The goal was to run faster or jump higher than your competition. Not to murder them.

And so I reported on the magnificent Olga Korbut, the diminutive, blonde, pony-tailed Russian gold-medal gymnast whose smile could light up the gymnasium and hands down was the sweetheart of the Games. I saw the US men's basketball team, with future NBA players such as Doug Collins and Tom McMillen and Tom Henderson, wipe out Japan, 99–33, and appeared surely on their way to a gold medal. (In fact, Russia took the gold in a controversial 51–50 win.) I saw the American George Woods, all 312 pounds of him doing the Kugelstossen, which only sounds and looks like the Dance of the Hippopotamus. Kugelstossen is the German word for *shot put*, and Woods accomplished it with an unsuspecting graceful twirl, and mighty heave. Woods would win a silver, his throw coming in half an inch short, at 69-5 ½ feet, to Poland's Wladyslaw Komar, who set the Olympic record.

My national syndicate required a week's advance in order to produce the articles. So with a week to go in the Olympics, my work essentially was done. I left Munich and went to Berlin—sportswriters were given access to a tour of East and West Berlin. I decided to take the tour and the next morning, September 5, fly back to New York. I was glad for the experience of seeing the difference the Berlin Wall, with its barred wire and turrets manned by armed and helmeted soldiers to keep the

East Berliners from escaping to the West made. This was made most salient at night. Going from dark and dreary East Berlin, lights seemed in very limited supply, to West Berlin alive with neon signs and traffic and crowds enjoying night life was startling. It certainly made one grateful for the freedoms we often take for granted in a democracy.

I woke early the next morning for a very early flight. I didn't read German but bought a German newspaper just to see if it appeared there was news of consequence regarding the Olympics—you could tell by coverage and headlines. There wasn't. In the cab, the radio was on. It was in German. I asked the driver, who spoke English, if there was any news of importance from Munich. He said no. Had there been, I'd have returned immediately to Munich to cover it.

I boarded the plane, and some eight hours later landed at JFK Airport in New York. As I went through customs, the official behind the glass enclosure looked at my passport, saw I was coming from Germany and said, "What do you think about what happened?" I said, "What happened?"

He told me. A Palestinian terrorist organization called Black September was holding Israeli athletes, coaches, and officials hostage in their adjoining apartments in the Olympic Village. It had begun before dawn, not long before I was boarding the plane, and wasn't announced until several hours later, when I was soaring over the Atlantic Ocean. The entire world would see photos of white-hooded terrorists with weapons standing on the balcony of the Israeli team's rooms. I had wanted to return, but my organization felt that it wouldn't be necessary, that it would all be over quickly.

It went on for 18 hours. Two Israelis were killed in the Olympic Village, the other nine hostages were killed at the airport when the German police confronted the terrorists who were going to board a plane to an unknown destination, and mishandled the situation. Five terrorists were killed, the three others captured.

Reporting for ABC television from Munich, the sportscaster Jim McKay, following the murders, cast aside false reports and rumors, and said near tears, "Our worst fears have been realized tonight."

I felt I had missed one of the biggest stories of my lifetime. But I made several phone calls to Munich, and a painful significance was added to the tragedy. I had met the Wasserstein family and a Rabbi Grunewald when I had sought a synagogue to visit in Munich.

It was there that I met Itzchok and Shashana Wasserstein, and they invited me to a Shabbat dinner in their tidy apartment. I had made friends, and was delighted with them. We agreed to stay in touch. And now, back in the states, I called them and, adding reporting I had previously done but had not written, wrote the story the day after the catastrophe.

Olympic Disaster: Out of Beauty, Horror

September 6, 1972 / Munich, Germany

Saturday is the holiest day of the week for an orthodox Jew. It is a day devoted to solemn meditation and prayer. Phones are not answered. Money is not earned. But on Saturday, August 26, opening day of the Olympic Games, Shashana and Itzchok Wasserstein and their twenty-four-year-old son David call in the "Sabbath gentile," a neighbor, who usually does such chores as turning on the lights on Saturday. On this day, though, Shashana switches on the television set herself in their home in Garmisch-Partenkirchen, outside of Munich.

The Wassersteins risked desecration to watch the Israel team march into the Olympic Stadium.

"When I saw the Israeli flag walk into the stadium," she said, "my heart was springing out of my head. I cried to see Israel come as a free nation, into Germany, and with the Germans all around and making applause. It was worth living through the concentration camp to see."

This was a time of great pride, of profound satisfaction for the Jewish community. Israel was gloriously here, of course. So was Mark Spitz, an American Jew who ironically emerged in Germany as the most celebrated and triumphant athlete in the 1972 Olympics.

And there was such a friendly touch as the Helene Mayer Ring, the area leading to the main entrance of the Olympic Village. The "ring" was conspicuously named for the medal-winning German-Jewess fencer who was the center of controversy before the 1936 "Nazi Olympics" in Berlin. She was a token Jew, then an expatriate living in Los Angeles, who accepted Hitler's invitation to participate again for Germany, thus avoiding a boycott by some nations for racial discrimination.

The slogan in Munich now was Heitere Spiele—"fun and games"— a desperate attempt by the German Olympic Organizers to blot out the former memory of the '36 Games as a pageant for future slaughter.

If there was anything uncomfortable in the early going of the 1972 Olympics for the Jews of Munich, it was the telephone situation in the new synagogue building which replaced the one arsonists had burned down two years ago. No hookups have been made there, as in other buildings here. "Everything in town is for the Olympics," Rabbi Isaak Grunewald had told me with a resigned good humor. "No one has time for anything else."

Gone for a moment, even was the memory of the seven people killed in the blaze in the synagogue's adjacent old-age home. Police suspect the arsonists to be either neo-Nazis or leftist Arab sympathizers. The culprits are still at large. The local, state and national governments donated large financial sums for the resurrection of the temple.

Yet the Jews here generally consider themselves Israelis. "We have a saying that all Jews in Germany are sitting on their luggage," David Wasserstein told me. And on the first Friday night that the Israeli team was in Munich, several came to the temple at 27 Reichenbachstrasse and were joyfully embraced. Before the Nazis there were nearly 12,000 Jews in Munich and the suburbs, now there are about 4,000, out of a total population of 1.2 million. When the war ended in 1945 a quarter of a million Jews were liberated into Munich from concentration camps. Most went to the new nation, Israel. But some stayed on. Thousands, like David Wasserstein's parents, remained to search for lost relatives. Others were too sickly to travel. Many have found life livable here, but Israel is still the dream destination.

Shashana Wasserstein, in fact, was not chauvinistically taken by Spitz's seven gold medals. "It is not so important for me because when Spitz wins a medal they play the American hymn," she said. "I admire him like I admire the Russian gymnast. But he does not have my heart. Not like if the flag of Israel was raised when he won."

David, a tall and fashionably bearded pre-med student, is not of the same mind as his mother. "I remember sitting with a German friend who is gentile and all I wanted to do was tell him that Mark Spitz was a Jew," he said. "I didn't. I thought it was foolish, like a child would do. But you know, many Germans here still have the image of the Jew as dirty, long-nosed, short and weak."

Izhok had heard that Spitz's parents were staying in Garmisch-Partenkirchen. "We are the only Jewish family living there now," he said. "Usually when a Jew comes through town he finds out where we live and calls. Perhaps Spitz's parents are too busy. I can imagine, with seven gold medals!

But maybe they did not think to ask. I will find out where they stay and invite them to our home. After all, are not Jews all over the world a nation of brothers?"

Then, out of the most beautiful of times, disaster. Arab terrorists murder 11 Israeli Olympic team members.

One can hear the chanting murmur of prayer in Jewish homes here, I am told. And in some German homes. Candles of mourning flicker in night windows. A special prayer session is called at the synagogue. Rabbi Grunewald, elderly, white-bearded Holocaust survivor, in traditional black velour top hat and tallis, the traditional prayer shawl, offers sorrowful prayers, as he had during long nights in the Nazi regime.

I am told that some members of the congregation rumble to stage a protest march through downtown Munich. Rabbi Grunwald foresees only more bloodshed and cools heads.

At the university, David is about to take a final exam in child problems. His professor learns he is a Jew and cuts the session short. The police in Garmisch-Partenkirchen call the Wassersteins, express their horror, and offer protection.

It was feared that Mark Spitz might be a target of the terrorists, so he and his family are hurriedly returned to the United States under armed guard. They never see the Wassersteins.

Shashana Wasserstein, who was a teenager in serveral concentration camps, stares with her husband at the television set watching again the proceedings of the Olympic Games that have been resumed. She cries different tears from those of the opening ceremony. She has cried these tears before.

Mark Spitz, After the Glory

October 28, 1982

It has been ten years since Mark Spitz, swimming in the Munich Olympics, won a record seven gold medals, setting world marks in the seven events. When the medals, with thick gold chains, were all draped round his neck, he pronounced, "They're heavy."

Because of his triumphs before a world audience, Spitz, at age twenty-two, instantly became a leading celebrity. Just as suddenly, he found himself in a maelstrom.

On the morning after he had won his seventh gold medal, he was escorted to a news conference to discuss, he thought, his swimming. When he got there, he said, he found "pandemonium." He learned for the first time that Palestinian terrorists had invaded the quarters of Israeli Olympians.

"I was shocked and stunned," he recalled. "The press wanted my words because, first, I was Jewish, and second, they thought I was some kind of spokesman for athletes."

He was prepared neither to be a spokesman nor, later, to discuss authoritatively the political ramifications of the murder of eleven Israeli athletes and officials. Though he was a student at Indiana University, he had for years devoted himself to being a swimmer first, spending five or six hours a day in the pool.

"It was boring becoming the best in the world," he once said. At the time, the International Olympic Committee and the State Department thought it too dangerous for Spitz to remain in Munich. "Frankly, I was scared," he said. He was quickly returned home.

Some persons criticized him for not having made a meaningful statement about the event. He was also attacked for having endorsed many products and for his stiff appearances on several variety shows.

"Well, what did they expect without any training, Charlton Heston?" he said. "They thought I was a money-grubber. What's wrong with making a dollar?"

His life changed irreparably after the Olympics. "My biggest mistake was that I practically became a recluse," he said recently. "I didn't know how to handle it all."

Four years after Munich, however, Spitz was beginning to be more accessible. "One afternoon I was on a radio talk show in Miami," he said. "A woman called and really ripped into me. It was unbelievable. She said I was a rotten Jew, a rotten American, a rotten representative of the Olympics, because she said I had fled Munich.

"The engineers finally shut her off. The host on the show began to apologize profusely to me. I hadn't said a word. Then a call came in from a man who said he had just driven off the road to telephone. He said: 'I want you to know how much I disagreed with that woman. What did she expect you to do, grab a bayonet and singlehandedly fight the Arabs?'

"Then another call came supporting me. And another. Pretty soon the place was lighting up like a battlefield, with people coming to my defense. I felt like crying. It was fantastic. Nothing like that had ever happened to me before."

Spitz, though still retiring, is no longer reclusive. Recently he was among fifty athletes who gathered in Atlantic City for the 10th anniversary celebration of the television program, *Greatest Sports Legends*.

"The most important thing I've done in the last ten years," he said in a telephone interview, "was to make the transition from being an athlete back to being a normal person in the mainstream. I had never imagined all the attention I would get. It was mind-boggling.

"After Munich, I never swam competitively again. I felt I had done all I could do in my sport, and now I had to get off the podium. At first, it was a real adjustment. I mean, you no longer hear applause on a regular basis for every performance. You kind of get used to that."

Spitz, who lives in the Los Angeles area, became involved in several business enterprises. Today, at thirty-two, his primary financial interests are in a building-development company that he owns and in the licensing of sports apparel bearing his name.

Although he continues to make commercials, he still has difficulty being a public figure. "Some of the stuff that I read even today about me is trash," he said. "Like I was reading that I had been divorced. The truth is, I've been married to the same girl, Suzy, for ten years."

One of his recreations now is sailing. He competes every two years in a race from Los Angeles to Hawaii. Last year, he said proudly, he and his crew finished third.

Does he ever swim? "Barely," he said. About once a week he goes "through the motions" in the pool in his backyard. "And after only 20 minutes, I'm beat," he said.

Part V: The Furor, the Fuhrer, and Beyond

As the World Watches

Two of the most controversial individual Olympic track competitors, for different reasons, were Jesse Owens, in the 1936 Berlin Olympics (sometimes referred to as "The Nazi Olympics"), and John Carlos in the 1968 Mexico City Olympics, when both he and fellow medalist Tommie Smith raised black gloves in the Black Power salute on the 200-meter winners' platform, Smith having earned the gold and Carlos the bronze, for third place. I had an opportunity in later years to spend time with both Owens and Carlos and they recounted elements of their historic events.

Two other runners with highly significant achievements were Wilma Rudolph, (dubbed "America's Black Princess") who suffered a paralyzed left leg as a child and yet overcame it to become a gold medal winner in three sprint races in the 1960 Rome Olympics, and Abel Kiviat, the oldest American Olympic medal-winner, with intriguing insights. And then there was Kathy Switzer, a pioneer runner, who dramatically fought off a knife threat by a mugger while training for the New York City marathon. And soccer, once in the shadows in America in regard to popularity, has grown mightily; I explored just how great is that emergence from those shaded areas.

Aryan and Owens: Back to Berlin

March 25, 1968

The story of twenty-two-year-old Jesse Owens breaking three Olympic records and winning four gold medals, three in sprint races and one in the broad, or long, jump, in the 1936 Games is as tense, as touching, as thrilling today as it was then. The nationally televised documentary, *Jesse Owens Returns to Berlin* proves it again.

The setting for Owens' extraordinary feat was extraordinary, if not disquieting. Nazi leaders had boasted of Aryan superiority and disparaged the American team, especially its track contingent, which it termed a "black auxiliary." In the midst of goose-stepping military parades and throngs with arms thrust forward, booming "Heil Hitler," the Games resembled Armageddon.

It transcended pure sport and had an almost unreal aura of a morality play, fairy tale and soap opera lumped together.

Owens, now fifty-four years old, somewhat balding and still lean at 5-foot-10 in white turtle-neck sweater, dark slacks and black loafers, and still seemingly able to run 100 yards in record time if called on in a pinch, recalled in sonorous tones those times in the midtown Manhattan office of the film's producer and director Bud Greenspan.

"I don't think a lot of people knew the story of Luz Long and me," said Owens. Indeed, a little-known aspect of the unfolding drama in Berlin was the camaraderie developed between Owens and the blond, 6 foot, twenty-three-year-old Luz Long, Germany's top broad jumper. The pair continued their friendship through correspondence until the Nazis attacked Poland in September 1939.

Long joined the Wehrmacht during World War II and the lance corporal was killed in The Battle of St. Pietro in Sicily in 1943. Owens returned to Germany in 1951 and met Long's widow and ten-year-old son Kai. "I recognized the boy immediately," said Owens. "He looked exactly like his father." Owens and Kai struck up a correspondence, too, that continues to this day. "He's not a track man," said Owens. "He's a golfer, like I am."

When Owens went back to Berlin recently to film the documentary, he met Kai again. A sequence in the film shows Owens telling the young man about that Olympic experience. There is also a shot of Kai and Owens resting on their stomachs in the grass of what was called the Reich Sports Field Stadium, just as Luz and Owens had been photographed by a wire service photographer thirty-two years before. The Stadium, remarkably, was untouched by Allied bombing.

In 1936 the German team was housed apart from the rest of the athletes in the Olympic Village. One day before the Games began, Long came to the Village to meet Owens, the sprinter and broad jumper who had already earned an international reputation. Owens had never heard of Long.

Long spoke adequate English, and the two became friendly. A Mexican broad jumper—"I forgot his name," said Owens—became close with them, and the three often practiced together and aided each other when needed.

"This Mexican fellow had never jumped more than 22 feet," said Owens. "Luz and I were jumping 24 and 25 feet regularly. Qualifying was 23-51/2." (Despite the help of Owens and Long, the Mexican, Pascual Gutierrez, failed to qualify.)

Owens was favored to win that event easily. But, if not for Long, he might not even have qualified.

"Each contestant was allotted three jumps in the morning trials. Wearing his sweat suit, Owens fouled on the first try. He discarded the sweat suit on the second attempt, and improbably fouled again.

"Now I was ready to take off everything else," said Owens, with a wry smile. "At this point, Luz came up to him and said, 'Jesse, you should be able to qualify with your eyes closed. Why don't you draw a line a few inches back of the board and aim at making your take-off from there? You'll be sure not to foul, and you certainly ought to jump far enough to qualify."

Owens did so and qualified, with nearly a foot to spare. The finals were held the same afternoon. Long was Owens's stiffest competition. On his second jump, Owens set an Olympic record: 25-9 ¾. Incredibly, in that world of fractions, Long in his fifth of six jumps tied Owens. The black American bettered the mark on his next try. On Long's final effort, he fouled. Owens, in his last jump, catapulted 26-5 ¼, for a world record that would stand for twenty-five years.

As Owens lifted himself from the sawdust, Luz, as seen in the film, wearing black, ankle-length socks under his track shoes, bounded forward, embracing and slapping and congratulating him. A movie camera caught Hitler in his special box scowling with beetled eyebrows. His neck fidgeted as if his tie was too tight. Maybe that was why he broke custom and departed hastily without shaking the winner's hand. Long settled for a silver medal, to Owens's gold.

"I've had many moments in the sun," said Owens, "but none compare to the one of Luz Long beside me on the winner's platform."

"We climbed down and walked side by side around the stadium, our sweat suits tossed over our shoulders. It took a lot of courage for Luz to befriend me in front of Hitler. Each section rose as one as we passed. There were 110,000 people standing and cheering when we entered the shadows under the stands."

* * *

In his last letter to Owens, Long asked Jesse to contact his son after the war and tell him about his father and "what times were like when we were not separated by war. I am saying—tell him how things can be between men on this earth." Owens later served as the best man in Kai Long's wedding.

Marty Glickman: The Return Of the Old Sprinter

December 3, 1996

Jesse Owens on one leg could have beaten him in a race, he said. "But, I wasn't the only one," recalled Marty Glickman. Yet Glickman believed that he, and not Owens, ought to have run in the 400-meter relay in the 1936 Berlin Olympics. And Owens, who had already won three gold medals, had agreed, though when Owens expressed it to a coach of the United States track team, he was admonished. "You'll do as you're told," said Dean Cromwell.

So Marty Glickman, in one of the bleakest moments of his life, would become widely known for having not done something.

"If it hadn't been for that decision by our coaches," said Marty Glickman, who was then a freshman at Syracuse and already a track and football star, "no one would remember me as an Olympian. I mean, name another 400-meter relay runner. But I'd much prefer to have run and won a medal."

Glickman, who has recently published his autobiography, *The Fastest Kid on the Block*, with Stan Isaacs, became one of this country's finest sportscasters. He made a name for himself beyond the Olympics, when, on that August morning of the 400-meter relay trial heat in Berlin, the team got the news: Glickman and Sam Stoller, the only two Jews on the United States track team, were being scratched though both had qualified and were expected to run.

"We were heavily favored, but the two coaches, Lawson Robertson and Dean Cromwell, said that the Germans had been rumored to be hiding world-class runners," recalled Glickman. "I was steamed. I said to Cromwell, 'How can anyone hide world-class runners?'" The American team, with Owens and Ralph Metcalfe as replacements, won easily, while the Germans finished fourth.

"What I later heard is that Hitler made it known to Avery Brundage, the head of the International Olympic Committee, that he did not wish for the Jews to run. It was humiliating enough for Germany to have the black Americans winning gold medals, but giving Jews a chance to win was too much."

While Brundage and American officials denied the accusation, Glickman still harbors the notion. He thought the United States Olympic Committee might invite him to the Olympics in Atlanta, on the 60th anniversary of the Berlin Games. But it didn't. "I'm still an embarrassment to them," he said. "Only once in the 100-year history of the Olympics have any athletes who were fit and had qualified not been allowed to compete for the American team. And that was the two Jews on the 1936 track team."

Glickman was at the microphone for the first Knick game ever broadcast, fifty years ago, as well as college hoops. As a New York sportscaster for six decades, he was widely respected. "It was very satisfying to read in the paper one day," he recalled, "that a college basketball coach said he had scouted his next opponent by listening on the radio to my account of their game."

Glickman also broadcast Giants and Jets games—as well as Knicks games—before retiring four years ago. At seventy-eight, the still dark-haired, somewhat thicker former sprinter coaches HBO and Sports-Channel announcers.

Glickman believes that the Olympics have become so commercialized and inflated that they will self-destruct. "There's no point to the Games anymore except to sell products," wrote Glickman. "I predict that they will last for only a few more Olympics and die out."

But the incident in Berlin remains controversial. "It was crushing for Sam," said Glickman. "He was three years older than me and felt he'd never have another chance at the Olympics. I was eighteen and thought, 'I'll get 'em in the 1940 Olympics.' But the war knocked out the Games. I believe the letdown really got to Sam, and over time he became reclusive." Stoller died in 1983.

The 1936 Olympians ran throughout Europe and Glickman beat, among others, the best German sprinter, Erich Borchmeyer. One race took place in Scotland, at the Firth of Forth. Glickman returned this year.

"I mentioned to our cab driver, 'This is the first time I've been back here in sixty years,'" recalled Glickman. "The driver replied, 'Oh, was it something we said?'"

And Glickman laughed the rich laugh that many of his radio listeners will remember for as long as we do the time he was excluded from running in Berlin.

* * *

One American Olympian competing in the 1936 Games who actually met Hitler was Adolph Kiefer. I interviewed him in his suburban Chicago residence in 2000, when he was eighty-two years old.

An Olympic Swimmer Remembers the Fuhrer

August 5, 2000

There had been a commotion, Adolph Kiefer remembers, and everyone stopped what he was doing and looked around. There were German soldiers and an entourage surrounding Adolf Hitler entering the training-pool area in the Olympic village in Berlin. This was shortly before the start of the Games in 1936. Kiefer recalls Hitler taking a seat at poolside and watching some of the training session, and then the German Fuhrer asked to meet him and two other swimmers.

Kiefer, then seventeen, was already a record-holding backstroke champion and a cover boy on many magazines. At 6-foot-1, 175 pounds, he was strong and, with dark hair and blue eyes, handsome enough to have later been asked to audition to play Tarzan in a movie. But now Kiefer climbed out of the Olympic pool, soaking wet, and shook hands with Hitler.

"I remember him being a small man with a small hand," Kiefer said, "and his handshake wasn't a firm one. Then he spoke to the interpreter, and I was told he said something like, 'This young man is the perfect example of the true Aryan.'"

Kiefer wasn't sure, at that time, what Hitler was referring to. After all, he was an American—born and raised in Chicago. Yes, his parents, Otto and Emma, had immigrated to the United States from Germany some twenty years earlier, but there were no other ties to their homeland, or its new theories. "At the time, I was honored to meet this important head of state," Kiefer said. "But if I knew then what I know now about Hitler, I should have thrown him into the pool and drowned him. I even can't stand the name Adolph now. But I'm stuck with it."

* * *

Kiefer continued to make a name for himself. He won the gold medal in the 100-meter backstroke in the Berlin Games, setting the Olympic record of 1 minute 5.9 seconds, though he didn't break his own world record of 1:04.8. The Olympic record stood for twenty years and the world record for twenty-five. In his career, racing the backstroke from 50 feet to 1,500 meters, Kiefer lost just two races in 2,000 meets from 1935 to 1944, setting 17 world records. Last January, he was voted one of the 25 greatest male swimmers of the twentieth century by a panel for *Swimming World* magazine.

John Carlos: "All Because I Stuck My Fist in the Air"

August 25, 1972 / Munich, Germany

"What's it been like the last four years? Miserable. I beg here, borrow there, steal here. Hustlin'. When you grow up in a ghetto like Harlem you learn how to hustle," said John Carlos. "Nobody'll hire me. I'm an *untouchable*. All because I took my fist and stuck it in the air."

"Say, what you want, an interview? I need money. I got a wife and two little kids that I been making promises to. Then I show up empty. Come across with some bread, huh?"

Carlos, twenty-seven years old, slumped slightly in his chair in the Puma athletic shoe store in the Olympic Village here in the midst of the '72 Olympics. He stroked his beard, stretched his long legs (he's 6-foot-4) and agreed tacitly to talk.

Athletes in a rainbow of sweat suits came in to look at shoes, joke and slap palms with Carlos. He is not here as a participant because a short-lived pro football career ended his amateur standing. He is in fact working in the store. He says the shoe company paid his transportation and room here. But that's all. He says he must pick up all other expenses.

He had wanted an executive job with the company, whose shoes he has been wearing and promoting for ten years ("before other cats had even heard of 'em"), but says he was refused. "They said I give 'em a bum image in Mexico City."

In what has been variously described as an heroic, dumb, humanitarian, evil act, John Carlos and Tommie Smith each gave black-gloved Black Power salutes as they received their bronze and gold medals respectively after the 200-meter race in the 1968 Olympics. They were immediately expelled from the Olympic Village in Mexico City. Carlos said that Tommie Smith has had to "hustle," too, until he recently became assistant athletic director at Oberlin College in Ohio.

"I tried to do something for mankind," Carlos said. "I wanted to make some kind of statement about the injustices all over the world, not just America. I wanted people to wake up to what's happening in the world. One half the world is rich, the other half is starving. It should be balanced."

Is he involved in any kind of Olympic boycott action here?

"No, and I don't think there will be any from an individual standpoint. The athletes seem younger now, and not so socially conscious. I'm not talking about the nation-to-nation thing. That's something else.

"But that's part of the whole political thing about the Olympics. Don Schollander, the swimmer, told it straight. He said the Olympics are more political than the presidential elections. You know, why do you have to wear the uniform of your country here? Why do they play national anthems? Why do we have to beat the Russians? Why do we have to beat the East Germans? Why can't everyone wear the same colors but wear different numbers to tell 'em apart? What happened to the Olympic ideal of man against man?"

Has anything concrete come from his action in 1968?

"I think some people, maybe even guys in our government, got their heads together better about some issues, like race."

Did he learn anything from the experience?

"I learned that the only difference between America and the other countries is that the other countries are not preachin' this freedom of speech jive. In the States, if they don't dig what you're sayin', you're an outcast.

"I see that 'cause I can't get hired. I got a degree in business from San Jose State. It means nothing. I wanted something in public relations. Nothing. I wanted to make a State Department track tour. They took Bill Toomey, not me. In so many words they told me I was *undesirable*.

Would he do the Black Power salute again if he had it to do over again.

"I felt I had to."

Is he disappointed in not being able to compete here?

"I go down to the track every day and work out. I ran a 10-flat 100 meters the other day. And I see this Russian, Borzov, who people are talkin' about. They call him the White Blitz. But that's cool. I'd like to run against him man to man, not black against white. For the competition. But a good white sprinter comes along once every eight, ten years, like tht German a couple years back, and that Italian, and people fuss over 'em.

"Borzov saw me on the track the other night. I was in my sweats. I knew he was wondering if I was eligible."

And the future?

"Maybe I'll be a track coach. I've had offers from Africa. I may be forced to leave my own country."

* * *

Valery Borzov won the 200-meter race with a time of 20.00 seconds. Carlos's time in Mexico City for the bronze was 20.10. (Smith's was 19.83.) Carlos went on to coach track and field at Palm Springs (California) High School, and later worked for the US Olympic Committee.

Wilma Rudolph: Forever the Regal Champion

November 13, 1994

She became America's black Cinderella. But her early dreams were not to find Prince Charming, or to be Queen of the Debutante's Ball. Or even to be adored, as she would be, and cheered lustily and mobbed around the world, with her fans sometimes even stealing off her shoes—while she wore them.

"The only thing I ever really wanted when I was a child," Wilma Rudolph once told me, "was to be normal. To be average. To be able to run, jump, play and do all the things the other kids did in my neighborhood."

Wilma Rudolph's life, however, became the stuff of fairy tales, the crippled girl at age eleven who became an Olympic sprint champion at twenty, whose charm and elegance captivated millions.

She was born in 1940 in a small house in Clarksville, Tennessee, the twentieth of twenty-two children to the combined two marriages of her father, Ed Rudolph, a railroad porter, and her mother, Blanche, a domestic.

And yesterday early in the morning, in Brentwood, Tennessee, not far from her birthplace, Wilma Rudolph died, having succumbed to a malignant brain tumor.

"She was beautiful, she was nice, and she was the best," said Bill Mulliken, winner of an Olympic gold medal in swimming and team-mate of Rudolph's on the 1960 American team in Rome Olympics. "I can still see in my mind's eye a photograph of her gracefully crossing the finish line first in the 200-meter dash in Rome, her head back, her outside leg raised. To me, that picture symbolized what Wilma Rudolph was all about—the epitome of athletic femininity."

When Wilma was four, suffering simultaneously from double pneumonia and scarlet fever, her left leg became paralyzed. At age six, she was fitted with a special shoe, which enabled her to walk haltingly. She wore that shoe until she was eleven.

"I remember the kids always saying, 'I don't want to play with her. We don't want her on our team,'" she said. "So I never had a chance to participate. And all my young life I would say, 'One day I'm going to be somebody very special. And I'm not going to forget those kids.'"

Whatever spurs are needed to drive a champion, one of those must be a need to continually prove oneself to others, as well as to oneself. Talent, while, significant, is not enough.

"I was competitive from the very first moment I heard that girls were allowed to run track," she said. "And from that moment, that was my world. I trained daily. I was forever skipping class, and would climb over the fence and be the only girl in the stadium."

Tall and slender—she grew to 6 foot and 130 pounds—she was also greatly gifted. She became a track and basketball star in high school, and then at Tennessee State University in Nashville. As a high school star, she won a bronze medal in the relays in the 1956 Olympics in Melbourne. Good, but perhaps not enough to make those kids in her old neighborhood never forget her.

Four years later, she won three gold medals, in the 100-, the 200-, and the 400-meter relay, the most track and field gold medals won by a woman since Babe Didrikson in 1932.

"The '60 Olympics was my greatest thrill," Rudolph said. "And when I think back on it, I still get frightened, to remember a capacity crowd in the stadium all standing and chanting my name."

She returned to America and earned a teaching degree from Tennessee State. Her life took on a frequently mundane quality. She tried a few jobs, from teaching school to coaching. She was human, sometimes self-involved, and making decisions that turned out poorly. Had tax problems. Was married twice and divorced twice.

But she remained Wilma Rudolph, Olympic champion. She set up the Wilma Rudolph Foundation for minority youngsters. She gave speeches, she reaped honors for long-ago achievements. And, like other black Olympic champions, she returned to an America that could be hostile. When, once, she went for a bank loan, she experienced rejection because, she believed, of her color. And while she might not have had the same reaction to racial slights as her fellow 1960 American Olympian,

Cassius Clay, who threw his gold medal into a river, she remained aware that, in effect, the playing field outside of the playing field was uneven.

But none of that diminished her beauty, or her stature. When she entered a room, she commanded it immediately, walking straight and tall, invariably wearing a stylish hat and a generous smile, all warmth and majesty.

She retired from running in 1962 because, she said, she wanted to be remembered "at her best." And her legacy, her inspiring story, is a model of all the cliches turned truisms in sports. For boys as well as girls. For any color. From any culture. With any handicap.

"When I was running," Wilma Rudolph said, "I had the sense of freedom, of running in the wind. I never forgot all the years when I was a little girl and not able to be involved. When I ran, I felt like a butterfly. That feeling was always there."

Abel Kiviat: "America's Oldest Olympic Medal-Winner"
June 24, 1991

Abel Kiviat, born on the Lower East Side of Manhattan, was one of "a trio of great milers" from America competing in the final of the 1,500-meter run in the 1912 Olympic Games in Stockholm. Norman Taber and John Paul Jones were the other two outstanding American runners referred to by Dick Schaap in his book, *An Illustrated History of the Olympics*. The three, wrote Schaap, "waged a furious struggle as they stormed down the stretch, but in the final 30 meters, Arnold Jackson of Oxford and Britain uncorked a tremendous kick and, with his last ounce of energy, overtook the three Americans. He collapsed at the tape.

"The British star won by the narrow margin of one-tenth of a second over both Kiviat and Taber, with Jones only three-tenths of a second farther back. The first five finishers all broke the Olympic record by more than five seconds."

"Run, Abel, run," called a photographer. "One more time."

"If I have to run one more time," Kiviat replied yesterday, "I'll need a pushcart to bring me back."

All these years have passed and Kiviat now was back in running gear, on Fifth Avenue on a slow Sunday afternoon. He is America's oldest living Olympian and he was celebrating his 99th birthday.

A party was given in his honor at the New York Road Runners Club on East 89th Street, but in the late morning on this overcast summer day he had been asked to give a little sprint for the cameras. With the help of Fred Lebow, president of the Road Runners, Kiviat had changed from blazer and vest into a white Road Runners sweatshirt, fluorescent green shorts ("Don't you have a bigger pair?" he asked. "These are choking me.") and gray running shoes.

Kiviat, who stands about 5-foot-4, retains a wiry look. His hair and mustache are white, his eyes are still blue and knowing, his tongue is often sharp, if not at times a little testy, and, when put to the challenge, he can still pump his wrinkled knees and bowed legs for several strides.

"Catch me if I fall," he whispered on the street to a young woman from the Road Runners who stood nearby. And then, to the cheers of several, including some curious passers-by, he jogged his jog. He needed help from neither the young woman nor a pushcart. "Oh, it's cold out here," he said.

"OK," said Lebow, "let's go inside."

Kiviat, a widower who retired several years ago after thirty-nine years as a clerk in the United States Federal Court in Manhattan, lives now in a senior citizens' home in Lakehurst, New Jersey. "He still takes care of himself and cooks for himself," said his seventy-eight-year-old son and only child, Arthur, "and he still smokes a couple of cigars a day—enough to louse up the apartment."

Any advice on running? Kiviat was asked.

"Don't run on the roads," he said.

Any advice about diet?

"Don't eat condiments. Like salt and pepper and chili sauce."

Do you have any vices?

"Mind your own business and you'll never get a bloody nose or a black eye," he suggested.

In the balloon-laden room where his birthday party was held, there are several trophies that have been given by Kiviat to the Club. He lost his Olympic silver medal, however. "Haven't seen that thing in sixty years," he said. "I think one of my brothers took it. I used to give 'em all my medals."

Some of those medals were awarded for such triumphs as winning national championships in middle-distance running, beginning in 1911, and setting the world record for the 1,500 meters, at 3:55.8, which he held for six years, and which was the American record for 16 years. He loved running, and, says his son, never chose to become a coach because he wanted to retain his amateur status. "Kind of dumb, if you ask me," he said. "Dad just didn't want to make money from track. You know, he never took under-the-table money. Even back then it was being done."

The most famous athlete in the 1912 Olympics was, of course, Jim Thorpe. "My roommate, or I was his roommate, on the boat," recalled Kiviat. "But it only lasted a couple of days. They moved me after one night when Jim got loaded and kicked in the door of our room. But I think the King of Sweden was right: Jim was the greatest athlete in the world."

Another member of the American Olympic team that year was Avery Brundage, who competed in the decathlon, and later became the controversial head of the International Olympic Committee. "Everyone hated him, even then," said Kiviat. "He was very bossy, and had a big mouth. He was always abusing people."

There was a big birthday cake rimmed with strawberries for Kiviat, and several gifts, and a framed letter was read by his friend Stan Saplin, which wished him the best of health. It concluded: "God bless you. Sincerely, George Bush."

Kiviat smiled. "I once met Teddy Roosevelt," he said. "In aught-eight."

Kiviat was asked again about that 1,500-meter race in the 1912 Olympics: "Was it the highlight of your career, winning a silver medal, or a disappointment, in that you didn't win the gold?"

"Once in a while," he said, "I think about that. And think about my mistake."

What was your mistake?

"Letting him win," he said.

Kiviat was born in 1892, before automobiles came on the scene, before radio came into living rooms, and eleven years before the Wright brothers took off. He was a modern man, though, and only a few years ago was he forced to give up his driver's license. He says he's now looking for a woman to take up with.

"She doesn't have to have teeth," he said, "she just has to have a driver's license."

* * *

Abel Kiviat died in 1991 at age ninety-nine.

It's A Long Way Home

The Marathon's Other Side

November 8, 1989

You see a lot more people than usual wobbling along the streets of New York lately. You see them limping, as if they've been kicked in the shins, or listing to the left or right, as if they've been battered in the ribs. Sometimes, they'll clutch a lamp post to steady themselves, then slowly move on up the avenue.

You see this a lot at this time of the year; it's the season, the several days following the marathon.

About 25,000 people were at the cramped starting line for the New York City Marathon on Sunday, all 26 miles and 385 yards of it. Some 20,000 finished. That's a terrific amount of sore muscles and bruised feet and aching chests. Doctors all around town can't believe their luck that the marathon has become such a big deal.

What's amazing to me is that people do it at all. It's true in many instances that, as Adlai Stevenson said, there's no gain without pain. But this is taking a nice little adage to extremes. I never heard of Adlai Stevenson running a marathon.

On Sunday, a crisp fall day, the runners, at the end of the long route through the five boroughs, came heaving into that loose-leafed park. All along the way race officials laud the bystanders who cheer the runners on. What isn't noted is that the bystanders are standing, and not running. And they seem absolutely thrilled about this. Maybe that's why they're clapping, for themselves.

They figure if you want to go to Central Park, stroll, or take public transportation, why run 26 miles and then have to call for a stretcher when you arrive?

Acquaintances often ask if I'm going to run the marathon. This passes for small talk around here at this time of year.

I say, "No." They ask, "Why not?" I answer with brutal honesty, "Too far."

Fact is, I do run, or jog. I run three miles a few times a week up, up and down city streets. I don't run for medals, or personal bests (I don't keep track of time), or to beat women with buggies to a corner (though I admit to putting on a spurt occasionally and whizzing past them just at the light).

No, I run primarily for blueberry cheesecake. Or pineapple cheesecake. Or strawberry cheesecake. And sometimes for banana cream pie, seven layer cake or chocolate blackout.

Mostly, I run to get it over with. There is nothing so good as digging a fork into a piece of cheesecake that you feel you richly deserve.

I run to keep what I call a "balance." The balance is that I can often walk up three flights of stairs without having to drape myself over the banister after the second floor. The balance also involves the attempt to keep the same notch on my belt. Marathoners talk about a "high" at the 20-mile mark, something like that. Others talk about a high of accomplishment. My high comes when I sit down with a utensil and tuck my napkin in my shirt.

My friend Dave the Carp said he began running because a woman he was interested in was a runner. He pursued her all over town. He has since gone beyond her, and now is smitten by another who he sees running regularly in the park, someone he describes as having "a beautiful haughty stride." "I have," he said, 'Runner's Crush.'"

So people run for many reasons. One person runs for health, one person runs for romance, and someone else runs from the posse.

A few years ago, an inmate from the Fort Pillow (Tennessee) State Prison, who had trained by running 25 miles a day around the yard, escaped on foot while on a detail.

A ten-state search by National Guardsmen, aided by tracking dogs, pursued the convict. The question became, which would tire first, his dogs or theirs? As I recall, his did.

Why do I run three miles instead of 10 or 15 or 25? Because, as the saying goes, you've got to listen to your body. My body states, "Three miles, and not a foot more!" Somehow my body and I agree that my normal three miles is enough of an exercise to keep my juices coursing through the old rivulets.

Meanwhile, I've developed certain personal rules of the road. One is, don't think too much about running beforehand, or you'll go lie down. I run facing the traffic; I don't like surprises. And I don't stop to give change for a parking meter. I did once, to a woman with a dog, and she said: "Sir, would you mind? You're dripping on Freddie."

Like many who run, I was guilty of proselytizing. It was with a man named Gene in my building. He was sitting outside in a folding chair and smoking a cigar. He had been under the weather lately.

I stood in front of him after my run, sweating and breathing heavily. "You know, Gene," I said, "you might be able to use a little running." He slowly took the cigar out of his mouth. "Damn little," he said.

I slunk off to my cheesecake.

Kathy Switzer, Marathon Pioneer, and the Knife

October 10, 1974

The sun's morning rays were already growing warm as they spilled in an orange stream across Manhattan's East River, and then onto the concrete promenade where Kathy Switzer ran. A boat horn sounded; birds were heard in the trees. She felt easy and light. It was a beautiful morning. And when she became aware of the footsteps behind her she turned and looked, more out of instinctive curiosity than alarm.

A hundred yards or so behind, she saw a man in sweatshirt and sweat pants in a leisurely trot—obviously a fellow jogger. Subconsciously, she felt relieved about that.

Kathy has had some uncomfortable experiences while jogging alone. Now, she always clips a pencil-thin aerosol can of "dog spray" to the drawstring of her sweat pants, to ward off some dogs and some people.

One afternoon several months ago, while jogging through Central Park, five tough-looking youths jumped out of the bushes. As Kathy came up hill in her 18th mile, the boys made lip-smacking sounds and said how they liked her long legs and supple body. She recalls now that she was too tired even to be scared, paid them no heed, jogged around them and continued down the hill. They were too stunned by her insouciance to follow.

While she runs on the promenade, she runs along the iron barrier beside the river, as opposed to running close to the adjoining park area. It is similar to the precaution of the gunfighter who always sits in a saloon with his back to the wall.

The footsteps were coming closer behind her. She did not turn around this time. Just another case of fragile male ego, she said to herself. Men often pass her, she believes, because they don't like the feeling of running behind a woman.

Anyway, she did not want to think further about those footsteps. Kathy was in training for an important race for her, the New York City marathon. In the last year she has made tremendous progress in her times. She says, sitting with me in a coffee shop on Second Avenue, that she has cut 20 minutes, over the 26-mile, 285-yard distance run. With blue eyes smiling, she adds that she has lost 20 pounds, too.

The marathon event is important because she hopes to run it in less than three hours, a feat that equates to a miler breaking the four-minute barrier. And the satisfaction of such improvement over the year has been euphoric, she says. "The feeling –that you are doing all you can to be the best you can—is incredible," she has said.

Switzer received national attention when she became the first female to run in the Boston Marathon, in 1967, when she was a nineteen-year-old student at Syracuse University. She had signed the application form "K. V. Switzer" and wore a hooded sweatshirt on that rainy day. She was finally discovered when the day brightened and she removed her excess clothing while running. The Marathon's co-director, Jock Semple, a white-haired Scotsman, believing she was desecrating the, until then, all-male event, gave her hell with his brogue and tried to rip the bib number off her sweatshirt. Fellow runners came to her aid, and she remained in the race to the finish.

Later, the Amateur Athletic Union barred her and other women from competing with men (she had run distance on her college team, too). She successfully fought that ruling with the help of others. In 1972 she was running in the Boston Marathon again, but this time legally.

Kathy Switzer has been striving since the 1967 Boston Marathon to earn a place for herself and other women athletes in the male-dominated sports world. She feels women, even in athletic events, are always looked at as women first and athletes last, by officials, some participants, and many spectators. She recalls in her first Boston Marathon when, after some 20 miles, she was so fatigued she could hardly keep her eyes open. Strangely, she heard clapping. She opened her eyes and saw an elderly couple alongside the road, and the lady was applauding.

Kathy figured the lady was cheering her perseverance. As Kathy jogged by, she held her head high and overheard the lady say, "Look, dearie, isn't that cute—it's a girl and she's wearing earrings!"

The slapping steps behind Kathy got closer, louder. A sudden wash of panic came over her. The man shot his arm around her neck. He stuck a steak knife under her ear. Kathy couldn't scream; the sound was caught in the pit of her stomach.

"Gimme your money," he said. "I'm gonna cut you."

He was about 5-foot-8, an inch or so taller than she. He weighed about 160 pounds, some 35 pounds more than Kathy. His arm around her neck was viselike.

She heard her voice, coming from some distant place, saying so absurdly rational in this monstrous moment, "But you can plainly see I have no money."

"Come with me," he said. He began pulling her toward the cluster of trees and bushes. "I'm gonna cut you."

Sights and sounds and thoughts swirled for Kathy. The trees, the sun, the concrete, the smell of the man, the pressure of his muscles, the squashing of her neck, the sparkle of the river, the knife point jabbing the flesh behind her ear. Thoughts of rape, of no help nearby, of being slashed, and, how crazy it seemed later in the telling, the rage at how unfair that all her vigorous training for the marathon could be washed away in a pool of her own blood.

She knew she had to get her hand on the aerosol can clipped to her sweat pants, and hidden under her warmup jacket.

The man wasn't aware of Kathy's attempt to get the can. She knew even under this great pressure that she could not make a mistake, had to be precise, couldn't drop the can, had to get the hole pointed in the exact direction.

She touched the can. And now everything went fantastically slow, like a dream sequence. She brought the can up, spraying all the way. She remembers seeing the stream of spray—the sun filtering through it—rising from the man's waist to his chest to his neck to his chin and into his eyes.

The man clutched his eyes and ran blindly off. Kathy dashed in the opposite direction. She got to a phone and called her friend Phillip at their apartment. He called the police.

Kathy, shaken, soon pulled herself together and a couple hours later was in her office, working at her public relations job at AMF, a sports equipment company.

And after work, before dark, she jogged her regular route of 10 miles. Kathy Switzer still had a marathon to run.

Part VI: When the Rubber Hits the Road

O ne of the first interviews as a cub reporter I conducted, so to speak, was in 1965 with Johnny Rutherford, a Texan who became a three-time winner of the Indianapolis 500 motor race. Many years later, I did the same with Gil de Ferran, a Brazilian who won the race in 2003. And again, later, I had the pleasure, truly, of sitting down with Richard Petty, the NASCAR king. Finally, I had my own adventures behind the wheel, in which in my odd way I might identify with the hazardous occupation of Johnny, Gil, and The King.

The Strange Vocabulary of Johnny Rutherford

May 31, 1974

The first question I ever put to Johnny Rutherford, one of the favorites in an upcoming local auto race I was to cover, he answered with "Vroooom, vroooom."

The answer was startling that now, nine years later, I can't even remember the question.

It was all the more disconcerting because this was one of my first assignments as a cub reporter for the Minneapolis Tribune. And on this late August day in 1965, in the infield at the Minnesota State

Fairgrounds, as cars sped around the oval track, I was attempting to conduct an interview.

I asked Mr. Rutherford—this was before I knew sports reporters ought to be on a first-name basis with their subjects—another question.

"Vrooom, vroom, vroom,'" he reiterated.

I was getting worried. Maybe he didn't hear me too well since he was wearing a helmet. Either that or he didn't speak English or I didn't speak racing. Language, in fact, was one reason I was interviewing Rutherford. I needed an advance story for the upcoming big race, and Rutherford and the other favorite in the race, Mario Andretti, were the obvious choices. I eliminated Andretti after he rather eliminated me. I spoke to him in the infield briefly. He spoke very briefly back. Perhaps he was shy with English, having grown up in Italy, or maybe he was surly, since he was not given to smiles. I tried Rutherford next. He smiled.

By now, however, I was beginning to lose my equilibrium. First, there were Rutherford's weird replies, and second the incredible clamor of the zooming cars.

I decided to try one more question, and then quit the newspaper business. This time, as in a dream, Rutherford spoke clearly and in a language I recognized. Not a single vroom. And it hit me why. For this one shining moment, the track was uniquely silent. It seemed there was some kind of break in the action, and I realized the vroom was not Rutherford's vocabulary. It belonged instead to the limited vocabulary of cars.

All this came back to me recently when Rutherford made headlines with his victory in the Indianapolis 500. His win for me was a kind of sentimental journey. We go back a long way together, though I'm certain he doesn't know it. And though I barely follow racing because I consider it a sport like jumping out of windows is a sport, I have followed Johnny Rutherford.

And I've been rooting for him. First, because he was courteous and helpful to a callow club who knew nothing about racing—I may have been the only man covering an auto race who didn't know how to fix a flat tire.

Second, I've been rooting for Rutherford because in some macabre way, I admired his professionalism.

The year before our interview, Rutherford was almost killed at Indy. He crashed into Eddie Sachs's car on the second lap. Sachs and another driver were killed. Rutherford suffered minor burns. He wanted to continue but his auto was too badly damaged. A few days after the disaster Rutherford took a practice spin around the Indianapolis track.

We talked about this on that Minnesota State Fairgrounds infield. He was beginning to speak in vroom again, so I virtually placed my ear as close to him as though it were a living microphone.

"When I went by the scene I got cold chills," he said, recalling that practice run. "But I felt no fear before or after about racing. If I did I'd quit.

"Sure, you feel terrible when something like that happens, but it's kind of like being in a war—you keep going." He shrugged his shoulders.

Rutherford went on to explain his technique for avoiding crashes. He follows what he calls his "Daytona rule-of-thumb." "At the Daytona Beach Speedway in Florida," he said, "they've got a saying that, if there's a crackup ahead of you, go straight for it because it'll probably have moved up or down by the time you get there."

The following year I was horrified to see a picture on the wire of Rutherford's car making a spectacular flip over the wall at an Ohio racetrack. Two years later he was seriously burned in a crash at Phoenix.

I wondered if he wasn't following his Daytona rule-of-thumb. I thought, too, that he ought to think of something more safely sedentary than sitting behind the wheel of a race car.

"When you're hurt so badly and you see so many others killed," he said, "there is some thought to quitting racing. But I tell myself, 'What the hell else would I do?'

What he did was win the Indy 500, the greatest accomplishment in his dangerous profession.

I was happy to hear of his triumph, but not nearly so ecstatic as the moment I discovered that Rutherford's vocabulary possessed more than just the verb vroooom.

* * *

Rutherford went on to win two more Indy 500 races, in 1976 and 1980. He retired from race-car driving in 1994, at age fifty-six. He was inducted into several auto racing Halls of Fame, including the Indianapolis Motor Speedway Hall of Fame.

De Ferran Keeps His Cool in the Heat of Competition

May 28, 2003

Gil de Ferran mulled the question about the difference between driving in the Indianapolis 500—which he won Sunday, reaching speeds of over 200 miles an hour during the 200-lap race—and riding in a New York City taxi. "Well," he said yesterday, "everything has a little danger to it."

De Ferran smiled. He has been smiling a lot in the last 48 hours, going from the famous bricks at the Motor Speedway to, as he said, "floating 40,000 feet in the clouds," to publicity functions in Manhattan, where a cab trip may indeed precipitate one's descent back to Planet Earth.

De Ferran has been smiling, that is, when he isn't crying. When the race was over—it was his first victory at Indy in four attempts—de Ferran, a thirty-five-year-old Brazilian, climbed out of the cockpit, the winner by 0.2990 of a second, the third-closest finish in race history.

And there were tears in his eyes when he met his wife, Angela; daughter, Anna, eight; and son, Luke, six.

"Daddy," he said his daughter asked when he hugged her, "why are you crying?"

"Crying for happiness," he explained.

De Ferran, who, with his short dark hair and gentle looks, can pass for a graduate student, had now exchanged his white Roger Penske team driving garb for a black business suit and said that winning the Indy 500 remained a huge thrill, despite the race itself admittedly being somewhat less of an event.

"I know that the outside perception is that Indy is not what it used to be just eight years ago," de Ferran said, "but I can tell you this: All I saw was that the stands were packed with people."

Yet he is, of course, enough of a realist to add that Indy, "if not still the biggest prize in international racing, is one of the biggest."

It was unquestionably the most popular race in the United States until 1996, when there was a split between some of the top drivers in Indy-car racing—Championship Auto Racing Teams raced on various tracks and the Indy Racing League was formed as an all-oval series.

The split diluted the competition, though in recent times there has been shifting from one to the other. The Penske Racing team, for one, switched last year from CART to the IRL, exclusively.

"What I would like to see in the sport is a concentration, not a dilution," he said. "I want to race against the best all the time. I want people like Jeff Gordon and Tony Stewart to be part of the competition. I'm optimistic that it will happen."

For the fans and surely for the drivers, the most interesting development would be for the best people to challenge one another. Imagine having baseball league championships but no World Series.

De Ferran has his own issues, regarding primarily health and performance. He broke bones in his neck and lower back in an accident during a race in Phoenix on March 23.

After diligent exercises, especially in a swimming pool, he climbed back into a racecar for the first time May 4. And during Sunday's race he said the pain, particularly in the shoulder, got worse and worse as the race went on.

"I remember at one point I looked up at the scoreboard and it read that I was on the 100th lap," he said. "I thought, 'Oh no, 100 more to go!' This was not a good sign."

Also, somewhere perhaps about that juncture, or a little before, he recalls fighting for position with Tomas Scheckter, and "not being given much room."

De Ferran added: "I thought to myself: 'You go now. I'll catch up with you later. I can wait. I'm in no particular hurry.'"

An odd thing to say in a race, it would seem, but de Ferran said that he had learned early in his career, when he was racing a car for Jackie Stewart, to cool his emotions in the heat of battle.

"There was a race in England in 1992," he said, "and I was leading, but my car started having trouble. I pulled into the pit and I was in a rage. Steam must have been coming out of my helmet. Jackie saw this and got on the radio to me and said: 'Gil, only two things can happen at this point. One, they don't fix the car, which you can't do anything about, or, two, they do fix it and then you have to race like nothing happened and do the best you can.' It was like a bucket of ice thrown on me."

The mechanics fixed the car, and de Ferran won.

He said that a great performer must have the "fire in the belly" but that the head must stay "rational." He said he admired tennis players like Ivan Lendl and Pete Sampras, and the Brazilian soccer player Dunga, who were masters in their sports but kept their composure.

And then there was an aging Carl Lewis, who won the gold in the 100-meter race in the Seoul Olympics in 1988. "The professional way he handled himself brought shivers to me," de Ferran said. "He was able to find something within him. And he wasn't running in a club meeting."

De Ferran added that his aim was not to make history—"I don't want to be Napoleon"—but said that the challenge of continually improving as a driver was paramount to him.

"Perfection is not achievable," he said, "but the pursuit of perfection is very achievable."

As for New York City cabbies, they can take heart. "They are not as scary as taxi drivers in Rio," de Ferran said. "Those drivers have a sense of the four corners of the car." The eyebrows of this very daring young man rose in awe. "I don't know how they do it. It's supernatural."

Taking a Detour from the Indy 500

May 28, 1990

The big motor race yesterday, which I wouldn't watch, reminded me that as a driver I was on my way to Indy the first time I got behind the wheel of a car. This is a true story, and in its way, a story of risking life and limb, as they do in that bizarre race.

I was sixteen years old in the summer of 1956 and my family was on vacation in Michigan City, Indiana, a popular resort area for people like us from Chicago. I had obtained a driver's permit, so I could have a licensed driver teach me to drive. That someone was supposed to be my father, who was reluctant to go this extra mile. After all, we had only one car in the family, a 1956 cream-and fire-engine red Chevy, and he used it for business. So of what use would the car be to him if his eldest son wrapped it around a telephone pole during an exercise?

But one summer's day in Michigan City, I prevailed upon him in a weak moment, and he located a lonely dirt road. Then I, unsteadily, and behind a steering wheel that seemed too large, began to drive the car. When we got to the bumpy end of the road after just missing a couple of trees, my father said, "Turn right." It happened that the dirt road ended at a huge eight-lane highway, with the deafening sound of semis rumbling by.

"Turn right?" I asked. "How about just backing up?"

"Go ahead," my father said. "You can do it."

So I turned right. And in a sweat I began to weave the car. "Stay in your lane!" my father shouted, as cars and trucks roared by. Eventually we made it off the highway. All this can be verified by an impeccable source, the honorable Judge Ian H. Levin of the Cook County Circuit Court. He was a sixteen-year-old kid then and my first cousin, and was in the back seat of the car that day screaming his head off.

When I thought about that time recently, I realized that a route going south from Michigan City is heading for Indianapolis. And I didn't miss not going to the mecca of car racing.

That first driving experience could have been disturbing enough for anyone to lose interest in cars, and in the hazards of automobile racing.

So naturally when I got my first newspaper job at the *Minneapolis Tribune* in 1965 I became the auto racing writer. I got the assignment on merit, and because no one else on the staff wanted it.

And that's how I came by the name Wheels. It was a short-lived nickname, but for a time it was all mine.

One of the first stories I did was an interview with Johnny Rutherford, who over the years I've noticed was either in the winner's circle or in the hospital.

I also read that he was again a scheduled starter yesterday in the Indy 500, which was on national television, though not in my home.

Through the years, I'd talk to other drivers about the dangers and the thrills in racing.

I asked Mario Andretti, "After all these years, do you still get nervous before a race?"

He said: "It hasn't changed in twenty-five years. You still get butterflies because you never know how it's going to come out. I can't wait till it's over."

And a driver named Pete Hamilton said: "There are very few sports in which someone can see a man put his life on the line. It's akin to bullfighting."

Johnny Rutherford, who understood the risks, said, "What else would I do?" I had some suggestions, but don't think he would have been very interested to hear.

Maybe that's the attraction for spectators. When a car hits a wall and 40 or 50 pieces of metal and several tires fly in the air, not to mention the driver himself, people roar. One of the great things about auto racing, though, is that a lot of people come out alive.

As Wheels the Racing Correspondent, meanwhile, I never got excited about seeing cars run around and around and around an oval. And when you figure in the pit stops, you never know who's ahead, and who lapped whom.

In 1957, just out of high school, I went with my father to buy my first car. I liked a black 1950 Plymouth, with a running board, a rattling metal visor over the front windshield, and a radio. It also had a stick shift. I had driven only an automatic shift, and was concerned about learning a standard shift. The price of the car, however, was right—$250.

"Go ahead," my father said. "It's not hard to learn." The words sounded familiar.

"Remember," my father said, as I got behind the wheel, "just don't ride the clutch." He explained that I should "let up on the clutch" after shifting gears.

I drove the car home, all 12 miles, down one of the busiest streets in Chicago, Western Avenue. I drove it the way I would have ridden a bucking bronco. I threw the car into first gear and the back leaped up. I threw it into second and the front jumped.

My father, driving in and out of the traffic alongside me, hollered out his window: "Don't ride the clutch! Don't ride the clutch!" I finally arrived home, exhausted. Sort of like the winner of the race yesterday.

* * *

The Dutchman Arie Luyendyk won the 1990 Indy 500. Rutherford had problems. In a practice run a few days before the race itself he endured his second crash of the month. He spun in turn three, and crashed hard into an outside wall, suffering a concussion and a knee injury. Otherwise, it must be assumed, he was compos mentis. But his speedy auto wasn't quite speedy enough, and he was "bumped," which is an official designation of the Indianapolis 500 for not qualifying for one of the 33 starting positions in the race.

"King" Richard Petty: Dealing with Defeat Away from NASCAR

December 6, 1996

It turned out that even for King Richard of North Carolina, who campaigned in his familiar feather-dominated cowboy hat and snakeskin boots and with stump speeches of about five minutes in duration, political office was not a divine right.

Richard Petty, generally known by the monarchical label accorded him by his legion of stock-car-racing fans, had run in the November election as a Republican for Secretary of State of North Carolina, and lost to Elaine Marshall by a hefty margin, gathering only about 45 percent of the vote.

"If I knew I was going to lose," Petty said afterward, "I wouldn'ta run."

From his remark, it seemed from afar that Petty might have been deluded by his fame and the adoration with which he is showered wherever he goes in his home state, and throughout much of the South, where stock-car racing is a passion.

It would not be an uncommon mistake that an athlete has believed the world—or at least his home state, surely—is his oyster, and that he could do and get about anything he pleased, and, in fact, was owed it.

Petty in person, however, does not carry himself in an imperial fashion, and maintains the common touch. "Lotta people ask me to sign their autograph with 'King Richard,'" he said, in his distinctive drawl. "But I won't. I ain't no King." He laughed. "Elvis is the King."

Yesterday, Petty, now fifty-nine and retired as a race driver for four years, was in town to receive an award for his record 200th—and last—Nascar victory, which was chosen by a national poll of racing fans as Mastercard's Greatest Moment in Nascar history. On July 4, 1984, at Daytona, in the Pepsi Firecracker 400, he nosed out, or bumpered out, Cale Yarborough, winning by about two feet.

With a pair of sun glasses perched atop his dark, curly hair, and wearing a sweater and lizard boots, he recalled that race with pleasure. "President Reagan was there," said Petty. "We met after the race. Cale and I had been runnin' side by side at about 200 miles an hour down the home stretch and bangin' against each other and the smoke was flyin' high, and the President had never seen nothin' like it in his life. He said it blowed his mind."

Petty also remembered raising his voice somewhat to speak to the President, because both of them wore hearing aids in each ear. For Petty, thirty-five years of having engines roar in his ears have caused such damage that, unless he wears hearing aids, he is nearly stone deaf.

When asked about his injuries over the years, he said: "Well, let's see. Let's start at the top. I broke my neck a couple times, broke my shoulders, my arms, my fingers, my ribs about 12 or 14 times, my legs, both feet." He paused. "But that's not as bad as it sounds, because I done all that over a period of thirty-five years. But it was a job, and I had to do it, and I had a lot of fun at it."

Petty retired in 1992 because, he said, "an athlete has to stay focused. When I got married, I told Linda, racing is No. 1. And there ain't no No. 2. Well, family became No. 2. And my businesses—I got seven of 'em, from T-shirts to hats—and pretty soon racing was competin' for No. 1." He remains some 100 victories ahead of the second-best driver in Nascar history.

As for life on the pedestal, Petty believes that the voters did not knock him off it. "It's the opposite," he said. "They kept me on it. The problem was, they didn't want me to come down from it and be involved in everyday problems. At least, that's what I've told myself. I guess you always try to find a reason for not winning a race, any race. And this makes me feel better."

Of course, many surely believed he had few credentials for political office other than his sixteen years on the Randolph County governing commission, and as a millionaire racing entrepreneur.

"I coulda thrown away my cowboy hat and put on a suit and said I'm now a full-bore politician and I'm not gonna be in racing no more," he said. "But I didn't want to lie to the people. I still work with my son, Kyle—he drives my cars—and I still have my racing businesses."

Would he ever run for office again, like Governor, as some have proposed to him?

He smiled. "Right now, no," he said. "But then circumstances can change. And how I've reacted to circumstances have dictated my life, and my races."

Part VII: Behind the Curtain—Four Unlikely Sports Executives

A s in *The Wizard of Oz*, sports teams and leagues have people working their magic, plying their marionette strings and/or sometimes poking meddling fingers into the affairs of the athletes. Those people are called "executives," from team presidents to general managers. I have chosen four such individuals, Bart Giamatti, George Steinbrenner, Jerry Krause, and one Donald John Trump, that I have covered to represent here this particular corner of the sports world, and in the best of all possible worlds to pull aside the cover where they had been ensconced.

Donald Trump's Forays into Sports

Personal Experiences With the Donald: December 2017

Some of the people who know Donald Trump best, surely, are those who have lived and worked in his hometown, New York City, and, more specifically, Manhattan, where I have lived for five decades and continue to work.

In the 2016 election, Trump lost the city to Hillary Clinton by close to 90 percent. When he went to vote at the polling place near his Fifth Avenue residence, Trump Tower, he was soundly booed.

It comes as no surprise to many of us that in the first nine months of his presidency, the *Washington Post's* fact checkers have determined that he told untruths or misleading statements some 1,200 times, or five a day. It did come as a surprise originally, for example, to the hundreds of people who paid thousands to "get rich quick" in real estate by enrolling in his scam and now defunct "Trump University," for which the courts ordered him to pay $25 million to the bilked.

One day in the 1990s, my colleague Mark Mulvoy, a low-handicap golfer and former managing editor of *Sports Illustrated*, tells this story: he was playing golf with Trump at Long Island's Garden City Golf Club. At the sixth green, it began to rain. They ducked under a nearby awning. Shortly, the rain let up. When they returned to the green, Mulvoy discovered a ball a short putt from the pin. He was sure that that ball wasn't there before the rain.

"Who the hell's ball is this?" he said.

"That's me," said Trump.

"Donald, give me a break," Mulvoy recalls telling Trump. "You've been hacking away in the (bleeping) weeds all day. You do not lie there."

According to Mulvoy, Trump replied, "Ah, the guys I play with cheat all the time. I have to cheat just to keep up with them."

Though Trump asserts publicly that he never cheats at golf, the Mulvoy story is consistent with another story (among others) that I heard about Trump and golf and fairy tales. A major businessman and Trump were going around a course not long ago. Aiming for a green, Trump hit over it. The businessman hit onto the green. When the two approached the green, Trump went over to the other man's ball, picked it up and marked the place with a coin, as is customary.

"Donald, that's my ball," the businessman said. "Your ball is in the grass over there."

"No, this is my ball," Trump said, according to the businessman.

"Do you mark your ball?" the man asked.

"No," said Trump,

"I do," said the man. "I put three ink dots on it."

Trump looked at the ball, with the three ink dots, and handed it to the businessman.

"Well," the man recalled Trump saying, "you can't blame a guy for trying."

Trump is famous around town for not paying his bills. Marty Appel, a Manhattan public relations man, tells of being hired by a representative in Trump's hands-on organization to do publicity for Trump's book, *The Art of the Deal*. He was to get $2,500. When he finished his work, he was mailed a check for $1,000. He called and said he was owed another $1,500. "No," he was told, "that's all we thought your work was worth."

"But I did everything that was agreed to, and more," said Appel.

"True," said the representative, "but that's all you're getting."

Appel sent back the check in disgust. He was, and is, now out a total of $2,500.

Trump is also famous around town for threatening to sue, or even following through, as a form of putting the muscle on an adversary. He's also famous for having a short attention span and not being an avid reader. An attorney of my acquaintance told this story: He was doing some legal work for Trump and brought several papers to his office for Trump to sign. Trump took out his pen to begin signing.

"Better first read what you're signing, Donald," said the attorney.

"I'm not going to read them," said Donald. "And if they get me in trouble I'll sue you."

When I was a sports columnist at *The New York Times*, I had occasion to spend time with Trump since he owned a professional football team in New Jersey in the short-lived United States Football League (of which he was integral in its demise) and he promoted major prizefights at his Trump Plaza casino in Atlantic City. He was often generous with his time with me, and other journalists. He admitted to liking to see his name in the papers. In the late 1990s, I was writing a book about basketball, and asked Trump, who was a basketball fan, for an interview. "Yes," he said, "but I'm doing it because I only get involved in best sellers."

"Donald," I said, "there is one way to ensure that my book is a best seller."

"What's that?" he said.

"That you buy 25,000 copies."

Donald didn't buy 25,000 copies. In fact, the only copy he may have received was the one I sent him. Oh, to make a sad story even sadder, my book, *Court Vision*, never saw the light of day on any bestseller list.

* * *

The first time I met Donald Trump was on assignment for *The New York Times*, in late December 1983. He had recently become the ownership face of the New Jersey Generals in the new United States Football League. He was already, at age thirty-seven, a known mogul around town, and famous for his buildings which are plastered in huge letters "TRUMP" on the front of them and for his publicity seeking. I hadn't personally known him before this, and when I entered his office his secretary insisted, despite my reluctance, to show a glorifying film of my subject. I found him to be a fine pitchman, and only occasionally believable.

Trump Building the Generals in His Own Style

January 1, 1984

One does not see Donald Trump right away, though; one first must see the eight-minute slide show about Trump Tower and Donald Trump.

One is ushered into a plush room—but everything about Trump Tower is plush, from the six-story-high atrium with waterfall in the marble lobby, to a pink marble football on a bronze tee in his office. (There is, however, a sense of style, and the lobby has a pianist and violinist playing in tuxedos, and the marble football has white cotton laces.)

"Can't I just skip the slide show?" a visitor asks Trump's pleasant secretary.

"Mr. Trump would like you to see it," says the secretary, pleasantly, firmly.

It runs: "This is Manhattan through a golden eye," says the film's narrator, "and only for the select few." The scenes of New York are, indeed, "breathtaking."

"Any wish, no matter how opulent or unusual, may come true."

All this leads to a pitch to buy condominium apartments—ranging from $600,000 for a one-bedroom to $12 million for a triplex—at Trump Tower, "created by a visionary builder."

Ninety-five percent of the 270 units have been sold, according to Trump, in the four months the building has been open for occupancy.

"Creating illusions, to an extent, is what has to be done," said Donald John Trump, sitting behind a wide desk and in front of a large window on the 26th floor that looks out on a panorama of Central Park. "But you have to give quality. And I've always gone first class."

He is, at thirty-seven, young to be the head of the $1 billion organization—he took his father's good real-estate business in Queens and Brooklyn and built it into a more profitable one, expanding to Manhattan and beyond. Trump has a collegiate look about him—sandy-haired, tallish at 6-2, and trim in dark business suit—and is enthusiastic and conversational.

"Two of the people I admired most and who I kind of studied for the way they did things," he said, "were the great Flo Ziegfeld, the Broadway producer, and Bill Zeckendorf, the builder. They created glamour, and the pageantry, the elegance, the joy they brought to what they did was magnificent. Others tried to copy them, and generally failed.

"In some ways, I think I've tried and succeeded with this in my buildings—the Trump Tower, the Grand Hyatt Hotel, the Trump Plaza, the Harrah-Trump hotel in Atlantic City, which opens in four months and will be the largest casino in the world—and I hope I can create some of this with the football team."

In the two and a half months since he bought the Generals of the one-year-old USFL—purchase price is estimated at $8 million or $9 million—he has created headlines on the sports pages and interest, presumably, among fans. It seems apparent that he has also stirred consternation among rivals of the National Football League.

He has done this by hiring or trying to hire or possibly hiring some of the most prominent members or former members of the NFL.

He tried to woo Don Shula from the Dolphins to coach his club, and replace Chuck Fairbanks. The news media was filled with speculation. He didn't get Shula but wound up hiring Walt Michaels, the former Jet coach, a popular New York figure, and a very newsy catch.

Last Wednesday Trump reeled in Brian Sipe, the standout quarterback for the Browns, for a reported $1.9 million for two years with an option for a third, and Dave Lapham, a veteran guard of the Bengals, to protect Sipe. The signings were announced at a news conference at Giants Stadium that drew a large number of television and newspaper reporters.

Earlier, he had acquired Gary Barbaro, a highly regarded free safety from the Chiefs, for a three-year, $825,000 contract, and on Friday he acquired two more National Football League players whose contracts had expired, Bobby Leopold and Willie Harper of the 49ers.

Then there is the report from a reliable source that he has signed Lawrence Taylor of the Giants to a contract that would begin when the star linebacker's current contract is up. In "1987 or 1988, he has an option year on it," says Trump.

"But no one knows if we signed him—actually only three people know, that's Lawrence, his agent, and me."

Have you signed him?

Trump smiles. "All I can tell you is, 'no comment.'"

He is clearly enjoying the mystery he has created, and the attention he is causing. "I guess it's been established that I have certain promotional characteristics," he said. The publicity he has created surrounding Taylor is, it seems plain, his idea of "creating illusion."

"Taylor is someone we'd very much like to have, the kind of person the Generals need," said Trump. "He is an established great player, defensive player of the year in the NFL for three years, and maybe the best player in the league. He's only twenty-three, and in three years he'll be in his prime." Actually, Taylor is twenty-four.

For Trump, this seems the kind of activity that made the Jets and Sonny Werblin, their former owner, so successful.

"Sonny created something," said Trump. "The AFL was new, like the USFL, and Sonny got Joe Namath, who had not only a star quality, but a winning quality, and built with that. I think Taylor would be in that mold for us."

And Sipe? "Sipe is a good quarterback, and the Generals were weak at quarterback last year. He will be a great plus for us. And he'll be able to help spring Herschel Walker for runs. It was a real coup getting Brian, and Cleveland still wanted him bad."

Trump admitted, however, that Joe Theismann, the Redskin quarterback, would be his idea of a star-quality quarterback. "But right now," said Trump, "he's taken."

Trump said he bought the Generals because it was a challenge, and "life is a challenge."

"I've always enjoyed sports, starting from the time I was a kid," said Trump. "I was always the captain of the teams in high school. I liked baseball, golf, tennis, football, all the sports."

He went to high school at the New York Military Academy in Cornwall-on-Hudson. In college, at the Wharton School of Finance and

Commerce, he said he had no time for sports. "I was already getting involved in real-estate deals. But I still maintain an interest in sports. My favorite, as a spectator, is football."

He also said he did not buy the Generals to make a lot of money. When he was on a recent sports forum with George Steinbrenner, the Yankees' principal owner, Trump said that everyone knows sports is a bad business and no one goes into it to make money. Steinbrenner piped up, "I did."

Trump laughs when this is recalled. "Well," he said, "maybe some of George's other businesses aren't doing so well. But in comparison to many other businesses, the profits from sports are relative peanuts."

So why get involved? For one thing, Trump admitted, the publicity that sports generate can help his other businesses. "I hire a general manager to help run a billion-dollar business and there's a squib in the papers. I hire a coach for a football team and there are 60 and 70 reporters calling to interview me."

"I could have bought an NFL team," he continued. "There were three or four available—that still are available, including, of course, the Dallas Cowboys.

"I could have bought an NFL club for $40 million or $50 million, but it's established and you would just see it move laterally. Not enough to create there."

But the Generals, he thought, were different. The league is in its infancy and could even be profitable—given that the less than $10 million he bought it for could help build a team that, he hopes, could challenge the NFL, and thereby be worth in the neighborhood of $50 million.

"I feel sorry for the poor guy who is going to buy the Dallas Cowboys. It's a no-win situation for him, because if he wins, well, so what, they've won through the years, and if he loses, which seems likely because they're having troubles, he'll be known to the world as a loser."

Meanwhile, the USFL is still a risky proposition. Can it make it in spring-time play? There are many who believe it cannot. "What I like is for people to tell me that something can't be done, when I think it can," said Trump. "In real estate, you deal with some very smart, very devious people. They're the sharpest wolves in the world. I've competed against them and I've come out fine. Sports is really small potatoes compared to that. I still have to devote 95 percent of my time to real estate, but if I didn't, if I spent most of my time on football like a lot of the NFL guys do, I think it would be cakewalk, I really do."

He believes that "in the couple months I've been with the Generals, we've already established a credibility gap we didn't have before." The team had a 6–12 record in 1983, but he believes it is stronger now. "Ticket sales are great—we've got 25,000 sold and we aren't even into training camp yet. We're hoping for 40,000 to 50,000."

Last year, though, ticket sales were 34,000. "Well, that was because of the Herschel Walker publicity. But when the team didn't win, it punctured enthusiasm."

Trump says that a winning team in the new league will fill Giants Stadium.

"People are hungry for a winning football team in New York," he said, "and I'm sure they'll support it. There's a void today in New York. And the NFL, with all its parity, it's become equal, and boring. I remember when I used to love to watch the Green Bay Packers, in their great years. You liked to watch excellence, not everyone being equal. And if you rooted for an underdog team to beat them, it was inspiring, gave you hope. It's like people going to watch Martina Navratilova play tennis. You know she's going to win, but go and you watch her for her excellence, and if someone beats her, it's a great upset, and that's wonderful, too."

For the USFL to succeed, he says, not only must New York have a strong franchise but first the league must be strong. "Like in building, you have to have a strong foundation," said Trump. "And you see other teams picking up players from the NFL. There is excitement for it in most of the cities that we're in. You also have to remember that we can afford to go after players. In general, the owners of the USFL teams are financially more solid than NFL owners."

The USFL appreciated Trump's flamboyant approach to business, and he was sought originally by the USFL for its New York franchise. "They wanted Trump," he said, "but I was immersed in the building of Trump Tower then, and, even though I had some good friends who had bought teams, like Al Taubman with the Michigan Panthers, and John Bassett with the Tampa Bay Bandits, I just couldn't find the time.

"Then when J. Walter Duncan found that being an absentee owner was too hard—he lives in Oklahoma City and every game was an 'away' game for him—he was up for selling the team, and now the league came to me and I was ready for it."

The interest of the USFL in Trump is confirmed by Steven E. Ehrhart, assistant to Commissioner Chet Simmons. It was believed that Trump's high visibility and the fact that he was not an absentee owner would stimulate a good New York franchise. "And a good New York franchise," said Ehrart, is of "paramount importance" to the league.

Trump has hopes that in two or three or four years the USFL will be competing with the NFL, and possibly moving from the spring-time schedule to fall and winter games. "And I'd like to challenge them to a championship game," he said. "That would be a lot of fun. Although I think a couple of our teams can play equally with some NFL teams, it will take a few years before this league, this entity, this entertainment is fully formed."

Meanwhile, Trump, the newest sports franchise owner, goes about becoming one of the most visible, and, in his way, candid.

At the news conference for Brian Sipe, for example, Sipe was telling about having been benched for a game. Trump stood up and said it came after Sipe, on an off-day, was in New York talking with Trump, and the Browns knew it, and reacted angrily to it.

"Brian is too much of a gentleman to say it," said Trump, "but I guess I'm not."

Trump was reminded of that recently. "That's the way I saw it, and perhaps honesty overrides gentlemanliness," he said. "But in the end we got him, we got results. I like results."

* * *

He never did sign Lawrence Taylor; there was no evidence that he could have bought an NFL team, ticket sales, it turned out, weren't great, among other claims. Things weren't working out so well for Trump and the USFL—for one thing the NFL thwarted his ambition to force a few of the USFL teams, primarily, for him, the Generals—to merge with the NFL. So, as it would be learned, Trump naturally sued. I covered some of the trial.

Donald vs. Goliath

July 25, 1986

It was close to noon Wednesday in the packed courtroom in the United States Court House in Foley Square, and Frank Rothman, a rather scholarly looking man in spectacles and gray suit and red tie, was concluding his two-and-a-half-hour summation in defense of his client, who is being sued for $1.69 billion in damages and sundry other items.

To the jury—a sextet of five women and one man who have been moored in that box for 10 weeks—Rothman now argued that the National Football League had done nothing to restrain the United States

Football League in its attempt to gain a television contract with one of the three networks to play ball in the fall.

And, he added, no matter what you'll hear this afternoon from the plaintiff's attorney, "this is not a case of the little guy versus the big guy, of David versus Goliath. It's more," he said, "like Donald versus Goliath."

That is, Donald Trump, the man with the golden slingshot, the real estate mogul and owner of the New Jersey Generals of the USFL. And the man who, according to memos by fellow owners, had devised a "grand plan" to get a handful of USFL teams merged with the NFL.

Trump is the most widely known of the well-heeled USFL owners, and the leader in this lawsuit, which is litigation by millionaires against millionaires seeking more millions, or billions.

In his summation in the afternoon session, Harvey Myerson, an appealing thespian and trial lawyer in longish dark hair, dark suit and yellow tie, and raspy voice, called on the jury to, in effect, save the republic.

It wasn't just the USFL—he always referred to it, for increased effect, as "the United States Football League"—that was at stake, but "the essence of competition is at stake." He said that the country is following this trial and expecting the jury to correct "these wrongs. . . . That's what this country is looking for you to do."

He added that the NFL—rarely calling it "the National Football League"—is "the most powerful monopoly in the country." His band of hardy entrepreneurs was being shut out because the NFL had a "stranglehold" on the three major television networks. And it is a fact of life that without a network outlet, a football league will disappear like cigar smoke in the wind.

Rothman had anticipated this argument, of course, and suggested that the NFL had worked for sixty-seven years to attain the position it now enjoyed, and that it had done it with honest toil and sweat. But the crux of the matter is, did the NFL conspire to prevent the networks, ABC, CBS, and NBC, from giving the USFL a spot during the fall?

ABC had given the new league—which began operations in 1983—a spot, but it was in the spring. The new league had an original premise that it would play football in the American springtime.

And it did. And it did it, more or less, before a hugely indifferent populace.

No matter how much the USFL teams spent on a handful of big-name players—Herschel Walker, Doug Flutie, Steve Young, the $40 million quarterback who helped sink the team that bought him, the Los Angeles Express—the league generated little excitement.

Perhaps the nation was dog-tired from a fall and winter menu of behemoths banging into one another. Perhaps this country wants nothing more from its spring than a lot of hope, a little lust, and baseball. Whatever, after three seasons, the USFL remained a virtual minor league of football to most fans. And the networks knew it.

Now, it became obvious to Trump and his handful of fellow owners that the USFL was not going to make it in the spring, and so they wanted to switch to the fall, where America has a tradition of football, of the sounds of boola boola and crunch.

And so they wanted to get a network to showcase their product. Or, short of that, they'd try to wreak a merger with the NFL, as three teams from the All-America Football Conference had accomplished in 1950, and 10 teams from the American Football League in 1966.

But for various reasons (the AFL, for example, did have a TV contract in the fall with NBC) the other leagues had a leverage that the USFL did not.

Now a lawsuit was the only way to get this leverage, it was apparently decided.

And if the USFL could prove that there was restraint of trade, that the NFL people used unfair business tactics to suppress the USFL, then that would be the pot of gold at the end of the rainbow. The USFL has attempted to prove this in several ways. The most damaging, perhaps, is that the NFL had sixty-five of its executives attend a seminar given by a professor from the Harvard Business School—the so-called Porter presentation—in which, the USFL contends, the executives were instructed in how to "destroy" the USFL.

The NFL contends that they were just trying to learn how to deal lawfully with competition.

Did the NFL, in fact, take the tack from the seminar and, among other things, try to "co-opt" influential USFL owners like Trump and Alfred Taubman of the Oakland Invaders, and promise them NFL franchises down the line?

It would not have been the first time that Commissioner Pete Rozelle of the NFL had "dangled" franchises.

And did he also twist the compliant arms of network executives to lay off the USFL? It doesn't seem unlikely, but is there concrete evidence that he did?

To these eyes and ears, the USFL has not given sufficient evidence that it has been wronged. And although the NFL is the big guy on the block, a big guy—even an acknowledged bully—must be proved wrong by conclusive evidence.

If the USFL loses, it will be gone. If it wins, it will also be gone, but a few of its teams will surely merge with the NFL, just what Trump and associates have striven and sued for.

And so the essence of competition in America, despite what Myerson contends, will not change. The NFL will continue to be what it was, a powerful monopoly, although somewhat heftier, and the football league of choice for most fans.

* * *

The result of the jury trial, NFL vs. USFL, was published on the front page of *The New York Times* on July 30, 1986, with the headline: "U.S.F.L Loses in Antitrust Case; Jury Assigns Just $1 in Damages."

The United States Football League suffered what both sides considered a resounding defeat in United States District Court in Manhattan yesterday when a jury found that the National Football League had violated antitrust law but awarded the USFL only $1 in damages.

Attorneys for the USFL, which had sought as much as $1.69 billion in damages, succeeded in proving only that the NFL had a monopoly power "to control prices or exclude competition" in the "relevant market" of professional football in the United States.

It was for that violation that the jury of five women and one man unanimously awarded $1, which is trebled in antitrust cases."

In winning, the NFL attorneys were able to convince the jury that the USFL's financial difficulties developed as a result of mismanagement and, in part, a "merger strategy," designed to take USFL teams out of major market cities and into smaller areas that the NFL might find attractive for merger possibilities.

As reported in the *Guardian*, there was a testimony on the witness stand by NFL commissioner Pete Rozelle, that is pertinent to an insight into Trump's version of truth. The two had a meeting in the Pierre Hotel in March 1984.

> "Didn't you tell Mr. Trump you wish he had been able to buy the Baltimore Colts and hadn't gone into the USFL?" asked Harvey Myerson, lead attorney for the USFL of Rozelle.
>
> "No," said Rozelle.
>
> "Did you tell him that if he hadn't gone to the USFL, the USFL would have died?" Myerson asked.

"No," said Rozelle. "Never."

Trump's testimony was decidedly different. He said the hotel rendezvous was Rozelle's idea, and recalled the commissioner saying, "You will have a good chance of an NFL franchise and, in fact, you will have an NFL franchise." The tradeoff, according to Trump, was that the USFL remain in the spring and "not bringing a lawsuit."

Trump insisted he and Rozelle were friends . . . Rozelle couldn't believe what he was hearing . . . Rozelle insisted he and Trump were certainly not friends. (There were other disagreements on the facts between Trump and Rozelle.) Unlike Trump, Rozelle was a meticulous note-taker, and he presented his documented recollections from the meeting.

* * *

The USFL, with Trump's Generals, disbanded shortly after the trial, and announced it had lost $163 million in its existence.

On November 8, 2016, Donald Trump was elected president of the United States.

* * *

Bart Giamatti was one of the most fascinating individuals that I had ever met in my five-plus decades on the sports scene. He was highly intelligent, as befitting a classics professor and later president of Yale University, and remarkably articulate. And I would learn, funny, when one might, given his background, expect a soupcon of dryness.

Bart Giamatti: From Dante to Darling

June 11, 1986

A. Bartlett Giamatti once described himself as a household name only in his own household. An apt description, perhaps, for someone who just six years ago was teaching college kids a course in Myths and Mythography in Renaissance Cultures.

In the nation's households, he may never be up there with names like Twinkies or Drano, but A., or "Bart," as he prefers to be called, may soon be making inroads.

Yesterday he was introduced in the Starlight Room of the Waldorf-Astoria to members of the news media as the 12th president of the National League, a unanimous selection by the owners of the 12 National League teams.

For the last eight years he toiled in what he apparently assumed was virtual obscurity as another kind of president. He was the head of a school in Connecticut that, most recently, is famous for having produced a pitcher for the Mets named Darling.

It is natural to wonder why a man who led the cheers for Eli Yale's scholars would decide to join the sweaty forces of the cleated and knickered. Was his leave-taking of academia reminiscent, in any way, of a scene he once recalled in a baseball article he wrote for *Harper's Magazine*? The scene was the "Expulsion of Adam and Eve" in the Brancacci Chapel.

He was asked, in other words, why a man of letters would gravitate to sports.

"Men of letters have always gravitated to sports," he said. "Witness yourselves." If ever a gravitator wished to ingratiate himself to a gathering, Dr. Giamatti found the perfect method.

This professor of Italian literature had swung smoothly and swiftly from Dante to Dale Carnegie. Dr. Giamatti has gray hair and a gray mustache and goatee, grayish eyes, and wore a gray suit, but his approach to these inquisitors was as many-hued as a Petrarch sonnet. When he made his reply to this assemblage of lettered men, the forty-eight-year-old scholar smiled a gentle and knowing smile. He conceivably was resisting the temptation to quote a line from dear Dante, who once remarked that "He listens well who takes notes."

But Dante was in the air. When asked what the author of *The Divine Comedy* would have thought about his move, Dr. Giamatti said, "He would have been delighted. He knew very well the nature of paradise, and what preceded it. After all, baseball was first played in the Elysian Fields—in Hoboken, New Jersey, in 1845, if I'm not mistaken."

He added that he was looking for changes and new challenges in his life, and it is no secret that he is a great baseball fan, and has been since he first began following the Red Sox in the middle 1940s.

It had been said that he was often seen wearing a Red Sox cap around the New Haven campus. Would he continue to do so? "No," he said, "I'll be wearing a lot of other hats in my new role."

He was asked about his own participation in baseball. "I had dreams of becoming a second baseman," he said. He paused, and then, as if to reveal a deep secret, he said, "OK, I wanted more than anything to be Bobby Doerr. There, and that's the last time I'll say it."

Dr. Giamatti said he played second base, as did his Red Sox Doerr, but he played it because "the throw was the shortest to first base."

The highest level of baseball he reached, he added, was as student-manager for the South Hadley (Masschusetts) High School team. And how did the team do? "As well as it could," he said.

"But maybe that was the beginning of my desire to be part of management."

He said that a president of a league does a number of chores that are not much different from that of a president of a university. There's keeping a hand in the financial end of the game, and surely in the public relations end. And though he has had no previous contact with professional organized sports, he said that he has had a lot to do with organized sports. "I had the ultimate responsibility for 33 varsity sports for undergraduates at Yale," he said.

He was asked if, in fact, he didn't attempt to de-emphasize sports at Yale. "No, I tried to affirm Ivy League principles," he said. He did have strong opinions on certain elements of baseball.

On the designated hitter: "I'll soften my answer by just saying that it's appalling."

Interleague play? "I favor the fundamental grid, the geometrical beauty, the fundamental structure of the history of baseball, and I think it ought to be tampered with very gingerly. I support the current autonomy of leagues, except of course for All-Star Games and World Series play, as exciting and meaningful."

On expansion: "I'm not instinctively pro-expansion. I'm for making strong and vibrant the franchises that exist. I'd first want to shore them up."

He added that "the challenges and issues that affect baseball to an enormous degree affect the country." He added that part of his job would be to maintain this "institution, this form of a public trust."

It seems to some casual observers, though, that a league president might be nothing more than a well-dressed figurehead.

Dr. Giamatti believes this will not be so. He must oversee the screening of ownership transfers and represent the league in legislation with television and lawsuits, and be responsible for the approval of player contracts.

None of which sounds particularly enthralling to at least one of the assembled flowers of American sports journalism. But there is no accounting for tastes. After all, a Renaissance man whom Dr. Giamatti studied once spent four years painting the ceiling of a church.

* * *

On April 1, 1988, Giamatti was named commissioner of baseball unanimously by the 26 baseball team owners. The one decision he will be most remembered for is his lifetime ban from Major League baseball of Pete Rose, one of the greatest baseball players in history, for gambling on games, something to which Rose first denied, but later confessed. Giamatti did offer Rose hope for eventual reinstatement if, Giamatti, said, Rose "reconfigures" his life, and abstains from gambling.

Giamatti only served 12 months as commissioner. He died unexpectedly of a heart attack on September 1, 1989, just one week after having banned Rose from baseball. Angelo Bartlett Giamatti was fifty-one years old.

Jerry Krause: The Man Who Built Jordan's Bulls

May 11, 1992

Would you have hired Jerry Krause?

When Jerry Reinsdorf, the chairman of the Chicago Bulls, did just that in 1985, shortly after he bought the Bulls and chose Krause as his vice president in charge of basketball operations, or general manager, he received a phone call from one of the top executives in the National Basketball Association.

"Why didn't you talk to me before you hired him?" the executive told Reinsdorf. "I would have told you not to."

Over the last seven years, some of Reinsdorf's business associates and close friends, as well as his star player, Michael Jordan, have counseled him fervently to fire the guy.

"What Do You Have to Do?"

Before the Bulls' first home game this season, each player and team offical was introduced to the capacity crowd of more than 18,000 at Chicago Stadium and presented with his championship ring, emblematic of the NBA title the Bulls won when they beat the Lakers, 4 games to 1, in the Finals in June. The only man to hear boos was Jerry Krause.

"What do you have to do to please them?" Krause asked his wife, Thelma, when he returned to his seat in the stands.

After all, this is Jerry Krause's team. Only one player and no coaches remain from the team he inherited on March 26, 1985.

Admittedly that one player is Jordan, but, says Krause, "no one has ever before built a team around a No. 2 guard, no matter who it was." Others, like his boss, echo that notion. It was Krause who maneuvered to make a trade in order to draft Scottie Pippen, and drafted Horace Grant, and traded for Bill Cartwright, and purchased John

Paxson. And he went after capable reserves like B. J. Armstrong and Scott Williams.

"One guy can't win a championship, never been done," said Krause. "We needed guys who could help take the pressure off Michael, and hit their shots and get the rebounds and hound on defense. And you needed a solid bench. We needed 'deep depth,' like Casey Stengel used to say. Now we got it."

While the Bulls are favorites to win their second straight NBA title—they beat Miami three straight in the first round of the playoffs and are tied 2–2 in their second-round series with the Knicks—Reinsdorf admits that Krause, now fifty-three years old, has his "foibles."

Reinsdorf says Krause can be, well, "abrupt," and sometimes "he doesn't shut up," and some of his decisions "haven't worked out so well." Fans haven't forgotten top draft picks like Brad Sellers ("a real nice guy, but I'll never again draft a guy who plays soft," said Krause), or trades he made, like Dennis Hopson ("the harder Dennis tried here, the worse he got"). Both Sellers and Hopson are now former Bulls.

Sports teams generally try to hire general managers who can court a good press. "The press in Chicago doesn't like Jerry," said Reinsdorf. "He won't give them the time of day. He's afraid that if some piece of information gets out, it'll hurt him in his basketball dealings."

Said Sam Smith of the *Chicago Tribune*: "He treats us like we're morons."

Some of Krause's fellow general managers around the league feel similarly. "Sometimes he calls you with deals that are ludicrous," said Red Auerbach of the Boston Celtics. "And he expects you to fall into his trap. The thing is, sometimes it works. Some people think Jerry's not too bright, but they're wrong. He can disarm you and fool you."

And another sports executive, who knew Krause when he was a baseball scout, said: "Ask Jerry Krause and he'll tell you that he discovered Willie Mays, Hank Aaron, and Roberto Clemente. And that was just on Saturday."

"Well," said Krause, "I admit that I used to toot my horn a little too much."

Nor does Krause appear the stereotype of a sleek sports executive. Pat Williams, the general manager of the Orlando Magic and the general manager of the Bulls when Krause was his director of scouting from 1969 to 1972, has another description: "He's short, fat, dumpy and disheveled and almost unconcerned with clothes. I call him the Prince of Polyester."

Said Reinsdorf: "That's maybe the way it used to be. But Jerry dresses better these days. It's just that nothing looks neat on him."

Krause's hair appears permanently ruffled, he is jowly to the point where the neck is nearly obscured, his left eye squints like that of the frazzled boss of Inspector Clouseau, his pants cuffs sag, and the owner of the team sizes him up at about 5-foot-5 and 230 pounds "or more."

Before he signed Krause to his current contract, four years ago, Reinsdorf offered to add $50,000 if Krause lost 50 pounds and kept it off for a year. "Not so much for looks," Reinsdorf insists, "but for his health." Krause refused. "When I'm ready to lose weight, I'll lose it," he said.

The best player on his team (the best player in the universe, for that matter), the sharp-tongued Jordan, has referred to him as Crumbs because of the doughnut flakings he had supposedly spotted on the lapels of Krause's sport jacket. And just last season Jordan went to Reinsdorf and asked that Krause be allowed immediately to find employment elsewhere. (Reinsdorf told him nicely to zip his lip and play basketball.)

Bulls Coach Phil Jackson said Krause reminds him of Joe Btfsplk, in the Li'l Abner comics. "You know, the guy with the cloud always over his head? That's like Jerry," said Jackson. "He always seems to park his car under a tree, and when he comes out the windshield is covered with bird droppings."

Said Pat Williams: "I pinned the nickname Sleuth on him. He's a classic. Slinking, suspicious, secretive, talking low and fast, plotting, planning, hiding behind potted palms, wearing disguises."

Said Krause: "I don't know if you call them disguises, but when I go to scout a player in college I often wear a hat pulled down and a raincoat and dark glasses and try to sit behind someone taller. Of course, I take off my glasses and look over the guy's shoulder in order to see the game."

To throw off would-be competitors—he's concerned another scout might see him at a game and thus heighten interest in a particular player—Krause confesses to buying a new hat every year (the current one is olive suede).

"He's been mocked, laughed at, scoffed at, kicked around, and written off more than anybody I know of in sports, and yet here he is, the general manager of the defending world champions," said Pat Williams. "He's like a rubber ball. He keeps bouncing back. And I'll tell you why. No one works harder. He works and works and works. He is relentless. He believes in himself and never has doubts about his abilities. And he does know talent. He also has a vision, a design for the future. I remember one day when he was a scout for the Bulls and he said, 'Pat, one day I'm going to run my own club.' He has had the same kind of plan for his team."

"I don't always agree with him," said Jackson, whom Krause fought for to become first an assistant coach and later head coach. "But you listen to him because you know he knows what he's talking about."

Reinsdorf discovered Krause for himself when Krause was a scout for the Chicago White Sox, a team Reinsdorf also owns. Krause had been hired by the previous team owner and a mentor, Bill Veeck.

"I remember in team meetings about ballplayers that Jerry would never get off a point when he believed in it," said Reinsdorf. "Some of the baseball people would roll their eyes. But I found that he argued from knowledge. He had spent days and weeks studying a prospect. He watched Ozzie Guillen in the Pacific Coast League for 17 straight games. He was convinced he'd be a big-league star, and fought for us to trade LaMarr Hoyt—the year after he was a Cy Young Award winner—for this minor-league shortstop. It turned out to be a great deal for us. I love a guy who has the courage of his convictions and puts his behind on the line and will be held accountable."

When Reinsdorf bought the Bulls, he had long talks with Krause and decided that their basketball philosophies coincided. "We both believed that the key to winning was defense," he said.

Reinsdorf also knew that Krause had an extensive background in basketball. He had been director of scouting of a one-man staff for the Baltimore Bullets in the late 1960s, where he was responsible for drafting Earl Monroe, Wes Unseld, and Jerry Sloan. He scouted for the Lakers and the Suns, besides having been a baseball scout for Cleveland, Oakland, Seattle, and the Cubs.

He even had a previous stint as a Bulls' general manager in 1976 and was fired because he supposedly tried to hire Ray Meyer of DePaul as the team's coach without first discussing it with the owner, Arthur Wirtz. Krause denies that he did that, but, he said: "I wanted the job too much then. I was too eager. I learned a lesson."

Krause grew up in Chicago, the son of the owner of a shoe store on the northwest side. He never played schoolboy basketball—he was, however, a backup catcher on the Taft High School baseball team—but at Bradley University he was so good at charting plays for the basketball team and analyzing players and teams that he soon quit school and wrangled his first job in 1961 as a "gopher flunky" in the office of the Cubs at $65 a week. Some thirty-five years later he earns more than $300,000 a year and has overseen a franchise that seven years ago was purchased by Reinsdorf and partners for $16 million and which is now worth upwards of $150 million.

Krause loves his work and is challenged by it to the point, Reinsdorf believes, where "the man is devoid of any other outside interests."

This certainly seems to be the case. In his memento-studded office on Michigan Avenue, Krause is calling Europe to keep the lines of communication open with Tony Kukoc, a star player in Italy, whom he has visited several times and hopes one day will be a Bull. On his VCR, Krause goes over game film after game film, of college and pro teams, forward and backward, to the point where he has suffered an occupational injury he calls "clicker thumb."

"I could never be an Elgin Baylor or Michael Jordan on the basketball court," Krause said, "but I try to be that good behind this desk."

"One scene I remember typifies Jerry best for me," said Pat Williams. "We went to scout a college game years ago and were given bad seats way upstairs. He wouldn't accept them. He ran downstairs and fought with the ushers so he could at least stand beside the bleachers seats and be closer to the court. You couldn't contain him. Then we had to leave early. And I'll never forget the sight.

"It was snowing and he was running to his car, his hair wet, his coat flapping behind him, papers that he was carrying flying out of his hands, red in the face, this overweight guy about to have a heart attack, and hollering for me to hurry up because he had to see another game that night in another town."

* * *

The Krause-Jordan Bulls went on to win five more NBA titles—making six in all in eight years—and Krause was twice named the NBA's Executive of the Year. He died in 2017 at age seventy-seven, shortly before the announcement that he had been elected to the Basketball Hall of Fame in Springfield, Massachusetts.

* * *

At the writing of the article above, Jerry Krause, general manager of the Chicago Bulls—and, essentially, the boss of Michael Jordan, arguably the best player in basketball history—after undergoing often withering criticism, had assembled a team that had just won its first National Basketball Association championship.

* * *

George Steinbrenner of the New York Yankees was one of the most controversial, and autocratic—yet to some somewhat even likable, if not lovable—owners in sports history. Also mercurial, and the hiring and firing of manager Billy Martin five times is a significant case—cases—in point. For a writer he was outstanding, ever available for a juicy quote. But I found as a columnist for *The New York Times* that he could also have a thin skin. I once ran into him at a charity event. "George," I said, "I have a question for you." He said, "Ira, I don't remember. Am I talking with you or not talking with you." I said, "George, don't you remember? You *are* talking to me." (Who remembered?) And he answered my question. At the point of the imagined column below, he had been suspended from baseball several months earlier for association with a known gambler.

The Man Who Missed George Steinbrenner

March 26, 1992

The good doctor was surprised to see me. After all, it had been quite a long time since my last visit. He led me to his couch.

"A terrible thing has happened to me, Doctor," I said, lying down and propping up my feet on his furniture, "and I need help."

"Terrible?" he said. "How so?"

"I've had a certain feeling, Doctor, which has created great guilt and angst and confusion in my mind."

"Does it have anything to do with love? Marriage? Business? The gross national product?"

"No, Doctor, the fact is, I think I miss George Steinbrenner."

The doctor sprang from his chair, rushed around his office, and returned with a cold compress, which he applied to my forehead. "No, Doctor," I said, "it's not physical. It's mental."

"You're telling me?" he said, with uncustomary sarcasm.

"Doctor, I saw in the papers where George went to a baseball game the other day. Like Elvis at 7-Elevens, there had been sightings of George at ball games, but this was the first one actually confirmed. And something stirred in me. 'Yes,' I said, 'it was right.'"

"Hmmm," said the doctor.

"And then I saw yesterday that he wrote some cockamamie letter to the other owners, saying he's tried everything he could to get back into baseball, and he wants justice, and so on and so forth. You know there's some ploy there, some subterfuge to maybe getting a suit going even though he had a signed document that he wouldn't do it. And, Doctor, I laughed to myself when I read it."

"How loud was the laugh? A chuckle? A guffaw? Or a kind of hysteria and rolling around on the carpet?"

"Something in between. You see, I don't think I've been fooled by George in the past. I mean, I know he's often been a bully, a knee-jerk jerk, a publicity hound, a twister of facts and arms, but for all his own misjudgments and failings, I miss him. He adds something to my life."

"Your life?"

"With all the bad news every day, from the front page to the sports page, George made me laugh. He is the master of the outrageous, the king of the bizarre. He is vaudeville, Doctor. Baseball is his stage."

"You think so?"

"No, doctor, please, no more compresses." I closed my eyes. "Yes, George Steinbrenner is vaudeville. He's a pie in the face, a kick in the pants, a pratfall on a banana peel."

"How about two fingers in the eyes?"

"That too. Listen, I wouldn't want to work for him. He berates. He screams. He makes people crazy. When you go home at night from him it's like being on a work release program. But he can also be generous, I understand, and he does a lot of charity work, especially with schools and minorities. But that's not why I miss him."

I'm not sure, because it was rather dark in the room, but I think the good doctor was now applying the compresses to his own head. I went on.

"For one thing, his teams had often been competitive. They've fallen on hard times, but that doesn't mean they won't bounce back. Even the Cubs have bounced back. OK, let's forget the Cubs. But I think, what's so important about winning? I mean, isn't entertainment the name of the game in professional sports? And George helps entertain us. He is by far the most recognizable owner in sports. The only one close to him is Gene Autry, and who would recognize him unless he's wearing a ten-gallon hat, strumming his gee-tar and warbling 'Tumbling Tumbleweeds'? And I'm sure that if you asked George, he'd jump up on his desk and sing for you, too. He's that kinda guy."

"Does he know 'Rudolph the Red-Nosed Reindeer'?" mumbled the doctor.

"Doctor, please, no jokes. Now, what other owner would enjoy the nickname some call him, 'Attila the Hun,' and go on to read some nutsy book titled, *The Leadership Secrets of Attila the Hun*? And underline passages, and quote it to people? One of George's favorites from the book is, 'Do not expect everyone to agree with you—even if you are King.' And here's another he liked to quote: 'Chieftains must teach their Huns well that which is expected of them. Otherwise, Huns will probably do something not expected of them.'

"And what other owner has been quoted as widely as George? Remember when Goose Gossage was complaining about something? The Boss said, 'Goose should do more pitching and less quacking.'"

The doctor cleared his throat.

"Doc," I said, "will I be all right? Can I overcome this affliction of missing Steinbrenner?"

"Hmmm," he said, opening his appointments book. "Will next Thursday at 6 p.m. be convenient for you?"

* * *

Steinbrenner returned to baseball, and led the Yankees to seven American League pennants and five World Series championships. He died in 2010 of Alzheimer's disease at age eighty.

Part VIII: How the Weather Was

Sports—quite like life—has four seasons to recommend it. Below are my reflections on that sweet—sometimes bittersweet—quartet of confounding nature in play.

On the Whole, He'd Rather Be in May

April 18, 1973

In the entry for April 1, Jim Bouton, diarist and former big-league knuckleballer, wrote in his seminal book, *Ball Four*, as his team ended spring training, "Four pitchers were cut today."

What a foreboding way to open April! It is doubtful that Bouton was consciously aware of T. S. Eliot's melancholy opening line from his poem "The Wasteland": "April is the cruelest month." The notion, though, is in the spring air.

The fragrant breezes of an early April day carry in hope as if on a magic carpet. Too often it is just an evil tease. The carpet runs afoul of the elements. It happened recently in the Midwest. The regular baseball season opened blithely, and immediately ran into a wall of mid-winter whiteness.

A most telling and terrible photograph was that of Norm Cash, the Tigers' first baseman, taking batting practice before a frigid game in Detroit wearing a woolen cap that covered his face like an executioner's mask.

April is the cruelest month, figured Eliot, because in "breeding/ Lilacs out of dead land, mixing/Memory and desire, stirring/Dull roots with spring rain," it also flushes up tendrils of disillusion.

There is a forward look of youth and aspiration in April that, for baseball, will end in October, will end for most in disappointment, and will end not with a bang, to paraphrase another Eliot line, but with a wither.

Once, April was the domain of baseball in American professional sport. Baseball must now share this mercurial month with hockey, basketball, golf, tennis and track.

The seasons grow into one another—the businessmen of sport seeing ever greater and greener billfolds in April. And so the cold shadow of winter sports such as hockey and basketball now falls across April.

To add another insult to the month, some people are exploring the idea of the college football season switching to spring, so that there would be no conflict with professional football in the fall.

Next, a batch of progressive buffoons will try to transplant the hepatica, the saxifrage and the arbutus to bloom not in April but in October. Fat chance.

It is hard to deal with the disenchantment of spring and all the glorious promises that are too soon exposed as being as bare as a late-fall dogwood.

There is, as recalled, the itchy pitcher throwing to his squatting dad on an Indiana farm field on a dreamy, snowy February day—and on an April morning in Florida being cut coldly from the team.

Or the group of lawyers who attended a New York Mets' home opener last year on an icy, wind-swept afternoon, and sued the management for allowing the game to be played. The lawyers had expected a public-relations-promised sun-kissed day. Good enough for the players, the judge decided, good enough for the fans. Case dismissed. April fools.

Yet, the trick of April is that sometimes what seems so forlorn now may indeed fulfill expectations.

Each spring some miracles occur, such as that of George Basil Theodore, lanky outfielder, the 717th draft pick a few years ago, being the only rookie to crack the Mets' roster this season.

Each spring a miracle happens among the rookie gray squirrels, too. They are born naked, toothless and blind, and must nuzzle their mothers through April and May. But in June, they go scampering off on their own four furry feet. And April? April, if considered at all, is nothing but a vinegary memory.

Rain Check

July 7, 1972

Raining harder. Pockets of puddles now cover the slick infield tarpaulin. Little hope that a ballgame will be played today.

The summer rain started earlier in the morning. There was a sudden, ominous appearance of dark clouds. It brought a shift of wind and bend of tree. Then, in rapid orchestration, a rumble of the kettledrum, the rise of the snare, a boom of the bass drum, and an ultimate clash of cymbals. Crackle of lightning. Rain.

How quickly cheeriness can become gloom. Bright prospects of a ballgame today swiftly drowning in the downpour. Yet there remains hope for the sun. The ballplayers come to the park, hustling from bus or car with newspaper covering their heads as they hop and dodge the wet splotches. They do not look up to the stadium roof and see flags sotted with rain, losing the struggle to flap in the wind.

Taciturn vendors and sullen ticket sellers are there. Some fans, with optimism as implacable as the rain, arrive.

Umbrellas pop up in the stands like mushrooms. Another jolt of lightning and a man with his son seated next to him lowers his black umbrella, as if he is pulling a bedcover tighter over their despondent heads.

One man under a poncho sits alone in the saturated bleachers. There is only a dark cavity where his face might be. A wet imitation of the Grim Reaper.

Rain everywhere. The big black scoreboard in center field is blacker for the wash. The outfield is soaked. Cops stand outside the dugout, their black slickers glistening in the deluge.

Lights are turned on; an ersatz sun which brings no relief from the rain. But the tarpaulin's puddles are now sprinkled with the stars. The geometric railings give a glassiness to the stands.

A few half-dressed players with shower shoes stand on the dugout bench, since the floor is already filling with water.

"Can you swim?" one asks another. "If not we'll have to cut you."

"The backstroke is my specialty," says the other.

The batboy has had to run from one dugout to the other. In that short desperate flight he has become matted with rain. He had to slosh through the sea of mud and water in front of the dugouts. He comes dripping, clattering in his spike shoes, and laughing breathlessly out of the rain. He brings into the dugout a smell of wet wool, shakes himself like a spaniel.

A couple of players return to playing cards in the quiet of the club-house. Pitchers will wonder what a rainout will mean to their routine and rotation. A slumping batter is thankful for a day of respite.

A second-line player is prepared for a drenching of ego in an unusual way, if the game goes on. He will probably be in the lineup since the manager does not want to risk injury to a star on a poor field.

But a team in a hot streak is afraid the rain may dampen its momentum.

And one remembers the Boston Braves of 1948, with the saying, "Spahn and Sain and pray for rain." (One wonders how Vern Bickford, the Braves' third starting pitcher behind Warren Spahn and Johnny Sain in that championship season, felt about that rhyme. Was it water off a duck's back?) And in Chicago that season the last-place Cubs had a soggy saying, too: "Kush and Rush and pray for slush." (The Cubs didn't have a third adequate pitcher behind Emil Kush and Bob Rush, with or without tender feelings.)

Raining, raining, raining. The hands of the scoreboard clock are seemingly sodden now, for it's an hour past game time. And still no game. The home team is forever reluctant to give up the ship, and the prospects of a miracle: sun and a good crowd. But soon the announcement: sorry, no game today.

The several thousand fans in the random stands boo. But boo whom? The management? The public address announcer? The turbulent gods? The snipping of hope?

And yet in their wet pockets these fans can clutch a rain check, a soggy but palpable symbol of a better day ahead. The rain check is a passport to sunshine.

On Sports in October

October 8, 1970

October is an odd month, combining the sober reality of a crisp afternoon one day with an illusory Indian summer the next.

It combines early on crack of bat against ball with the dreamed-up "fall classic"; and thus: the factual smack of shoulder-padded people with a complex playbook mystique.

October is the simplest month in sport. Summer sports are gone. Water is employed to carry a fallen golden leaf instead of a crew in a canoe. In November, the water will be swabbed with ice for skating.

In the North, golf courses begin to shudder with a ghostly gust. Flags atop pin placements flutter and snap. Only the most crusty, ruddy fellow, nose and eyes a-drip, fingers rigid, crunches along the fairway now.

With a bright sun that defies the breeze and belies the coming onslaught of snow, tennis players in shimmering white rush to embrace the fading glimpse of summer sun.

Overhead wild geese, mysteriously released, arrow southward. Perhaps they will elude the blunderbuss in the blinds below.

On a day that crackles with the brittleness of a twig, a World Series crowd sits collared and scarved and sends up smoke signals with a cheer.

But on a day that was misplaced in May, a football crowd sits amid the smell of burning leaves, and many sit in shirt sleeves and squint at the game from under the shade of their palms.

On such a day, a flask may contain the tang of apple cider instead of something conventionally harder.

The sky can be bright blue or mellow yellow or soft gray with a sharp relief of charcoal clouds. No matter the hue or whim of the October day, there is a purity that joins air and soul. On such days the world must stand still and let the hypocrisy of some sports, the dissembling in some sports, the authoritarianism in some sports pass.

Permit for a suspended moment a nation caught up, eyes raised, mouths agape at the overwhelming importance of a high fly, and whether when it decides to topple off a cloud it will thump into the hardening ground on the other side of the fence, or into a fielder's yawning glove.

Permit for a suspended moment the short flight of a halfback, dangling on a concealed string at the goal line, as a mass of men, waiting for him to descend, crouch with arms wide like the jaws of crocodiles.

Soon winter will commence with a different sense, a different chill, different sport, different thrill.

October ends. A month of reality and myth. It ends with eerie gaps in a Jack O'Lantern's grin.

The Pigeon Race

December 24, 1969 / Ocho Rios, Jamaica

If football is symbolic of the violent way of life in America, as some scholars tell us, then pigeon racing is what living is all about here in Jamaica.

For an American sports fan brought up on a strict fare of blood and mangled bones, it is startling, even here in the tropical sunshine between sips of rum beside the easy sea, to find a three-column story in the island newspaper about pigeon racing.

There is pigeon racing in America, too, but it is kept so far underground—or overhead—as to seem almost nefarious. A pigeon racer in Maine or Texas or Idaho, say, has as much social standing as the local chicken plucker and is perhaps a notch below your favorite noisy neighbor.

Jamaica, to the eyes of this beach umbrella-shaded tourist, is a very unhurried island, filled with bright smiles and languishing palm trees. The natives possess the kind of highly civilized, low-keyed carriage that would make the viewing of pigeon racing enthralling.

It is difficult for an American to watch a pigeon race. In fact, it is difficult for anyone to watch a pigeon race, unless one goes equipped with a helicopter.

The story in the paper noted that the Jamaica Racing Pigeon Club— not to be confused with the National Football League—"conducted an important race from Negril."

"Breaking from the boxes at 7:30 a.m. sharp," went the report, "the large flock of pigeons headed homewards."

A group of Jamaicans see the birds flutter off into the blue, then sit back and enjoy a splash of breakfast rum. At a similar time in many parts of America, this wintry December, coffee is being poured into thermos bottles, long johns are being wiggled into, mittens are being pinned to sleeves for the refrigerated afternoon ahead at the stadium.

"It seemed as if some of the bird diverted and circled some bad weather in the mountains, whilst the majority persisted through showers," gathered the article. "Apparently some came to a halt because quite a few pigeons arrived home during the latter part of the day."

It is one thing for participants to combat the elements, it is another for spectators to suffer through, as they do in such snowy pockets of frigid sophistication as Green Bay, Chicago, Cleveland, Minneapolis, and Buffalo, to select just a few, where a blizzard to some fans means nothing more than an additional coating, like new paint on a wall. The simulated war on the field takes precedence over creature comforts.

And in Jamaica, pigeon fanciers are on their second and third glasses of rum. (One note of similarity: in some thermos jugs in football stadiums, the liquid content is not always coffee.)

The average island newspaper reader is so excited by this pigeon sports story by now, that he may have been turned over onto his stomach on the beach, to get some shade on the article. He is anxious to know what happened in the race, but only after a customary dip in the sea.

"Cashoni, a beautiful blue-chequered hen, came home to Montego Bay first, displaying intelligence and true gameness," detailed the article.

Even partisans of the other racing pigeons must surely have appreciated the heart, the skill and the pulchritude of the winner. All spectators and participants in Jamaica then go off to savor more rum, and bread crumbs, as the case may be.

In America, fans file out of the stadium stiff as icicles.

Credits

All columns and feature stories in this book written between 1967 and 1977 appeared first in the Newspaper Enterprise Association syndicate and are reissued with permission of NEA. All columns and feature stories written between 1981 and 2007 appeared first in *The New York Times* and are reissued with permission from *The New York Times*. The article "Playing Pickup with Oscar" appeared first in *To the Hoop*, which was reprinted in the April 27, 1997 issue of *The New York Times Sunday Magazine*. The column "Jackie Robinson and Elston Howard" first appeared in The National Pastime.com. The column "Personal Experiences with The Donald" and "An Historic Sullivan High School Baseball Game" appeared first in the Sullivan High School Alumni *Sentinel* periodical.

Acknowledgments

With utmost respect and appreciation, I want to thank Jason Katzman who took an early interest in the idea for this book and edited it with not only tender loving care, but also with a fine, firm head, hand, and heart.

And a bow to the sports editors both at Newspaper Enterprise Assn. and *The New York Times* who were instrumental in work that appears in this book but first had to pass muster with them.

First among equals is Murray Olderman at NEA (based in New York), who hired me in 1967 from the *Minneapolis Tribune*. It was the esteemed sportscaster Beano Cook who said, "Working for Murray Olderman is like going to Yale." Murray, besides holding three college degrees including Phi Beta Kappa from Stanford, and being fluent in several languages—as an Army first lieutenant at the end of World War II in Europe he was assigned to interrogate German military prisoners—he was not only an award-winning writer but also a nationally recognized sports cartoonist.

Joe Vecchione hired me at *The New York Times* and, as at NEA, gave me, with much appreciation, considerable rein to roam the sports world, first as a reporter and feature writer and then as a columnist.

A special appreciation to Sandy Padwe, then the deputy sports editor, who recommended me to Joe.

It was a pleasure and honor to work alongside the terrific stable of "Sports of the Times" columnists over my twenty-six years at *The Times*:

Dave Anderson, Harvey Araton, Bob Lipsyte, Bill Rhoden, Selena Roberts, Red Smith, and George Vecsey.

Following Joe as sports editor was Neil Amdur, highly creative and with a vast knowledge of sports, under whom I continued on the path that Joe had established, and who recommended me for senior writer at *The Times*. Neil also made a great difference in my life when he suggested to executive editor Joe Lelyveld that I join the team that would produce the series "How Race Is Lived in America." I wrote the 8,000-word story that began on the front page of a Sunday edition—the lone sports-related article in the 15-part series—about the white quarterback, Marcus Jacoby, at the historically black Southern University and subsequently shared in the 2001 Pulitzer Prize for national reporting that was awarded to the *Times* for the series.

Other editors at the two organizations that I worked for and whose invisible but invaluable input are in the collected pieces in this volume include *The Times* deputy sports editors at various times Sandy Bailey, Bill Brink, Lawrie Mifflin, Arthur Pincus, and Rich Rosenbush. Other truly significant editors on the desks at both organizations were Jill Agostino, Harold Claasen, Bob Cochnar, Alan Finder, Joyce Gabriel, Ernestine Guglielmo, David Hendin, Geoge Kaplan, Hanna Umlauf Lane, Ralph Novak, and Mike Sisak. And a tip of the hat to the *Sullivan Alumni Sentinel* publisher Dick Hurwitz and the editor-in-chief Marilyn Addis Kaplow. And thanks to friends Rich Lerner and Rob Weissman for critical suggestions. And a deep bow to Tim Pratt for his careful and astute reading of the manuscript.

And, to be sure, a note of gratitude to Don Marquis, who inspired the dedication of this book with his inscription at the beginning of his beguiling 1927 book of verse, *archy and mehitabel*.

About the Author

Ira Berkow, a sports columnist and feature writer for *The New York Times* for twenty-six years, and awarded senior writer status there, shared the Pulitzer Prize for national reporting in 2001, was a finalist for the Pulitzer for commentary in 1988, and was nominated for a Pulitzer for international reporting in 1972. He was also a reporter and staff book reviewer for the *Minneapolis Tribune* and a columnist, sports editor, and senior editor for Newspaper Enterprise Association. He is the author of twenty-six books, including the best-sellers *Red: A Biography of Red Smith* and *Maxwell Street: Survival in a Bazaar*, as well as ten collections of his journalism. His work has been included in numerous literary and textbook anthologies, and has been cited for more than six decades in the prestigious anthologies *Best Sports Stories* and its successor *Best American Sports Writing*, as well as a column that was reprinted in the 1999 anthology *Best American Sports Writing of the Century*. He holds a bachelor's degree in English from Miami University (Ohio) and a master's degree in journalism from Northwestern University, and has been honored with distinguished professional achievement awards from both schools. In 2009, he received an Honorary Doctorate of Humane Letters from Roosevelt University in Chicago, a school he had also attended. Mr. Berkow lives in New York City with his wife Dolly.